The Labour Party and the world

VOLUME 1

Published in our
centenary year
∾ 2004 ∾
MANCHESTER
UNIVERSITY
PRESS

For Ceridwen

The Labour Party and the world

VOLUME 1

The evolution of Labour's foreign policy, 1900–51

Rhiannon Vickers

Manchester University Press
Manchester and New York

published exclusively in the USA by Palgrave

Published by
Manchester University Press
Oxford Road, Manchester M13 9NR, UK
and Room 400, 175 Fifth Avenue, New York, NY 10010, USA
www.manchesteruniversitypress.co.uk

Distributed exclusively in the USA by
Palgrave, 175 Fifth Avenue, New York,
NY 10010, USA

Distributed exclusively in Canada by
UBC Press, University of British Columbia, 2029 West Mall
Vancouver, BC, Canada V6T 1Z2

British Library Cataloguing-in-Publication Data
A catalogue record for this book is available from the British Library

Library of Congress Cataloging-in-Publication Data applied for

ISBN 0 7190 6744 8 *hardback*
     0 7190 6745 6 *paperback*

First published 2003

11 10 09 08 07 06 05 04 03   10 9 8 7 6 5 4 3 2 1

Typeset by Helen Skelton, Brighton, UK
Printed in Great Britain
by Biddles Ltd, Guildford and King's Lynn

Contents

List of tables

Acknowledgements

I would like to thank the following institutions for permission to quote from the documents of which they hold the copyright: the British Library of Political and Economic Science, London School of Economics, for the use of the following papers (Hugh Dalton, Arthur Lansbury, E. D. Morel); Churchill College, Cambridge (Ernest Bevin papers); the Modern Records Centre, University of Warwick (TUC, Keep Left and miscellaneous papers); the National Labour History Archive, Manchester (Labour Party papers); the Public Record Office (Foreign Office, Cabinet Office, Prime Minister's Office, Ramsay MacDonald papers, Ernest Bevin papers); the US National Archive, College Park, Maryland (State Department papers). In particular the archivists at the National Labour History Archive, Manchester, and the Modern Records Centre at the University of Warwick were, as ever, of great assistance, and my Honorary Fellowship at the Modern Records Centre was much appreciated. I am also grateful to the British Academy for providing research grant number SG 8982, which enabled me to carry out my archival work.

I would like to thank friends and colleagues for reading draft chapters, and in some cases the whole manuscript, and for providing advice and support in the writing of this volume, in particular Robin Brown, Andrew Gamble, Caroline Kennedy-Pipe, Mike Kenny and Andrew Taylor. My thanks also go to Kevin Theakston for suggesting this project in the first place; to the reviewers for their comments and suggestions; and in particular to everyone at Manchester University Press involved in the publication of this book.

List of abbreviations

AFL	American Federation of Labor
CPGB	Communist Party of Great Britain
EAM	National Liberation Front (Greece)
ELAS	National Popular Liberation Army (Greece)
IFTU	International Federation of Trade Unions
ILP	Independent Labour Party
ITSs	International Trade Secretariats
LRC	Labour Representation Committee
LSI	Labour and Socialist International
MP	Member of Parliament
MRC	Modern Records Centre
NATO	North Atlantic Treaty Organisation
NEC	National Executive Committee (Labour Party)
PLP	Parliamentary Labour Party
PRO	Public Record Office
RILU	Red International of Labour Unions (also known as the Profintern)
SDF	Social Democratic Federation
TUC	Trades Union Congress
UDC	Union of Democratic Control
UN	United Nations
WFTU	World Federation of Trade Unions

Introduction

Labour's election victory in May 1997 was closely followed by the new Foreign Secretary, Robin Cook, launching his department's mission statement in which he made a commitment to an 'ethical dimension' to British foreign policy. Cook declared that he was going to implement a new kind of foreign policy, which 'recognises that the national interest cannot be defined only by narrow realpolitik'. The aim was 'to make Britain once again a force for good in the world.'[1] This sparked a debate on the nature of Labour's foreign policy, which has seen a return to some of the arguments within the Labour Party from much earlier in the twentieth century, such as whether a Labour government should conduct foreign policy in the national interest or the international interest. Indeed, according to Blair, 'We are all internationalists now, whether we like it or not.' This is because 'Interdependence is the core reality of the modern world. It is revolutionising our idea of national interest. It is forcing us to locate that interest in the wider international community.'[2] These ideas of a moral dimension to foreign policy, of membership of an international community and of the need to think of the international interest, are not new. Rather, they reflect a particular world-view that has been prevalent throughout the Labour Party's history and which is the focus of this study.

Foreign policy under 'New Labour' has stimulated a renewed interest in the nature of Labour's approach to the world.[3] Not since a proliferation of studies of foreign policy under the Attlee governments has so much been said and written about Labour and international affairs.[4] However, foreign policy is in general an under-researched area of Labour Party policy and history. While there have been many studies of British foreign policy in the twentieth century,[5] remarkably little has been said about the development, formulation and nature of the

Labour Party's foreign policy. Studies of the Labour Party tend to focus on domestic policy, in particular social and economic policy, both in terms of policy-making and in terms of ideology.[6] This is partly because many academics who study the Labour Party come from a domestic British politics or economics background, rather than from an International Relations background, whereas International Relations scholars tend to focus on the state as a unitary actor, rather than unpacking it into constitutive parts. Undoubtedly, it is difficult to identify the extent to which parties can have an impact on foreign policy. States have to operate within the opportunities and constraints provided by the international system and so governments do not necessarily have much power to take a different policy stance, and opposition parties have even less. There are also the constraints provided by domestic state institutions, political culture, geographical location and economic resources. In the case of Britain, foreign policy is rarely made by bills passed through Parliament, and this tends to isolate it from the kind of scrutiny and legislative control that other policy areas are subject to. There is also a particular oblique British style of conducting foreign policy, which mitigates against a radical redrawing of foreign policy, that Kenneth Waltz described as:

> To proceed by a sidling movement rather than to move directly toward an object, to underplay one's hand, to dampen conflicts and depreciate dangers, to balance parties against each other, to compromise rather than to fight, to postpone decisions, to obscure issues rather than confront them, to move as it were by elision from one position of policy to another: such habits, anciently engendered and long crystallized, form the style of British foreign policy.[7]

In addition, foreign policy tends to be made in reaction to external events rather than as a result of internal policy development. As a result, Labour's policy on Britain's external relations is treated as a side issue, used to demonstrate the tensions between the different factions within the party,[8] or as evidence of the failure of the left to produce a foreign policy reflecting the ideological roots of the party,[9] rather than as a topic of interest in itself. Research that does focus on Labour's foreign policy, both published and unpublished, focuses on quite specific time periods,[10] on individual administrations – in particular the 1945 Labour government – or on particular issues.[11] There has been some work on Labour's defence and security policy since the Second World War, but this has not covered foreign policy as such.[12] None of the major studies of the Labour Party subject Labour's foreign policy

to sustained analysis. David Howell argues that both the Attlee and
Wilson governments emphasised bi-partisanship in foreign policy and
had an enduring attachment to nationalism and *real-politik* over a
socialist foreign policy or even liberal idealism, but his analysis is very
limited in depth.[13] Research that does provide any kind of overview is
in desperate need of updating, for example Miller's examination of
Labour's foreign policy up to 1931, Naylor's study of Labour's international policy in the 1930s, Gordon's analysis of Labour's foreign
policy between 1914 and 1965 and Windrich's study of Labour's
foreign policy published in 1952.[14] This dearth of material occurs
despite the fact that foreign policy has always been an area of
contention within the Labour Party, providing the arena for some of
its most intense tribal warfare.

This dearth of material has also contributed to the myth that
Labour has been insular in its outlook, not much interested in international affairs and has made little contribution to British foreign
policy in terms of ideas or policies. Nye Bevan, while opposition
spokesman for foreign affairs, told the 1958 Labour Party annual
conference that,

> When I first entered the House of Commons there was a myth, a preva-
> lent myth. It was to the effect that although the Labour Members of
> Parliament could reasonably be expected to know something about engi-
> neering, or about mining, there were two subjects on which they were
> completely ignorant: foreign affairs, and how to make war. It was always
> understood that those were the special prerogatives of the Tories, and
> their attitude has not changed very much. Despite an appalling series of
> blunders, they still assume that it is altogether a good thing to be able to
> talk international nonsense in several languages.[15]

This myth was promoted by the Labour Party's political opponents
keen to emphasise that Labour was not fit to govern. Somewhat more
surprisingly, it has also been encouraged by writers on the left. Some
have argued that, in its early days, the Labour Party was insular and not
concerned with either international affairs or the fate of the working
class overseas. Kenneth O. Morgan has said that 'The political labour
movement in Britain as it emerged in the later nineteenth century was
almost entirely insular in outlook.'[16] James Hinton that 'Socialism, as
it developed in Britain, had little distinctive contribution to make to
the formulation of foreign policy.'[17] In particular, 'The incapacity of
socialists to develop an independent position in foreign policy reflected
both theoretical weaknesses and the lack of interest in foreign affairs
shown by their predominantly working-class constituency.'[18] This

study, therefore, seeks to rectify this gap in the literature on both the political ideology and the history of the Labour Party's foreign policy and to demonstrate that the Labour Party has, from its very beginning, been involved and interested in international policy and with Britain's relations with the rest of the world. International affairs have been a major cause for concern for many in the Labour Party, not least because of its fundamental understanding that domestic and international politics were part of a whole that could not be treated as mutually exclusive. Indeed, the two Labour Party leaders who resigned during the time period under consideration for this first volume, namely Ramsay MacDonald in 1914 and George Lansbury in 1935, both did so over foreign and security policy disagreements with the party, demonstrating the great depth of passion aroused by foreign affairs.

This study provides an in-depth political history of the evolution of Labour's foreign policy in the twentieth century, with volume one based on extensive archival research, using Labour Party, Trades Union Congress (TUC), and government papers.[19] While giving centre-stage to Labour's foreign policy, it also includes an assessment of certain aspects of Labour's defence policy. Studying foreign policy is itself no easy task, given that definitions of foreign policy range in their scope.[20] For certain issues and for certain time periods, foreign and defence policy are inextricably linked and so any analysis of foreign policy involves an analysis of defence policy also.

In addition, this book does not simply seek to provide a narrative of events, but to construct a framework through which Labour's foreign policy and its outlook on the world can be analysed and interpreted. To date, this has been done within the context of developing a typology of a 'socialist' foreign policy. The most interesting attempts to do this are by Michael Gordon in *Conflict and Consensus in Labour's Foreign Policy: 1914–1965*, which was published in 1969, and Eric Shaw, who focused on the more limited time frame of 1945 to 1951. Gordon's typology of Labour's 'socialist' foreign policy had the following four main principles: internationalism, international working-class solidarity, anti-capitalism and anti-militarism or antipathy to power politics.[21] Eric Shaw, in his unpublished thesis, outlined two ideal types of socialist approach to foreign policy, a social-democratic Marxist doctrine and a radical democrat doctrine, based on the following principles of a socialist foreign policy: the rejection of power politics; liberal internationalism; socialist internationalism; social democratic solidarity; and the facilitation of the building of socialism at home.[22] Kenneth Miller, in *Socialism and Foreign Policy*, which was published in 1967, set out to determine the influence of socialist ideology on Labour's foreign policy up to 1931, but ended up emphasising the liberal influence on Labour's perspective instead.

In contrast, this book does not seek to assess the extent to which Labour's perspective was socialist, or evaluate the extent to which Labour has tried to apply socialist theories to foreign policy actions. This is because the Labour Party did not offer a radically alternative view in terms of providing a socialist foreign policy. Indeed, it has never been self-evident as to what such a policy would look like. As far as foreign policy was concerned, it is not clear that the Labour Party ever had any socialist ideology as such. Labour did seek to offer an alternative to the traditional, power politics or realist approach of British foreign policy, which had stressed national self-interest, and to provide a version based on internationalism, which stressed co-operation and interdependence, and a concern with the international as well as the national interest. In this, by far the most important influence on Labour's foreign policy were liberal views of international relations. While the Labour Party did at various times in its history call for a socialist foreign policy, it never really explained how it would be possible to implement a policy based on socialist ideology in a world where the existing nation-states were capitalist nation-states. Conversely, the Communist Party did appear to offer a particular version of a 'socialist' foreign policy that could be implemented in the existing international system. This was based on realist assumptions, namely that a socialist policy should be in line with the interests of a particular nation-state, the Soviet Union. This was one of the major reasons why the Communists were so distrusted by the Labour Party, because their position was seen to be not genuinely internationalist, but another variant of power politics, in service to the national interests of the Soviet state rather than the British state. What the Labour Party did not tend to fully comprehend was that for a socialist foreign policy to be practicable, there first had to be a transformation of the existing state form; to expect a capitalist state to pursue a socialist foreign policy was never feasible.

While it is difficult to develop an overall analytical framework within which to outline a typology of Labour's foreign policy, there are certain meta-principles, such as a belief in progress and an optimistic view of human nature, which reflect an internationalist perspective. This study argues that internationalism has been the underlying basis of Labour's world-view and foreign policy. Internationalism, broadly defined, is the desire to transcend national boundaries in order to find solutions to international issues. However, there are different strands of internationalism and it is not a world-view that is the preserve of the Labour Party or of socialist or social democratic parties. Much of the party's thinking on internationalism was shaped by radical liberal thinking as well as being influenced by a Christian-socialist, Nonconformist streak amongst party members. The Labour Party's own particular brand of internationalism has emphasised certain aspects of internationalist thought. These are first, that while states operate within a system of international anarchy, reform of the system is possible because states have common interests and values. This change is only likely to be secured through the construction of international institutions with which to regulate economic, political and military relations between states. Second, linked to this is a sense that states belong to an international community and that each state has a responsibility to work towards the common good of the international system, to work in the 'international' interest rather than purely in what it perceives to be its national interest. These two principles are closely intertwined. It was the belief in internationalism and an international community that underpinned Labour's demand in 1916 for an 'international authority to settle points of difference among the nations by compulsory conciliation and arbitration, and to compel all nations to maintain peace'.[23] This led Labour to support the establishment of the League of Nations following the First World War and to pursue its 'League of Nations' policy under Ramsay MacDonald and Arthur Henderson in the 1929–31 minority government, even if the party was at times critical of the form that the League of Nations took and the way that it operated. Belief in the international community was even written into the Labour Party's constitution, with the commitment 'for the establishment of suitable machinery for the adjustment and settlement of international disputes by conciliation or judicial arbitration and for such other international legislation as may be practicable.'[24] The Labour Party was the most wholehearted supporter amongst the British political parties for the establishment of international organisations to regulate and arbitrate world affairs, and it spent the years during the First and Second World Wars thinking about the post-war settlement and the maintenance of peace through international institutions.

The third aspect of Labour's internationalism was that international policy and governance should be based on democratic principles and universal moral norms. For Labour, domestic and foreign policy were seen as parts of a whole, as inextricably linked and as impacting on each other. Arthur Henderson said that there is an 'intimate' connection between Labour's home and foreign policy.[25] Policies pursued externally should help, or at least not hinder, the kind of society being built domestically. In addition, principles valued domestically, such as democracy and human rights, should be reflected externally and pursued in relations with other states. The key to international peace was social justice at home and abroad. This was strongly emphasised during the Second World War, with Attlee arguing that 'the world that must emerge from this war must be a world attuned to our ideals.'[26] Linked to the idea of universal moral norms was a belief in a democratic foreign policy and a rejection of secret diplomacy. This was an issue that was particularly popular within the Labour Party in the years just before and after the First World War, and Labour was strongly influenced in this through the involvement of radical Liberals such as E. D. Morel. The war was seen as the result of secret diplomacy, as 'Instead of taking advantage of the marked growth in the pacific inclinations of the peoples of the world', statesmen 'have insisted on encouraging between the Governments of Europe the most deadly and determined competition in preparation for war that the world has ever known.'[27] One of the achievements of the 1924 minority Labour government was that it fulfilled its manifesto pledge to end secret diplomatic agreements by presenting all new treaties to Parliament for ratification.

The fourth aspect of Labour's internationalism was the belief that collective security is better than balance of power politics, which is self-defeating in terms of generating conflict. The League of Nations, it was hoped, would by-pass the need for balance-of-power politics, and Labour had envisaged a League that was 'so strong in its representative character and so dignified by its powers and respect that questions of national defence sink into the background of solved problems.'[28] The belief in collective security was one of the reasons that Labour tended to vote against the government's defence estimates, preferring a national military capability which formed part of an international military force that could used for international intervention. Linked to this was the fifth principle of Labour's internationalism, its belief in 'anti-militarism'. This has been manifested in many different ways, including a commitment to collective security, arms control and disarmament, regulation of the arms industry, opposition to conscription, support for arbitration and a suspicion of the use of force as a foreign policy instrument. The annual conference regularly passed resolutions

condemning militarism and war, and many in the party believed that
war could be avoided through the avowed rejection of armaments and
the use of force. The preparation for war was seen as one of the major
causes of war, as this destabilised the international system by causing
suspicion between states. The Labour Party was strongly influenced by
the pacific outlook of the Independent Labour Party (ILP), who
believed that 'War is the result of the preparation for war.'[29] Labour's
anti-militarist tendencies manifested themselves in a number of ways,
such as attempts to control the arms industry and implement tighter
regulations on the sale of arms. In particular, there was a commitment
to controlling the proliferation of weapons, especially weapons of mass
destruction, through multilateral negotiations. Labour supported the
organisation of disarmament conferences and presented itself as the
party able to reach disarmament agreements internationally because of
its moral leadership.

In addition to these five principles was one further aspect of
Labour's international thought that did develop more directly out of
its socialist ideology, and this has been a belief in international
working-class and socialist solidarity. This was expressed in Labour's
early years through a commitment to the international socialist and
trade union movements and through Labour's campaigns for labour
movements overseas. Feelings of kinship with workers overseas were
engendered not only from a socialist belief in the need for international
working-class solidarity, but also from the impact of Nonconformist
beliefs in the brotherhood of man. This led to a concern with imperialism and of conditions in the British empire and, at times, support for
nationalist movements and for national self-determination, which was
often at odds with Labour's belief in Britain's continuing world and
imperial role. Indeed, Labour's policy on colonial affairs was usually
confused and inconsistent.

Within the Labour Party there have always been divisions over
how these internationalist principles should be interpreted, which of
these principles should be prioritised and which of these principles
were achievable in the real world. These divisions are at the heart of
this study, which argues that Labour never really came to an ideological agreement over how to be internationalist within an international
system dominated by nation-states. Labour did not question the existence of a world of sovereign nation-states, but its internationalist
perspective led it to look for ways to control relations between states
and ameliorate the inherent conflict in the international system. The
tension between national sovereignty and internationalism lay behind

many of the battles over Labour's foreign policy, and the party often found itself unable to transcend national barriers in order to meet its commitment to internationalism. These are themes that are explored throughout the following chapters and returned to more directly in the conclusion.

Outline of study

Due to the huge breadth and depth of material to be covered, this study consists of two volumes. The first volume outlines and assesses the early development and evolution of Labour's foreign policy up to and including the Attlee governments, and provides the analytical framework for this study. The second volume examines Labour's foreign policy from its 1951 defeat to the present day and concludes with an analysis of the importance of the party's contribution to British foreign policy.

The first two chapters of this volume introduce the analytical framework within which we can understand Labour's foreign policy. Chapter 1 provides the context within which the Labour Party emerged, that is, to represent the working class of the most powerful nation in the world. This was to shape the way that the party thought about foreign policy and Britain's role in the world. It also outlines how the party developed, namely as a loose federation of organisations rather than a party with a specified ideology, and with a commitment to internal democracy in its structure and ethos, and how this has given rise to competing perspectives on foreign policy. Chapter 2 completes the framework for this study by analysing the main influences on the party's attitudes towards international affairs, namely the ILP; the trade union movement; the Social Democratic Federation and various Marxist groups; the Fabian Society; and the radical Liberals, epitomised by the members of the Union of Democratic Control (UDC). Each of these five main influences had their own particular impact on the development of Labour's foreign policy. The radical Liberals contributed greatly to Labour's liberal internationalism, while the Marxists, the trade unions and the ILP each contributed to Labour's socialist internationalism. The Fabians provided in part the rationalist underpinning of Labour's views on international relations, while the ILP provided the impulse towards common fellowship with other states. The ILP and the radical Liberals reinforced each other in their beliefs that militarism and secret diplomacy lead to war. Some of the radical Liberals shared with the Marxists the assumption of the economic basis of inter-capitalist rivalry. These different contributing streams to Labour's foreign policy also often pulled in opposing directions. Nothing revealed this more than the split over attitudes towards pacifism and war, brought to a head with the outbreak of the First World War in 1914, but it is also evident in the other major debates of the time, over the Boer War and imperialism. What was agreed, however, by all the contributing groups, was that foreign policy could not be viewed in isolation, as domestic and international policies were inter-related, and also because foreign policy was affected by economic relations as well as political ones. Chapter 2 also begins the historical narrative of Labour and the world, focusing on the response to the Boer War and attitudes towards imperialism.

The first major test of Labour's developing world-view was over the response to the outbreak of the First World War, and this is examined in Chapter 3. Internationally, the First World War demonstrated that socialist parties had yet to find a way to overcome their national perspectives, resulting in the collapse of the Second International. At home, the war led to a widening gulf between the ILP and the Labour Party. As the ILP declined in its importance within the Labour Party, the UDC, established in opposition to the war, went on to have a resounding impact on the development of the Labour Party's views on the need for a League of Nations, open diplomacy and arms control, and a renewed optimism in internationalism. In addition to the First World War and its aftermath, this time period was extremely influential in the development of the Labour Party's foreign policy because of the events in Russia. The February and October 1917 revolutions in Russia were to have a resounding impact on Labour, both in terms of temporarily raising hopes for a future based on international socialist solidarity and then in terms of deepening divisions between left and right as the Soviet Union offered a competing world-view to that of the British Labour Party.

Chapter 4 examines the post-war period and the two Labour minority governments of 1924 and 1929–31, which saw a number of foreign policy achievements. As a result, the Labour Party had some considerable impact at this time on British views of internationalism, the arms trade and the League of Nations. From the early 1920s to the late 1930s, the internationalist, anti-war section of the party, strongly influenced by the UDC, dominated Labour Party thinking on international affairs. While this wing of the party had initially been highly critical of the League of Nations, they came to see it as the institution through which peace could be maintained. Despite, or possibly because of, the trauma of the First World War, the post-war years saw a period of remarkable optimism about the ability to banish war and conflict through the rational application of international law and the operation of the League of Nations.

Chapter 5 focuses on the years 1931 to 1938. This period saw significant transformations in Labour's foreign policy, with the optimism of the 1920s being replaced by the growing pessimism and fear of fascism in the 1930s. The initial reaction to the perceived weakness of the League of Nations due to its failure to prevent the use of force by Japan in 1931 and then by Italy in 1935 was, paradoxically, to increase support for the League in the short term, for there appeared to be no alternative to this policy. However, this period then saw Labour's foreign policy shift from a fairly anti-militaristic and almost pacifist stance in 1933, to support for rearmament and a policy of strength in the face of the threat posed by fascism by 1937. This was quite a remarkable shift in policy in a short space of time, resulting in the resignation of George Lansbury as party leader and an increase in the influence of the trade union movement over foreign policy through the work of the TUC on the National Council of Labour. It meant that when the Chamberlain government was replaced in 1940, the Labour Party was ready to join forces with Churchill in a coalition government to support Britain's war effort, which is examined in Chapter 6. Whereas other authors have seen the Attlee governments as marking a turning point in Labour's foreign policy,[30] this study traces the shift to the late 1930s and the fight against fascism. The Second World War marked a decisive break with the past for the Labour Party, pointing to the way that Labour governments in the future would approach foreign and defence policy. Labour had rejected appeasement as it did not think that there was any chance of a peaceful settlement with Hitler, thus ending its flirtation of the 1930s with pacifism and its traditional rejection of the use of force. The war also seemed to vindicate the necessity of policies that Labour had been advocating, such as state planning. The Labour Party spent much of its time thinking about what would happen when victory was won, and the party's apparatus of committees focused on developing ideas about the future international order. Labour wanted nothing less than the radical restructuring of British society and the radical restructuring of the international order that had brought about both the world wars. Their vision of a post-war international order was to be based on the acceptance of the idea of subordinating national sovereignty to world institutions and obligations, and on the need for international economic planning.

Chapter 7 examines foreign policy under the Attlee governments. The central conundrum that Labour faced when gaining power in 1945 was how to cut back expenditure while continuing to have as powerful a role in the world as possible. Labour was often just as reluctant as its opponents to admit to Britain's decline, or to be open about its inability to afford a world-wide role in security issues. Its response to its problems was to turn to the USA for support, as Britain could no longer afford to maintain its world role unaided. Rather than subordinating national sovereignty to international institutions in any substantial way, the Labour government linked Britain's national interest to that of the USA. Ernest Bevin in particular predicated his foreign policy on a close relationship with the USA, and America's involvement in Europe became institutionalised through the Marshall Plan and NATO. To a certain extent the Labour government's foreign policy of 1945–51 was Bevin's foreign policy, with Attlee allowing him a remarkable degree of freedom. No other Labour foreign secretary has had the impact that Ernest Bevin had, either on the party's foreign policy or Britain's role in the world. However, while Bevin was implementing what he saw as Labour's foreign policy, his critics on the left felt that the party had wasted its opportunity to change the nature of British foreign policy. For many in the rank-and-file of the party, their hopes for a post-war policy were based on a continuation of the wartime alliance with the Soviet Union, and internationalism and international solidarity meant working with Russia, not capitalist America. The criticisms over the Labour government's foreign policy were muted by the onset of the Cold War, but they never really went away, and this period saw the division between left and right of the party on foreign policy solidify into a division between Atlanticists and those suspicious of the USA, which continues to this day.

This volume concludes by outlining the principles underpinning Labour's foreign policy in order to construct a framework through which the policy and the party's outlook on the world can be analysed and interpreted. These principles will be returned to in the second volume of this study, which begins with Labour's loss of power in the 1950s. At the core of this study is the conviction that the past is an integral part of the study of the present, and that in order to understand Labour's foreign policy today, it is necessary to place it within the historical context of both the history of the Labour Party and the recent history of Britain's role in the world.

Notes

1 Robin Cook, 'Mission statement for the Foreign and Commonwealth Office', FCO, London, 12 May 1997.

2 Tony Blair, 'Doctrine of international community', speech to the Economic Club of Chicago, 22 April 1999; Tony Blair, 'At our best when at our boldest', speech to the Labour Party Annual Conference, 1 October 2002.

3 John Kampfner, *Robin Cook* (London: Victor Gollancz, 1998); Richard Little and Mark Wickham-Jones, eds, *New Labour's Foreign Policy: A New Moral Crusade?* (Manchester: Manchester University Press, 2000); Nicholas Wheeler and Tim Dunne, 'Good international citizenship: a Third Way for British foreign policy', *International Affairs*, 74:4 (1998), 847–70. There are also chapters in the following overviews: David Coates and Peter Lawler, eds, *New Labour in Power* (Manchester: Manchester University Press, 2000); Steve Ludlam and Martin Smith, eds, *New Labour in Government* (London: Macmillan, 2001).

4 On the Attlee governments there are various chapters in the following books; Kenneth O. Morgan, *Labour in Power 1945–51* (Oxford: Oxford University Press, 1985); Henry Pelling, *The British Labour Governments, 1945–51* (London: Macmillan, 1984); Nick Tiratsoo, ed., *The Attlee Years* (London: Pinter, 1991). Work that focuses more specifically on foreign policy includes Michael Dockrill and John Young, eds, *British Foreign Policy, 1945–1956* (London: Macmillan, 1989); Ritchie Ovendale, ed., *The Foreign Policy of the British Labour Governments, 1945–1951* (Leicester: University of Leicester Press, 1984); John Saville, *The Politics of Continuity: British Foreign Policy and the Labour Government, 1945–46* (London: Verso, 1993); Jonathan Schneer, 'Hopes deferred or shattered: the British Labour Left and the Third Force movement, 1945–49', *Journal of Modern History*, 56:2 (1984), 197–226; Peter Weiler, 'British Labour and the Cold War: the foreign policy of the Labour governments, 1945–1951', *Journal of British Studies*, 26:1 (1987), 54–82, and Weiler, *British Labour and the Cold War* (Stanford: Stanford University Press, 1988). See also Alan Bullock, *The Life and Times of Ernest Bevin, vol. 3: Foreign Secretary, 1945–1951* (London: Heinemann, 1983). There are also some excellent unpublished theses on this topic, in particular Richard Rose, 'The Relation of Socialist Principles to British Labour Foreign Policy, 1945–51', D.Phil. thesis, Oxford, 1959; and Eric Shaw, 'British Socialist Approaches to International Affairs, 1945–1951', M.Phil. thesis, University of Leeds, 1974.

5 For example, C. J. Bartlett, *British Foreign Policy in the Twentieth Century* (London: Macmillan, 1989); David Dilks, ed., *Retreat from Power: Studies in British Foreign Policy of the Twentieth Century, vols 1 and 2* (London: Macmillan, 1981); Laurence Martin and John Garnett, *British Foreign Policy: Challenges and Choices for the 21st Century* (London: Pinter/RIIA, 1997); Michael Smith, Steve Smith and Brian White, eds, *British Foreign Policy: Tradition, Change and Transformation* (London: Unwin Hyman, 1988); Donald Cameron Watt, *Succeeding*

John Bull: America in Britain's Place, 1900–1975 (Cambridge, Cambridge University Press, 1984).

6 For instance, Henry Pelling and Alastair Reid, *A Short History of the Labour Party* (London: Macmillan, 11th edn, 1996); Eric Shaw, *The Labour Party since 1945: Old Labour; New Labour* (Oxford: Blackwell, 1996).

7 Kenneth Waltz, *Foreign Policy and Democratic Politics: The American and British Experience* (London: Longmans, 1968), pp. 7–8.

8 For example, David Coates, *The Labour Party and the Struggle for Socialism* (Cambridge: Cambridge University Press, 1975); Eric Shaw, *Discipline and Discord in the Labour Party: The Politics of Managerial Control in the Labour Party, 1951–87* (Manchester: Manchester University Press, 1988).

9 Ralph Miliband, *Parliamentary Socialism. A Study in the Politics of Labour* (London: Allen and Unwin, 1961).

10 For example, Henry Winkler, 'The emergence of a Labor foreign policy in Great Britain, 1918–1929', *Journal of Modern History*, 28:3 (1956), 247–58.

11 On policy towards Russia, for example, work includes Bill Jones, *The Russia Complex: the British Labour Party and the Soviet Union* (Manchester: Manchester University Press, 1977); Andrew Williams, *Labour and Russia: The Attitude of the Labour Party to the USSR, 1924–34* (Manchester: Manchester University Press, 1989).

12 Dan Keohane, *Labour Party Defence Policy since 1945* (Leicester: Leicester University Press, 1993), and Keohane, *Security in British Politics, 1945–99* (London: Macmillan, 2000).

13 David Howell, *British Social Democracy: A Study in Development and Decay* (London: Croom Helm, 1976), pp. 144–9 and 267–74.

14 Michael Gordon, *Conflict and Consensus in Labour's Foreign Policy 1914–1965* (Stanford, CA: Stanford University Press, 1969); Kenneth Miller, *Socialism and Foreign Policy: Theory and Practice in Britain to 1931* (The Hague: Martinus Nijhoff, 1967); John Naylor, *Labour's International Policy: The Labour Party in the 1930s* (London: Weidenfield and Nicolson, 1969); Elaine Windrich, *British Labour's Foreign Policy* (Stanford, CA: Stanford University Press, 1952).

15 *Labour Party Annual Conference Report* (hereafter *LPACR*), 1958, p. 186.

16 Kenneth O. Morgan, *Keir Hardie: Radical and Socialist* (London: Weidenfeld and Nicolson, 1975), p. 178.

17 James Hinton, *Protests and Visions: Peace Politics in Twentieth Century Britain* (London: Hutchinson, 1989), p. 33.

18 *Ibid.*, p. 19.

19 These sources inevitably mean that this work is influenced by the view from the top of the party. The perspective of the rank-and-file of the party on foreign policy is difficult to trace, and the impact of the rank-and-file even more difficult to assess, but the author has taken into account discussions at conference, and correspondence from party members held in the Labour Party archive.

20 Useful discussions include Kim Richard Nossal, *The Politics of Canadian Foreign Policy* (Scarborough, Ontario: Prentice-Hall, 2nd edn, 1989), pp. 2–5; Smith, Smith and White, eds, *British Foreign Policy*, ch. 1.

21 Gordon, *Conflict and Consensus in Labour's Foreign Policy*, ch. 1.

22 Eric Shaw, 'British Socialist Approaches to International Affairs, 1945–1951', M.Phil thesis, University of Leeds, 1974, ch. 1.

23 *LPACR*, 1916, p. 32.

24 *LPACR*, 1918, p. 141.

25 Arthur Henderson, *Labour's Way to Peace* (London: Methuen, 1935), p. 30.

26 *LPACR*, 1940, p. 125.

27 Arthur Ponsonby, *Parliament and Foreign Policy* (London: UDC, pamphlet no. 5, 1914), p. 1.

28 J. Ramsay MacDonald, *A Policy for the Labour Party* (London: Leonard Parsons, 1920), pp. 131, 161 and 172.

29 J. Ramsay MacDonald, *Labour and International Relations* (Derby: Derby and District ILP Federation, 1917), p. 5.

30 Denis Healey, 'Power politics and the Labour Party', in Richard Crossman, ed., *New Fabian Essays* (London: Turnstile Press, 1952), p. 178; Kenneth O. Morgan, *Labour People: Leaders and Lieutenants, Hardie to Kinnock* (Oxford: Oxford University Press, 1987), p. 154.

Chapter 1

Context: the emergence of the British Labour Party

The Labour Party emerged in a very specific context, namely to represent the working class of the most powerful nation of its day. At the beginning of the twentieth century, Britain's dominant position in the world, her economic, military and political power, were largely taken as given, and Labour's world-view and foreign policy developed within this environment of Britain as global hegemon. This is not something that the founders of the Labour Party necessarily appreciated, but they and the party they created were marked by Britain's position in the world. Britain had been the first state to industrialise, and this too affected Labour's outlook and its perception of itself as a world player in the international socialist and trade union movements. This chapter starts by giving a brief introduction to the international context within which the Labour Party emerged in terms of Britain's role in the world, before turning to the historical sociology of the development of the Labour Party itself.

Britain's role in the world

British foreign policy in the twentieth century is itself a story of change, of Britain's attempts to come to terms with the consequences of it relative decline in the world. In 1900, Britain possessed the largest empire in history and ruled one-quarter of the world's population.[1] As the global superpower of the time, many assumed that Britain's destiny was to be a world leader, with a vast imperial outreach. Britain had been the world's foremost trading nation during the nineteenth century, and its export-based economy relied on its naval power to keep open trading routes and protect Britain's enormous colonial empire. Its security was based on the superiority of Britain's navy, which was then the dominant form of military technology.[2] This superiority was due to Britain's early industrialisation and its lead in steel production. Britain's naval dominance was based on the strategy that the Royal Navy should always be superior in power to the combined forces of the next two largest fleets. In addition, Britain had an unrivalled network of naval bases around the world, including Gibraltar, Malta, the Cape, Alexandria, Bombay, Singapore, Sydney and Halifax, and by far the largest merchant navy.[3] Thus, British foreign and security policy was based on isolationism, in terms of its ability to depend upon its own strength to repel any attack on it or its colonies through its naval dominance.

However, the reality was that by the turn of the twentieth century Britain was a declining superpower. Britain's economic power was already being challenged by its competitors, as it lost its economic lead with the rapid industrialisation of other states.[4] As the table below demonstrates, the United States of America had overtaken Britain in terms of its share of world manufacturing output, a key indicator of economic strength. Whereas in 1860, at the height of its dominance, the UK had almost three times the share of world manufacturing output of its nearest rivals, by 1900 the USA had raced ahead with 23.6 per cent of world output compared with 18.5 per cent for the UK. The British were 'no longer absolute masters of the markets of the world'.[5] Britain's relative share of steel production was declining, at a time when steel production was the best single indicator of industrial power and hence of military potential.[6] The USA, Germany and France were all expanding their naval capabilities. In addition, Britain had a relatively small standing army, at a time when armies were gaining in importance relative to naval power with the opportunities provided by the opening up of vast tracks of land through the development of the railway. For example, Russia expanded its standing army from 647,000 in 1890, to 1,119,000 in 1900, whereas the whole of the British empire expanded its standing army from 355,000 troops in 1890 to 513,000 in 1900.[7]

Thus, at the turn of the century, 'both the Pax Britannica and the concomitant foreign policy of "splendid isolation" were brought to an end with incredible swiftness.'[8] The growth in economic and military power of the United States, France, Germany, Italy, Russia and Japan, and the increased interest in overseas markets and international power-politics of Germany and the US in particular, posed threats to Britain's position as global hegemon and posed risks to Britain's ability to stand

Table 1.1   *Relative shares of total world manufacturing output (%)*

	1860	1880	1900	1913
United Kingdom	19.9	22.9	18.5	13.6
United States	7.2	14.7	23.6	32.0
Germany	4.9	8.5	13.2	14.8
France	7.9	7.8	6.8	6.1
Russia	7.0	7.6	8.8	8.2

Source: Adapted from Paul Bairoch, 'International industrialization levels from 1750 to 1980', *Journal of European Economic History*, 11:2 (1982), table 10, 296.

alone. The growth of the German navy in the early 1900s was seen as a particular threat to Britain's global position, leading to a naval arms race and a spiralling military and naval budget at a time when Britain was losing its economic advantages.

These factors led to a debate at the turn of the century about the relative merits of 'isolation or alliance'.[9] The Conservative government reluctantly agreed to form alliances with Britain's European neighbours, and to pursue a foreign policy based on a balance of power in Europe. Britain only joined this system of alliances out of necessity: 'it was the problems caused by her imperial commitments which brought England, gradually and unintentionally, into the European alliance system.'[10] Britain entered into a limited treaty with Japan in January 1902, and less formal *ententes* with France in April 1904 and Russia in August 1907.[11] The concern was that France was vulnerable to German expansionism, and that if France could not rely upon substantial British support, then it might in desperation become a political satellite of Germany.[12] As Foreign Office official Eyre Crowe explained: 'The general character of England's foreign policy is determined by the immutable conditions of her geographical situation on the ocean flank of Europe as an island State with vast overseas colonies and dependencies, whose existence and survival as an independent community are inseparably bound up with the possession of preponderant sea power.' However, there was always the danger of 'the momentary predominance of a neighbouring State at once militarily powerful, economically efficient, and ambitious to extend its frontiers or spread its influence.' Germany, for example, might indeed be 'aiming at a political hegemony with the object of promoting purely German schemes of expansion, and establishing a German primacy in the world of international politics'. Historically, 'The only check on the abuse of political predominance has always consisted in the opposition of an equally formidable rival, or of a combination of several countries forming leagues of defence. The equilibrium established by such grouping of forces is technically known as the balance of power'.[13]

This context of Britain's role in the world as a superpower, in gradual but not yet conspicuous decline, affected the way that the emerging Labour Party thought about itself and its foreign policy. The Labour Party was the representative of the workers of the world's leading power, of the first state to industrialise and of a state with a massive empire. It was internationalist in that it saw Britain as part of an interconnected world and had a socialist belief in the need for international working-class solidarity, but it also saw Britain and itself as world leaders. While the empire was viewed by many as a morally unjustified form of oppression, and imperialism in general was seen as a cause of war, Britain's export-based economy meant that many workers had an interest in the maintenance of the empire and access to overseas markets. Many also saw Britain as having a civilising mission in the world and, as the world's greatest democracy, as having a manifest destiny to act as a world leader. The empire was seen as a demonstration of, as well as a means of continuing, British influence in the world. Britain was not just another country, but the leading nation with a great empire.

These issues will be dealt with more fully in the next chapter, which outlines and assesses the main influences on the development of the Labour Party's attitudes towards international affairs, and focuses in particular on the Boer War and views on imperialism. First, however, it is necessary to provide a brief overview of the emergence of the Labour Party, before commenting on how the structure of the party has affected the way that policy has developed.[14]

The emergence of the Labour Party

The massive growth of British industry had meant that throughout the nineteenth century the size of the working class had grown dramatically. In the latter half of the century its political strength had also increased, with the expansion of primary education, a greater focus on social questions, increasing labour organisation and unionisation and the extension of the franchise, particularly by the Third Reform Act of 1884.[15] This increased the electorate from 2.62 million to 4.38 million men.[16] However, while the force of the working class in Britain was

growing, it largely expressed its political viewpoint through support of
the Liberals, and it only formed a party specifically to represent itself in
1900. This was later than its European counterparts; the German
Socialist Party was formed at the Gotha Congress in 1875, and in the
elections of 1890 gained about a fifth of all votes cast and returned
thirty-five Socialist members to the German Parliament.[17] The Belgian
Labour Party was formed in 1885; the Swedish Social Democratic
Party in 1887; even in the USA a Socialist Labor Party had been established in 1877.[18] In France, the development of trade unions occurred
relatively late, while socialist parties proliferated through a series of
splits and schisms in the late nineteenth century. The party that was to
emerge in Britain was also more eclectic in its intellectual and ideological positions than some of its socialist counterparts overseas, having
been more influenced by the British liberal tradition than by any
British socialist or Marxist tradition.

The political organisations that came together to form the Labour
Party consisted of the Social Democratic Federation (SDF), formed by
H. M. Hyndman, William Morris and Tom Mann, the main Marxist
grouping in Britain at that time;[19] the Fabian Society, a liberal-
influenced, predominantly middle-class debating society; and the
ethical socialists, whose main organisation was the ILP and who
worked closely with the trade union movement.[20] However, these
'socialist' societies were very small, and the main force behind the
establishment of a party to represent the British workers was the British
trade union movement. This was stronger and more influential than its
overseas counterparts as a result of British early industrialisation. In
1868 the TUC had been established as a federation of all British
unions, and while membership fluctuated widely, in 1874 just under a
million trade unionists were affiliated to it through their union
membership. By the end of the century, there was an increase in industrial conflict and the development of 'New Unionism' amongst the
un-skilled and semi-skilled. In 1900, trade union membership stood at
just over 2 million.[21] Following the Third Reform Act of 1884, the
trade unions had been able to sponsor a growing number of working-
men MPs. These 'Lib-Lab' trade-union-sponsored MPs co-operated
with the radicals on the left of the Liberal Party to press for further
measures of reform of particular relevance to organised labour, but did
not form their own party grouping.[22] The influence of British radical
liberalism was strong, as was the religious Nonconformist tradition,
and 'the British trade unions were far from being Socialist. Indeed,
most of their leaders saw in Socialism merely a utopia and in the theory

of the class struggle a dangerously destructive doctrine.'[23] Out of these four sets of organisations, it was the ILP and the SDF that were the most enthusiastic about founding a new political party, whereas the Fabians and the more established trade unions had been largely content to work with the Liberal Party.[24]

At the meeting of the 1899 TUC, a resolution from the Amalgamated Society of Railway Servants proposed holding a special congress of trade unions, co-operative societies and socialist bodies, to 'devise ways and means for securing the return of an increased number of labour members to the next Parliament.' The discussion was a little more controversial than the proposal, for it became clear the supporters of the motion, such as Ben Tillet of the Dock, Wharf, Riverside and General Labourers Union, wanted to form a labour representative body in Parliament, which would be independent from the existing political parties. The motion was hotly debated, for some of the more established trade unions wanted to maintain their sponsorship of Liberal MPs, and miners' representatives argued that the British worker had little interest in direct Parliamentary representation and that the suggestion was impractical as trade unionists had different political opinions. Despite this, the motion was passed with 546,000 votes for the proposal and 434,000 votes against.[25] This conference was held in London on 27–28 February 1900. While some of the delegates were still reluctant to see a new grouping develop in Parliament, it was decided to establish a committee to promote and co-ordinate plans for labour representation, which was to be known as the Labour Representation Committee (LRC).[26] This occasion is seen as the birth of what was subsequently renamed the Labour Party in 1906, but very little was actually decided at this conference. There was no clear political programme or declaration of principles upon which the LRC was to be based, and it was not quite clear from the resolutions that were passed at this conference as to whether the LRC was to act independently as a party, or to work as a grouping within Parliament in collaboration with one of the existing political parties.[27] However, an Executive Committee was set up, which initially consisted of seven trade unionists, two ILP delegates and one Fabian Society delegate. Two SDF delegates were nominated shortly after the conference.[28] The membership of the Executive Committee did not reflect the membership or resources of the respective organisations, for at the conference there were delegates from sixty-five trade unions, representing half a million members, while the socialist societies had only a few thousand members each.[29] The ILP actually had a great influence on the development of the LRC in its early years, as member Ramsay MacDonald was nominated as its secretary – the only full-time, though unpaid, office holder – and it was the ILP that supplied the LRC with a network of local branches across the country.

At its first election in the autumn of 1900, the LRC sponsored fifteen candidates, but won only two seats, Richard Bell at Derby and Keir Hardie at Merthyr, with 1.8 per cent of the vote. As more trade unions affiliated to the LRC, it gradually grew in strength and resources. The Taff Vale judgement of 1901, when the House of Lords ruled that a trade union could be sued for damages resulting from industrial action, jeopardised the rights that the trade unions had won and exercised over the previous thirty years. Trade union membership of the LRC doubled in 1902 following a dip in 1901, as: 'The imperative need to secure a reversal by legislation of the effects of the Taff Vale Judgement and of other recent court decisions brought the Trade Unions into politics much more rapidly than any amount of persuasion by the Socialists could have done.'[30] At the 1903 annual conference the LRC increased its subscription rate and introduced a compulsory parliamentary fund for the payment of MPs. At the January 1906 election it put forward fifty-one candidates, winning thirty seats, and gaining 5.9 per cent of the vote.[31] When the 1906 Parliament assembled, the LRC renamed itself the Labour Party. However, it was still a very weak organisation, without a clear programme, and owing its electoral success partly to a secret agreement made in 1903 between Ramsay MacDonald and Herbert Gladstone, the Liberal Party Chief Whip, that the Liberals would not put up a Liberal candidate in the seats where Labour was standing.[32]

The context of the emergence of the Labour Party is important: it emerged out of the strength of the trade union movement rather than the strength of socialist societies, and it was greatly influenced by the British liberalism. It emerged at a time when the labour movement in Britain was expanding, but the British economy was already experiencing relative decline as it was being taken over by rapidly industrialising competitors, and Britain was finding it increasingly difficult to secure its empire in isolation from political alliances. The next chapter will deal with the main political influences on the development of the Labour Party's attitudes towards international affairs and British foreign policy. However, first it is necessary to highlight some of the aspects of the party's structure that affected the making of policy. The structure of the party meant that party activists had a voice at conference, which, while not necessarily deciding policy, certainly acted as a constraint on policy. It is worth considering this in a little depth, as the structure and ethos of the Labour Party has had an impact on its policy-making process and the way that the party's foreign policy has developed.

The Labour Party's structure and the impact on policy

The Labour Party developed as a party that was external to the existing parliamentary elite, designed to represent the interests of the British working class. As such, inherent within its organisational structure, its traditions and its ethos was an element of democracy and participation. In particular, this was manifested through the power of the annual conference to make policy, and one enduring area of controversy has been over the issue of conference sovereignty.[33] This has varied somewhat over time, with the annual conference assuming greater sovereignty and power when Labour has been in opposition, but the power of the annual conference has been, for much of Labour's history, a matter of interpretation and practice.

The issue of conference sovereignty was first raised when the 1906 party conference had asserted its right to 'instruct' Labour MPs. However, the following year the annual conference approved an executive proposal put forward by Keir Hardie which has remained the definitive statement on the relationship between the Parliamentary Labour Party (PLP) and the party as a whole. This was that 'Resolutions instructing the Parliamentary Party as to their action in the House of Commons be taken as the opinions of the conference, on the understanding that the time and method of giving effect to these instructions be left to the party in the House, in conjunction with the National Executive.'[34] This position became known as 'the 1907 formula', namely that party conferences could not bind the party in Parliament. This gave the Parliamentary Labour Party considerable leeway in its policy positions. The relationship between the Executive Committee (later known as the National Executive Committee, or NEC), which was established at the LRC's inaugural conference in 1900, and the annual conference, was left ambiguous. This relationship was laid out in more detail in the party's constitution of 1918, drawn up as part of the reorganisation of the party's structure to take account of the Representation of the People Bill. This Bill widened the franchise, and the purpose of the reorganisation was to widen access to the Labour Party and bring into its ranks the large sections of the electorate who were not members of a trade union, or members of the socialist parties affiliated to the Labour Party.[35] The new constitution stated that one of the objectives of the party was 'To give effect as far as may be practicable to the principles from time to time approved by the Party Conference.'[36] In terms of the party programme and election manifestos, it was the duty of the conference to decide what policy proposals the party would promote, but 'no such proposal shall be made definitely part of the General Programme of the Party unless it has been adopted by the Conference by a majority of not less than two-thirds of the votes recorded on a card vote'. It was the duty of the NEC and the PLP, prior to every general election, 'to define the principal issues for that Election which in their judgement should be made the Special Party Programme'.[37] However, no guidance was given as to what should happen if there were conflicts between the programme of Conference and the programme of the NEC. Further control was also exercised over the PLP and NEC, as each had to submit a report to the annual conference, which was then voted on.

Related to conference sovereignty was the issue of the control of the agenda at the annual conference. Trade unions, trades councils, constituency parties and other affiliated parties, and the NEC could all submit policy resolutions to the conference, some of which were then placed onto the conference agenda. As Lewis Minkin explains, on the right wing of the party there has always been 'considerable trepidation about the organisational energy and dexterity' of the left and a tendency to see the preliminary agenda as the product of left-wing planning. The left on the other hand has been 'inclined to see the whole process of agenda preparation as the product of a conspiracy of the Conference officials, the leadership of the Parliamentary Labour Party, the NEC and the Party bureaucracy.'[38] This is because non-decision-making can be an exercise of power and influence just as much as decision-making.[39] Whichever groups dominated the agenda-setting process, the annual conference provided an opportunity for activists to take centre stage, and since activists tended to be more ideologically driven than party leaders, this had an impact on the nature of Labour's foreign policy, the type of issues that were raised at conference and the subsequent policy proposals put forward. This was in sharp contrast to the Conservative Party, where foreign policy was pretty much left in the hands of the party leadership. In addition to this, activists in the Labour Party, in particular if also trade unionists, were sometimes given the chance to travel as part of visiting delegations, fact-finding missions overseas and membership of international organisations, and so built up a knowledge and experience of international relations at a personal level. Back-bench MPs also had a greater influence on policy than their Conservative counterparts through their involvement in the network of Labour Party policy committees and potential membership of the NEC.

In addition to the structural constraints arising from the role of the party conference, Labour had to deal with the issue of minority groups within the party and their impact on policy-making. This was particularly significant over the areas of foreign and defence policy. The Labour Party, unlike the Conservative Party, had to fight against parties within the party and factions within the party, as its more democratic organisational structures provided factions with more opportunities to exert their influence. One obvious occasion was the fight with Militant in the 1980s, but another was the tension that arose over the affiliation of the ILP during the First World War, when the Labour Party largely supported the war, and the ILP opposed it. These tensions extended into the 1920s and became particularly apparent during the 1929–31 minority Labour government, which culminated in the break with the ILP. However, perhaps the most significant arguments within the party over the threat of a 'party within the party', have arisen over the role of the Communist Party of Great Britain (CPGB). Marxist groups had been affiliated in the Labour Party's early years. For example, the SDF was involved in the establishment of the LRC in 1900, disaffiliated in 1901, and then split during the First World War with one section, the British Socialist Party, affiliating to the Labour Party again in 1916. However, later attempts by the CPGB to affiliate to the Labour Party in the 1930s were viewed with great alarm by the Labour Party's leaders, as was their application in 1946. Herbert Morrison spoke on behalf of the Labour Party's NEC against the motion. The arguments he used included that the CPGB was not democratic but a 'dictatorship', not a political party but a 'conspiracy', that the CPGB would be an 'embarrassment to the Government', and that 'they do only what Moscow wants them to do.' Not unsurprisingly, the motion on their affiliation was rejected by 2,678,000 votes to 468,000.[40] In addition, on Denis Healey's suggestion, Herbert Morrison successfully moved an amendment to the party constitution to prevent the situation arising again.[41] This stipulated that,

> Political Organisations not affiliated to or associated … with the Party on January 1, 1946, having their own Programme, Principles and Policy for distinctive and separate propaganda, or possessing Branches in the Constituencies, or engaged in the promotion of Parliamentary or Local

> Government Candidatures, or owing allegiance to any political organisa-
> tion situation abroad, shall be ineligible for affiliation to the Party.

The aim was 'to end the possibility of communist affiliation once and
for all'.[43] Since 'individual membership of the Party is not possible for
anyone belonging to an organisation which is deemed ineligible for
Party affiliation', this constitutional change 'provided the Party leadership with the means to control the extent of organised factionalism
within the Party.'[44] However, while the problem of affiliation was dealt
with, individual communists, who tended to be highly motivated,
could still cause problems with policy development and policy implementation. Denis Healey, the Labour Party's International Secretary,
noted later that 'communist influence in the Labour Party and unions
remained a major obstacle in my task of winning support for the
[Attlee] Government's foreign policy.'[45]

Indeed, concern over the ability of the communist minority to
influence the development or success of Labour's foreign policy during
the 1945 Attlee government led the party to instigate a concerted anti-
communist campaign within the labour movement in Britain. Of
course, one of the strengths of the CPGB was its affiliation to the
Cominform, in that they received support and funding from the Soviet
Union, though this was also their major weakness, for they could be
accused of attempting to further the Soviet Union's interests rather
than Britain's in their foreign policy positions. However, the wartime
alliance with the Soviet Union meant that the Soviet Union in particular, and communism in general, had gained a legitimacy that it had
not previously enjoyed in the eyes of the British public. Left-wing
unionists and Labour Party members, non-communists as well as
communists, were calling for a 'socialist' foreign policy, which they
interpreted as being based on co-operation with the USSR, and the
idea that 'Left understands Left'.[46]

However, mitigating against the power of minority groups and of
the annual conference to control the development of Labour's policies
were the conventions of the British parliamentary system. These
'require that Members of Parliament, and therefore parliamentary
parties also, must hold themselves responsible solely to the electorate
and not to the mass organization of their supporters outside
Parliament.'[47] This provided legitimacy to the arguments of the leadership of the Labour Party that it was the duty of the party to develop
policies that are acceptable to the electorate, and not merely to the
party. As McKenzie noted in his comparison of the Labour and

Conservative Parties, despite the Labour Party's origins as a gathering of trade union, co-operative and socialist societies, the PLP increasingly resembled its opponents, and 'By the time the Parliamentary Labour Party had taken office in 1924 its transformation was almost complete. By accepting all the conventions with respect to the office of Prime Minister and of Cabinet government, it ensured that the Labour Party outside Parliament would be relegated to a status not unlike that of the [Conservative Party's] National Union.'[48] In addition, the annual conference was not the only avenue through which policy proposals were made. The Labour Party established a network of advisory committees to the NEC following its reorganisation in 1918, which prepared policy and position papers, and advised MPs on party policy and its development. These committees had a tendency to proliferate, with the establishment of advisory committees and working groups on specific foreign policy and security issues. While the committee structure diffused some power from the NEC to the committee members, the deliberations of the committees were private, and could be used to control the development of policy in certain directions. In addition, particular to the Labour Party was its membership of the Socialist Internationals. The party was affected by decisions made by the Internationals, and it tended to be party leaders who made up the delegations to meetings of the Internationals. This too tended to concentrate power over policy-making while giving the impression of diffusing it.

Another factor that influenced the way that Labour's foreign policy developed was that the Labour Party was created out of the trade union movement to represent interests external to those of the parliamentary elite, and hence was an externally created, oppositional party.[50] This oppositional nature of the Labour Party meant that the party's foreign policy, unlike that of the Conservative Party, had for extensive periods in the twentieth century developed more as a response to the internal dynamics of the party, rather than as a response to actualities of the international situation. The advantage of being in opposition was that the party had more time for reflection and policy development, and was able to pursue more long-term perspectives than the party in office. However, 'this is strongly counterbalanced by its lack of responsibility for action and implementation, which breeds a certain air of unreality and makes it receptive to the extremist pressures within the party.'[50] This has been the case with foreign policy, which has tended to be more left-wing during long periods in opposition. An additional factor that has contributed to this tendency is that, as John

Young has pointed out, Labour leaders have usually appointed 'reli-able' individuals to the positions of Foreign Secretary and Defence Secretary, who have often been from the centre and the right of the Labour Party, such as Ernest Bevin, Denis Healey, and David Owen.[51] More left-wing appointments, such as Aneurin Bevan as foreign policy spokesman in the late 1950s, were less radical on foreign affairs than they were on domestic issues. This resulted in a certain pragmatism in foreign policy, and a tendency for the party leadership to preach bi-partisanship in an effort to disarm its critics and reassure Britain's allies.

In brief, there are three main factors that affected the way that the emerging Labour Party thought about foreign policy. First, it was marked by the British position in the world, and of the British way of doing things as a world leader. However, this was during the period of the end of Britain's world-wide predominance and the age of 'Pax Britannica'. This affected Labour's view of Britain's role in the world. Second, the Labour Party emerged relatively late compared with some of its European counterparts, and it was made up of an amalgam of different groupings (within which the trade unions were dominant in terms of numbers of members, finances and political impact, but were under-represented on the core executive) and was without a clear polit-ical ideology. It developed as an oppositional party, and the party had to gain power within a historically constituted situation. Third has been the impact of the party's ethos and structure. There has been a tendency, throughout the twentieth century, for the Labour Party's rhetoric on foreign policy in opposition to be significantly to the left of actions taken once in power. This is because when in opposition the party's leadership was circumscribed by the party members, and when in power by the realities of Britain's role in the world. Labour's foreign policy has been more affected by this than that of the Conservatives, because the organisation of the Labour Party has provided for more of a role for the party members and activists, and given them more oppor-tunities to state their opinions. The second and third of these factors meant that there were diverse influences on the development of the Labour Party's world-view and competing perspectives on foreign policy, which will be outlined in the next chapter.

Notes

1 Andrew Gamble, *Britain in Decline: Economic Policy, Political Strategy and the British State* (London: Macmillan, 4th edn, 1994), provides a useful historical overview of this.

2 See Aaron Friedberg, *The Weary Titan: Britain and the Experience of Relative Decline, 1895–1905* (Princeton, NJ: Princeton University Press, 1988), pp. 298–300.

3 Paul Kennedy, *The Rise and Fall of the Great Powers: Economic Change and Military Conflict from 1500 to 2000* (London: Fontana Press, 1989), pp. 197–8, 291.

4 See Eric Hobsbawm, *Industry and Empire: An Economic History of Britain since 1750* (London: Penguin, 1968), ch. 9.

5 H. M. Hyndman, *The Coming Revolution in England* (London: William Reeves, 1883), p. 22.

6 Robert Cox, *Production, Power and World Order: Social Forces in the Making of History* (New York: Columbia University Press, 1987), p. 153. See Kennedy, *Rise and Fall of the Great Powers*, p. 257, table 15, for figures.

7 Figures taken from Quincy Wright, *A Study of War* (Chicago: University of Chicago Press, 2nd edn, 1965), table 58, pp. 670–1.

8 Paul Kennedy, *The Rise and Fall of British Naval Mastery* (London: Allen Lane, 1976), p. 210.

9 Paul Kennedy, *The Realities Behind Diplomacy: Background Influences on British External Policy, 1865–1980* (London: Fontana Press, 1981), pp. 110–17.

10 James Joll, *The Origins of the First World War* (London: Longman, 1984), p. 40.

11 See Michael Howard, *The Continental Commitment* (London: Temple Smith, 1972), chs 1 and 2 for a useful overview of the defence aspects of this shift in policy.

12 Kennedy, *Rise and Fall of British Naval Mastery*, p. 233.

13 Eyre Crowe, 'Memorandum on the present state of British relations with France and Germany', 1 January 1907, FO 371/257, reprinted in George Gooch and Harold Temperly, eds, *British Documents on the Origin of the War 1898–1914*, vol. 3 (London: HMSO, 1928), pp. 402–3.

14 This is intended merely to provide some background on the party's emergence. For more detailed accounts see the readings listed below.

15 See Henry Pelling, *The Origins of the Labour Party, 1880–1900* (Oxford: Oxford University Press, 2nd edn, 1965), ch. 1.

16 G. D. H. Cole, *British Working Class Politics, 1832–1914* (London: Routledge, 1941), p. 5.

17 Julius Braunthal, *History of the International, vol. 1, 1864–1914*, translated by Henry Collins and Kenneth Mitchell (London: Thomas Nelson, 1966), pp. 200–1.

18 Lewis Lorwin, *The International Labor Movement: History, Policies, Outlook* (New York: Harper, 1953), p. 20.

19 It was originally formed in 1881 as the Democratic Federation, but reconstituted and renamed in 1884 to emphasise its increased socialist emphasis. William Morris left the SDF in December 1884 to form another organisation, the Socialist League, which initially comprised of a semi-anarchist wing under Morris, and a Marxist wing led by Engels.

20 See David Howell, *British Workers and the Independent Labour Party 1888–1906* (Manchester: Manchester University Press, 1983).

21 Hugh Clegg, Alan Fox and A. Thompson, *A History of British Trade Unions since 1889, vol. 1, 1889–1910* (Oxford: Clarendon Press, 1964), pp. 3 and 489. See also Henry Pelling, *A History of British Trade Unionism* (London: Macmillan, 1963), for information on the development of British trade unions.

22 Henry Pelling and Alastair Reid, *A Short History of the Labour Party* (London: Macmillan, 11th edn, 1996), p. 1.

23 Braunthal, *History of the International, 1864–1914*, p. 201.

24 Support for the establishment of a 'labour' party came from newer unions such as the Gas Workers, the Dock, Wharf, Riverside and General Labourers' Union, the Amalgamated Society of Engineers, and the Boot and Shoe Operatives.

25 *Trades Union Congress Annual Report*, 1899, pp. 64–6.

26 For information on the LRC, see Frank Bealey and Henry Pelling, *Labour and Politics, 1900–1906: A History of the Labour Representation Committee* (London: Macmillan, 1958).

27 *Report of the Inaugural Conference of the Labour Representation Committee*, (London: Labour Representation Committee, 1900), pp. 11–13.

28 *Ibid.*, p. 15.

29 Carl Brand, *The British Labour Party: A Short History* (Stanford, CA: Hoover Institution Press, revised edn 1974), p. 11.

30 Cole, *British Working Class Politics*, p. 169.

31 David Butler and Gareth Butler, *British Political Facts 1900–1985* (London: Macmillan, 6th edn, 1986), p. 224.

32 Pelling and Reid, *A Short History of the Labour Party*, p. 14.

33 The annual party conference is often referred to as 'Conference' by party members and officials, dropping the definite article and using a capital letter, but this study will usually refer to it as 'the conference' or 'the annual conference'.

34 *Keesing's Contemporary Archives*, vol. 12, 1959–60, p. 17744. See also Kenneth O. Morgan, *Keir Hardie: Radical and Socialist*, (London: Weidenfeld and Nicolson, 1975) p. 168.

35 *LPACR*, 1918, p. 15.

36 *LPACR*, 1918, appendix 1, p. 82, the Constitution of the Labour Party, section 3, clause 3.

37 *LPACR*, 1918, appendix 1, p. 83, the Constitution of the Labour Party, section 4, clauses 1 and 2.

38 Lewis Minkin, *Labour Party Conference: A Study in the Politics of Intra-Party Democracy* (Manchester: Manchester University Press, 1980), p. xii.

39 Stephen Lukes, *Power: A Radical View* (London: Macmillan, 1974).

40 *LPACR*, 1946, pp. 169–73 and 174.

41 Denis Healey, *The Time of My Life* (London: Michael Joseph, 1989), p. 75.

42 *LPACR*, 1946, p. 174.

43 Healey, *The Time of My Life*, p. 75.

44 Patrick Seyd, *The Rise and Fall of the Labour Left* (London: Macmillan, 1987), p. 7.
45 Healey, *The Time of My Life*, p. 75.
46 See for example, *Trades Union Congress Annual Report*, 1946, p. 469; *LPACR*, 1946, pp. 151–7.
47 Robert McKenzie, *British Political Parties: The Distribution of Power within the Conservative and Labour Parties* (London: Heinemann, 1955), p. 588.
48 *Ibid.*, p. 584.
49 See Maurice Duverger, *Political Parties: Their Organization and Activity in the Modern State*, 1st English language edn (London: Methuen, 1954); Angelo Panebianco, *Political Parties: Organization and Power* (Cambridge: Cambridge University Press, 1988).
50 Joseph Frankel, *British Foreign Policy 1945–1973* (Oxford: Oxford University Press, 1975), p. 33.
51 John Young, 'Foreign, defence and European affairs', in Brian Brivati and Tim Bale, eds, *New Labour in Power: Precedents and Prospects* (London: Routledge, 1997), p. 138.

Chapter 2

The main political influences on the development of the Labour Party's attitudes towards international affairs

The Labour Party was born out of domestic political discontent, and its policies – to a greater extent forged in opposition up until the 1940s – tended to reflect this. Because of these two factors, Labour's foreign policy reflected the party itself, the beliefs and standpoints of the various groups that came together to create it, and the dynamics between them, rather than necessarily the external world and experience and appraisal of international affairs. This issue will form a recurring theme throughout the next two chapters, which chart the early the years of Labour foreign policy, showing how Labour's foreign policy. It is worth briefly considering the main influences on, and groupings within, the Labour Party. This will, by necessity, be something of a cursory sketch, and it is worth remembering that conflicts over ideology and policy occurred within the different groupings almost as much as between them. Jupp points out that until 1918 the Labour Party was more of a movement than a party, 'in the sense of having little central discipline and being bound together by an agreement to accept all ideological positions critical of existing society and postulated on social change through political action. It had not orthodoxy, unlike the European social-democratic parties.'[1]

The main groupings within the Labour Party and their influence on Labour's world-view

As noted in the last chapter, when the LRC was set up in 1900 there were four main progenitors, each bringing their own influences on domestic and foreign policy: in no particular order of importance, the trade union movement, the ILP, the Fabian Society, and the SDF and various Marxist groups. In addition to these, a fifth grouping had a remarkable degree of influence over Labour's developing foreign policy, and this was composed of radical Liberals, epitomised by the members of the UDC. Each of these groups had its own particular influence over the way that foreign policy and international affairs were thought about. Each had their own particular analytical framework for understanding relations between states, and each their own way of responding to concrete situations. These different influences provided a rich source for ideas on international politics, but also produced impulses towards Labour's appropriate response to particular foreign policy issues that were sometimes antithetical to each other. This has added to the problems of developing a typology of the British Labour Party's foreign policy, while also explaining in part the depth of the some of the intra-party conflict on international affairs.

The first main group and influence within the Labour Party, the trade unionists, tended to have a more materialistic viewpoint than some of their political colleagues in that they were at times more aware of the tensions between aims, such as international working-class soli-darity, and the desire to protect British jobs; between anti-militarism and concern to protect the substantial British arms trade. The trade unions had a massive influence on the Labour Party's foreign policy in the first half of the century. This was because they had an international department that was sometimes more extensive than that of the Labour Party, because they were better financed than the Labour Party and because they had more international experience than the Labour Party. In particular, the British trade union movement already had a history of involvement in labour affairs overseas, and in the interna-tional trade union movement.[2] This was partly due to Britain having been the first highly industrialised nation, and partly due to Britain's position in the world with its extensive empire.

Historically, there had been two forms of international trade union organisation, both of which emerged around the turn of the twentieth century. First, there were the International Trade Secretariats (ITSs). These were transnational associations of unions in a given industry, which tended to focus their activities in areas directly related to their industrial sector. The second type of international trade union organi-sation consisted of federations of the national trade union centres of various countries such as the TUC in the UK and the American Federation of Labor (AFL) in the US.[3] While the ITSs tended to focus their activities on industry-specific questions, the federations had a more active political role. This was largely because the federations of national congresses tended to parallel the division of the labour movement into communist and non-communist camps. Before the Second World War, the two main federations were the International Federation of Trade Unions (IFTU), a non-communist federation consisting of some European centres and the AFL, and the communist Profintern, also known as the Red International of Labour Unions (RILU), which had been set up in the early 1920s. This organisation was in direct competition with the IFTU, and as the RILU affiliates were charged with the task of infiltrating and taking over their national trade union centres, great hostility existed between the two. At the end of the Second World War there was a doomed attempt to establish one international, the World Federation of Trade Unions (WFTU), but this split due to the developing hostilities of the Cold War and the enduring suspicion and inability to agree between the communist and non-communist unions.

Because of the important role of British trade union leaders in the international trade union movement, in the early years it was often they, rather than Labour Party politicians, who were the most experienced on the international stage. The union leaders tended to be critical of the intellectual wing of the party, and felt that they lacked real experience of dealing with matters at the international level. The man who represented the apogee of this viewpoint was Ernest Bevin. While it might have seemed remarkable that a trade union leader became the first Labour foreign secretary to operate within a majority Labour government, Bevin was highly experienced in the international arena. As with many of the union leaders in the first half of the century, Bevin was to the right of opinion within the Labour movement, and was instrumental in shifting the Labour Party from a position of pacifism to one of rearmament in the 1930s. The relationship of the trade union leadership being to the right of the party leadership on foreign and defence policy continued until the 1970s, when it was reversed.

The second of the main influences, the ILP, was founded at a conference in Bradford in 1893, where delegates included Ben Tillet, George Bernard Shaw, and Keir Hardie, and at which Eduard Bernstein of the German Social Democratic Party made an address. Ramsay MacDonald, in a short history of the ILP, described it as a product of the failure of liberalism to meet the new phase of conflict between capital and labour – where the struggle was no longer for political liberty but for economic enfranchisement – which challenged capitalism as a system.[4] Indeed: 'The socialism of the ILP was based partly on egalitarian and pacifist beliefs of Nonconformist religious origins.'[5] It believed strongly in international and working-class solidarity, and saw the British empire as exploitative. For the ILP, domestic and foreign policy were parts of a whole, with social reform at home requiring the projection of democratic ideals abroad. It was largely pacifist, believed in international co-operation, was against overt militarism and war, and believed that an end to secret diplomacy could mean an end to international conflict.[6] Both Kenneth O. Morgan and A. J. P. Taylor note that its leader, Keir Hardie, took an independent line on social questions from the moment he entered parliament in 1892, 'But he kept quiet about foreign affairs until driven to explosion by the Boer war'. This was 'lest he compromise his essential commitment to the cause of labour at home'.[7] Despite this, the ILP was influential over issues of foreign policy in the early years through the role played by its leaders Keir Hardie and Ramsey MacDonald. MacDonald visited South Africa in 1902 shortly after the end of the Boer War, writing of the devastation that he saw in a series of articles for the *Echo* and the *Leicester Pioneer*. Following his tour of Canada, Australia and New Zealand in 1906 he wrote a short book on *Labour and the Empire*.[8] Hardie visited India as part of his world tour of 1907, publishing his impressions of British rule in the ILP's journal, the *Labour Leader*, and then in collected form in 1909 as *India: Impressions and Suggestions*. His criticisms were widely read and raised awareness of the less positive aspects of British rule in India. Lenin wrote that 'the whole of the English bourgeois press raised a howl against the "rebel"'.[9] Ramsay MacDonald visited India in 1909, and published his findings as *The Awakening of India*, the following year. Morgan notes that these publications 'began the process of giving Labour a viable imperial and colonial policy, one which bore fruit in 1947.'[10] In 1912, MacDonald was part of a royal commission sent to investigate the Indian public services. Its findings were published in 1917, and he published his own book on *The Government of India* in 1919. These experiences led to the Labour Party giving an explicit commitment to freedom for India in its 1918 general election manifesto, which also said that Labour would 'extend to all subject peoples the right of self-determination within the British Commonwealth of Free Nations.'[11]

Ramsay MacDonald had a unique impact on the developing foreign policy of the Labour Party, as he was not only a leading member of the ILP, but was also a member of the SDF for a short period, was on the executive of the Fabian Society (he attended international conferences in that capacity) and was secretary of the Labour

Party from 1900 to 1911, and as such in charge of its organisational development. In 1906 he succeeded Philip Snowden as chairman of the ILP. He of course also became Labour's first Prime Minister and Foreign Secretary, and 'one of the central themes of MacDonald's career as prime minister and as leader of the Opposition is to be found in his concern for, and knowledge of, foreign policy.'[12] Both he and Hardie travelled widely and were closely acquainted with the socialist leaders on the continent.

The ILP was keenly involved in the Second International, and both Keir Hardie and Ramsay MacDonald attended its congresses, Hardie as an ILP delegate, MacDonald as delegate for the Fabian Society and then for the LRC/Labour Party.[13] Here they joined in with their French and German comrades in attacking Tsarist Russia, one issue which united the European socialists. MacDonald was bitterly opposed to the British government's friendship with Russia, and protested against the King's visit to Reval in June 1908.[14] Hardie also vociferously condemned it, arguing that 'For the King of Great Britain to pay an official visit to the Czar of Russia was to condone the atrocities for which the Czar's Government, and the Czar personally, must be held responsible.'[15] He also declared at the 1912 Labour Party Conference that 'if he was called upon to choose between the autocracy of Russia and the present German Government he would most unhesitatingly cast his lot on the side of Germany as against Russia.'[16] The Second International provided MacDonald and Hardie with an opportunity to make more strenuous denouncements of foreign policy than they tended to do at home, agreeing with the continental Marxists that capitalism was the cause of war, and international socialism the only alternative. However, the Second International rejected revolutionary means, and had a rule that only socialist parties and trade unions favouring parliamentary action should be admitted to its ranks.[17] The Second International also provided ILP delegates with the opportunity to interact with their continental counterparts, and both men struck up friendships with many leading socialists, such as Jaurès in France and Eduard Bernstein and August Bebel of the German Social Democrats. In particular at this time, Hardie attempted to work against the rising tide of militarism and anti-German sentiment in the UK by strengthening links between the British Labour Party and the German Social Democrats through the Second International. MacDonald believed that the key to peace was through joining forces with the German Social Democrats, who were opposed to the growing German militarism, and argued that one of the primary aims of British foreign policy should be to 'cultivate their friendship, and to help them in their struggle to democratize Germany.'[18] Both men differentiated between the German government and the German public. A recurring theme for Ramsay MacDonald was the need to educate the public about foreign policy in order to curb government's tendency towards secret diplomacy and militarism.

The third influence on the fledgling Labour Party was its intellectual wing, epitomised by the Fabian Society, which had been founded in January 1884.[19] Its most prominent members in its early years included George Bernard Shaw, Annie Besant, and Sidney Webb, who had joined in 1885 while working as a clerk in the Colonial Office. The Fabians initially contained both an anarchist wing and a wing that supported reform through constitutional means. In 1886 they voted to follow the parliamentary route, rejecting anarchism and revolution, and thus embraced a form of socialism that had much in common with French 'Possibilism', a type of Marxism which believed in gradual parliamentary reform.[20]

Margaret Cole described Fabian thinking as being characterised by eclecticism, taking ideas from many thinkers including Marx, John Stuart Mill, and De Tocqueville; by a belief in democracy and parliamentary reform as the political agent of socialism, rather than revolution and class war; and gradualism.[21] Sidney Webb wrote in the first collection of Fabian essays that,

> All students of society who are abreast of their time, Socialists as well as Individualists, realize that important organic changes can only be (1) democratic, and thus acceptable to a majority of the people, and prepared for in the minds of all; (2) gradual, and thus causing no dislocation, however rapid may be the rate of progress; (3) not regarded as immoral by the mass of the people, and thus not subjectively demoralizing to them; and (4) in this country at any rate, constitutional and peaceful.[22]

The Fabians did not have strong links with the trade unions, and were predominantly middle-class, London-based, and somewhat exclusive, if not elitist. For them, the main role for the working class was in terms of electing representatives who could then act as a check on the running of the state by expert administrators from the civil service. Thus, 'Fascinated by the prevailing doctrines of Positivism, with its belief in a gradual evolution of a harmonious and well-ordered society guided by an educated elite, Webb's Civil Service background reinforced his collectivist belief that individuals must subordinate themselves to the common good.'[23] The Fabians, while having links with the ILP, were initially committed to working through the reformist wing of the Liberal Party, rather than calling for the establishment of a new party. Indeed, Beatrice Webb, who in partnership with her husband Sidney came to have considerable influence within the Fabians, not least through their role in establishing the London School of Economics in 1895, proposed a policy of 'permeation.' This involved converting to Fabian socialism, or at least to parts of the immediate Fabian programme, people in positions of influence, whether as politicians or as advisors.[24] Such people could remain members of whatever party they wished, as long as they were convinced of the superiority of the Fabians' proposals – a sort of very English Trotskyite entryism in reverse.

Of all the groups on the left in Britain at this time, the Fabian Society were the least interested in foreign policy and international affairs. Issues of war and peace were not of immediate concern to them, and they had few links with overseas socialist organisations, apart from sending delegates to the Second International. The one issue that did impinge on their consciousness was British imperialism, and this was only because it became impossible not to discuss it once the Boer War had broken out. As will be demonstrated below, the Fabians were divided over the Boer War, to the extent that they declined to even make a public statement on it. Instead, in October 1900 they published a manifesto intended to clarify their views on imperialism, called *Fabianism and the Empire*, but this document was rather ambivalent. They accepted as 'a matter of fact' that the world was being divided up amongst the Great Powers, and took 'the problem before us' as being how this could be 'ordered'. They implied that they supported imperialism, as long as it was carried out by *civilised* countries, such as Switzerland, rather than uncivilised countries, such as Russia. Free trade was seen as a civilising influence across the globe, and states had a right to trade, which involved 'a right to insist upon a settled government which can keep the peace and enforce agreements.' Where a 'native government' could not be relied upon to do this, as in China, then 'the foreign trading power must set one up'. They were, however, against 'pure piratical conquests of weaker states.'[25] Thus, they 'not only recognized that the world was being divided up amongst the Imperialist powers, but in a general way they approved and justified the tendency. They seem to have been of the opinion that the states of Western Europe could and would benefit "less developed" communities by taking over or ruling them, at least for a while.'[26] Foote notes that 'The elitism which came so naturally to the Fabian leaders went hand-in-hand with a commitment to a socialist Empire.'[27] It was proclaimed that, 'In the Socialist view, the guardianship of the non-Adult races of the world must be undertaken as a corporate duty by the Eight Great Powers, either jointly or separately.'[28]

Following their first foray into imperialism, the Fabians wrote more widely about the British empire, and the need for successful and productive management by Britain. They provided a Fabian gradualist ideology of reform, and the Fabian Colonial Research Bureau had a particular impact on the party's plans for imperial reform post-1945.[29] Much more cautious in their assessment of the chances of international working-class solidarity than some of the other component parts of British socialism, they tended not to be concerned about any possible conflict between class interest and national interest. The one issue where they did overcome their particular British perspective on world politics was in their opinion of the Soviet Union. Many of the high-profile Fabians supported strong relations with the Soviet Union, discovering much in their fact-finding missions to recommend about Soviet planning.

The fourth main influence on, and grouping within, the Labour Party were the Marxists. Many of the people who joined the party had a basic Marxist belief in terms of capitalism being an exploitative class mode of production, but did not necessarily see Marxism as a political ideology that should determine policy. The main Marxist grouping at the time in Britain, the SDF, was involved in the establishment of the LRC in 1900, and key future Labour Party leaders such Ramsay MacDonald, George Lansbury and Herbert Morrison were influenced by their time spent as SDF members.[30] Under the autocratic leadership of Henry Mayers Hyndman, the SDF had a 'penchant to split on doctrinal grounds',[31] and many prominent figures on the British left tended to have only a short stay in the organisation. The SDF disaffiliated from the LRC in August 1901 because it would not accept the SDF doctrine of class war.[32] The SDF had moved from a position of supporting parliamentary reform at its establishment in 1884, to a semi-revolutionary attitude by 1888, back again to reform by 1890, and then to supporting a form of revolution rather than peaceful change by 1900. The SDF argued that war and conflict was brought about by the capitalist system, and that this was to be resisted through the means of a general strike, or even revolution. Hyndman had been greatly influenced by Marx's *Capital*, to the extent that Marx felt that Hyndman had plagiarised him in his work, *The Text-book of Democracy: England for All*.[33] However, Hyndman was also a very British Marxist,

being seen by many on his contemporaries as 'jingoistic', and tending
to support an independent nationalism rather than any creed of international working-class solidarity. He strongly supported the British
empire while at the same time advocating Indian self-government, and
published many articles, books and pamphlets criticising British rule
there.[34] Hyndman also supported the campaigned for Irish Home
Rule. He was unusual on the left in Britain in that he had started off
as a Conservative radical and was strongly anti-Liberal. The SDF
renamed itself the Social Democratic Party in October 1907, and then
formed the largest section of a newly created British Socialist Party in
1911, which included some rebels from the ILP and representatives of
other socialist societies.[35] The British Socialist Party split during the
First World War, when the more nationalistic faction led by Hyndman
broke away to form the National Socialist Party. The internationalist
section of the British Socialist Party opposed the war and, in 1920,
became one of the elements in the British Communist Party.[36] While
the SDF and then the British Socialist Party remained relatively small
organisations, Marxism and Marxists to the left of the main political
Labour Party grouping continued to have a massive impact on it. This
was not only through their involvement in the trade unions and party
as, alienated by Hyndman and the SDF they sought to build the
Labour Party into a Marxist party with its basis in the mass labour
movement, but also because of their impact on the left as it sought to
delineate itself as distinct from the far or hard left inhabited by the
Trotskyite and communist groupings.

The fifth grouping, not involved in the actual creation of the
Labour Party as such, but relevant for its influence upon Labour
foreign policy, is the Liberals.[37] While the Labour Party led to the
demise of the Liberals, the Liberals in turn had a much greater impact
on the party than tended to be appreciated at the time. There was a
strong radical tradition within the Liberals, particularly on the issue of
foreign policy and international peace, which is wonderfully outlined
in A. J. P. Taylor's book *The Trouble Makers*. The radical Liberals,
working within the Parliamentary system at the end of the nineteenth
century, argued against secret diplomacy with its disregard for any
form of popular control of foreign policy, proposing instead that
treaties should be subjected to Parliamentary ratification before being
signed. They tended to see foreign policy as 'a conspiracy run by the
old order' that 'would disappear with the triumph of Radicalism'.
However, when in power the Liberals tended to vote to increase
the defence estimates and to intervene overseas, and so 'Imperialism

was a product of Radical enthusiasm', as well as being bitterly critiqued by it.[38]

In August 1914, following the outbreak of the First World War, Ramsey MacDonald joined with radical Liberals E. D. Morel, Norman Angell, Charles Trevelyan and Arthur Ponsonby, to establish the UDC.[39] The UDC was particularly important during the First World War and the inter-war period for its role in shaping Labour's foreign policy. Morel, for example, was editor of the influential journal *Foreign Affairs*. His pamphlet, *Morocco in Diplomacy*, contained the secret clauses of the Anglo-French *entente*, documents that revealed the secret diplomacy at the heart of foreign policy. A. J. P. Taylor points out that this pamphlet 'had an influence without parallel.'[40] Ramsay MacDonald said of it: 'From that time I suspected our diplomacy, and ceased to believe the assurances given by Ministers in parliament or out of it.'[41]

The UDC joined the Labour Party, but members such as E. D. Morel and Arthur Ponsonby had entered the party 'mainly because it gave a hearing to their ideas on foreign policy. Their private attitude toward the party appeared frequently to be conditioned by a conviction of their own superiority to rank and file and leaders alike.'[42] For instance, Morel, while trying to explain the nature of the British Labour Party to Count Max Montgelas, wrote that the British Labour Party 'has never contained among its leaders intellectuals of even second-rate or third-rate type ... The British Labour Party has never thought internationally; has never been developed intellectually.' Though he claimed that 'In the last six years we have acquired a prodigious moral influence upon this vast mass [of ignorance].'[43] These radical Liberals believed in the extension of national law to the international arena and the operation of international organisations, with many of them calling for a League of Nations. Foreign policy should not be pursued by individual states, aiming at creating alliances for the purpose of maintaining a balance of power, but through a supranational body with the capability of securing international agreements. It was argued in the House of Commons by Lees-Smith during a discussion on German peace proposals that 'I believe security can only be obtained by a scheme by which the nations of Europe and outside agree together that all will guarantee each and each will guarantee all ... we shall achieve the purposes of this War not according to whether or not we obtain a military decision, but according to whether or not there is created out of it a league of nations' with 'an absolute and decisive veto upon any mere aggression'. This was not Utopian, for

'We are standing upon the threshold of a new order of the world ... If Christian Europe does not now make up its mind to make an end of war, I do not see how civilisation as we have known it can go on.'[44] This was to be realised more fully by the United Nations (UN), rather than the settlements following the First World War. Members of the UDC, such as Hobson, Brailsford and Woolf, published detailed schemes for a League of Nations. However, not all the UDC agreed on the need for such a League: 'Morel ignored the agitation for a League. Ramsay MacDonald did more: he dissented from it. The League, in his own favourite word, was "quackery".'[45] For them, disarmament, open diplomacy and the democratisation of foreign policy were more important.

The UDC also had a great impact in terms of expressing and generalising pacifism, though their belief in pacifism was more complex than often presented. Norman Angell, for instance, railed against his critics who accused him of arguing in *The Great Illusion* that war was impossible; rather, he had argued that a modern nation cannot profit by conquest, 'the argument is *not* that war is impossible, but that it is futile.'[46] These issues are explored in more depth below. Many in the UDC supported Britain's role in the First World War, while denouncing the war itself.

Each of these five main influences had their own particular impact on the development of Labour's foreign policy. The radical Liberals obviously contributed greatly to Labour's liberal internationalism, while the Marxists, the trade unions and the ILP each contributed to Labour's socialist internationalism. The Fabians provided in part the rationalist underpinning of Labour's views on international relations, while the ILP provided the impulse towards common fellowship with other states. The ILP and the radical Liberals reinforced each other in their beliefs that militarism and secret diplomacy leads to war. Some of the radical Liberals influenced the Marxist perspective on the economic basis of inter-capitalist rivalry. These different contributing streams to Labour's foreign policy also often pulled in opposing directions. Nothing revealed this more than the split over attitudes towards pacifism and war, brought to a head with the outbreak of the First World War in 1914, but it also evident in the other major debates of the time, in particular over the Boer War and imperialism. What was agreed, however, by all the contributing groups, was that foreign policy could not be viewed in isolation, as domestic and international policies were inter-related and also because foreign policy was affected by economic relations as well as political ones.

The Boer War

The Boer War is significant because it raised the profile of foreign policy within the Labour Party from the very start of its organisational life. At the first annual conference of the LRC on Friday 1 February 1901, a resolution on the Boer War forwarded by the ILP was unanimously agreed to. 'This Congress, believing the harrowing war in South Africa to be mainly due to the corrupt agitation of the Transvaal mineowners, having for its object the acquisition of monopolies and a cheap supply of coloured and European labour', urges the government to seek the termination of hostilities and arbitration in South Africa.[47] Keir Hardie argued that 'The [Boer] war is a capitalist war. The British merchant hopes to secure markets for his goods, the investor an outlet for his capital, the speculator more fools out of whom to make money, and the mining companies cheaper labour and increased dividends.'[48] Hardie 'became passionately absorbed by the Boer War', denouncing the war in the *Labour Leader* between 1899 and 1902.[49] He drew on both Marxist explanations of the Boer War as the result of the inevitable decay of monopoly capitalism, and radical explanations of the war as the result of a small band of gold speculators. He became a member of the Stop-the-War committee, along with Liberals such as Lloyd George. However, some of the Fabians endorsed the British position on the war. 'They supported war with the Boer republics as a means of achieving "national efficiency" at home and a secure imperial relationship overseas.'[50] When it was suggested that they make a statement condemning the war, the leadership of the society was divided. Ramsay MacDonald and sixteen other members of the Fabian Society resigned in protest when the Fabians voted by 259 votes to 217 against supporting the issuing of a such a statement.[51] This was the most serious division to occur in the Society, and had an impact on the LRC, where, overall, the Boer war roused much passion:

> The socialists were divided; the Fabians were inclined to support it, but the ILP and the SDF came out on the side of the 'pro-Boers' and incurred great unpopularity. MacDonald and Hardie, in deploring the attack of a large nation on a small, were hardly to be distinguished from the Liberal Radicals. With the latter they accepted the Marxist analysis of the SDF – the war had been brought about by the machinations of international armament rings sponsored by international financiers.

Indeed, 'In general the episode revealed many naiveties in the Labour Party's approach to foreign affairs.'[52]

The Boer War also raised the profile of foreign policy and war more generally within the fledgling Labour Party. It highlighted all that was wrong with British imperialism, and became an argument against it, as the war appeared to be 'contrary to all our ideals of national political justice'.[53] While during its first year 'critics of the war were a distinct minority and ready targets for abuse and persecution', as information about Kitchener's concentration camps filtered through, the 'anti-war critics gained a new respectability'.[54] Before the Boer War the imperialists had appeared to win the moral argument over British imperialism, claiming that they brought about the abolition of slavery and the creation of schools, railways and health services to the colonies. The Boer War turned the tables of morality against the imperialists, as their claim to be fighting for the sake of the native peoples in South Africa 'was no good'.[55] Campbell-Bannerman's attack on the 'methods of barbarism' in fact 'switched the argument from the causes of the war to the way in which it was being conducted.' The 'muddles and disappointments' of the war 'discredited not only the competence, but also the principles, of those who had run it.'[56]

Furthermore, the Boer War raised questions that would later cause so many divisions at the outbreak of the First World War, such as the legitimate role of a political party at odds with government policy during times of conflict. A. J. P. Taylor argued that these issues receded following the end of the Boer War, and the overall domestic focus of the fledgling party is evident in their annual congress reports and election manifestos in terms of how little is said on foreign affairs. However, the early manifestos were themselves remarkably short, so the small amount of attention given in them to foreign policy does not necessarily indicate a lack of interest.[57] The annual conference reports do contain a significant number of resolutions on international affairs, suggesting that the issues of war, militarism and imperialism had not receded. For example, the party held a special party conference on disarmament at Leicester in 1911, and attended annual congresses of the Peace Association.[58] At the 1911 annual conference a proposal to inquire into 'the utility of the strike' was defeated, but was passed the following year when Bruce Glasier of the ILP moved a resolution that stated that Conference 'expresses its approval of the proposal to investigate and report on whether and how far a stoppage or work, either partial or general, in countries about to engage in war would be effective in preventing an outbreak of hostilities'.[59] The issue of a general strike in response to the outbreak of war was remitted to the International Socialist Bureau, with Keir Hardie and Arthur

Henderson writing to ask each affiliated organisation their views on the issue, in particular whether they were 'in favour of the organised Working Class Movements of all countries being asked to come to a mutual agreement whereby in the event of war being threatened between any two or more countries, the workers of those countries would hold themselves prepared to try to prevent it by a mutual and simultaneous stoppage of work in the countries affected'.[60] While little came of the inquiry, with the outbreak of the First World War inter-rupting the International's efforts to garner support for a general strike, in Britain the issue was returned to at Labour's annual confer-ences in the 1920s.

The Labour Party and the trade unions became increasingly involved in international affairs in the years leading up to 1914, as evinced by the conferences and meetings they attended and the increasing volume of resolutions and writings on international affairs. Militarism and rearmament involved trade unionists in particular on two levels. On the one hand, militarism and a concomitant focus on military strength was something to be deplored as a signal of an increase in hostilities between countries. On the other hand, rearma-ment and an arms race provided jobs and a steady wage. Hence, 'there was pressure from the dockyard towns, and to a less extent from the ports, against any opposition which might reduce the number of jobs.'[61] This tension has existed throughout the twentieth century. However, it has been argued by some that it was not until the outbreak of the First World War that the Labour Party really took seriously ques-tions of foreign policy. Attlee noted that 'The Party ... had no real constructive foreign policy, but shared the views which were traditional in radical circles.'[62] The lack of a 'constructive foreign policy' reflected the problems of pulling together the diverse influences on Labour's foreign policy rather than a lack of interest in it. Many in the party did pay attention to foreign affairs, particularly those from the ILP. At the 1912 annual conference, Keir Hardie moved a resolution on foreign policy, stating 'That this Congress, believing the anti-German policy pursued in the name of the British Government by Sir Edward Grey to be a cause of increasing armaments, international ill-will, and the betrayal of oppressed nationalities, protests in the strongest terms against it.' This diplomacy had led the government 'to risk war with Germany in the interests of French financiers over Morocco, to condone the Italian outrage in Tripoli, the Russian theft in Mongolia, and, above all, to join hands with Russia in making an assault on the national independence and freedom of Persia.' This resolution was passed unanimously. The next resolution was forwarded by J. Bruce Glasier of the ILP:

> That this Conference, realising the menace to social progress and working-class welfare involved in War, and the terrible suffering, sacrifice of life, and waste of material resources which it involves, hereby, as in previous years, expresses itself against the growing burden of armaments and protests against Militarism and Compulsory Military Service in all its forms; and declares that national disputes should be settled by arbitration ...[63]

This resolution caused concern to those in the armament industry, who were concerned about the 130,000 workers directly employed in armaments, but was unanimously carried.[64] These statements, forming Labour Party policy, were unequivocal on their stance on foreign policy, and were strongly supported by the party despite its still disparate strands.

Imperialism

One of the major issues discussed by those on the left at the beginning of the twentieth century was that of imperialism. Ramsay MacDonald and Keir Hardie had long spoken against imperialism, and MacDonald had argued that 'Further extensions of the Empire are only the grab-bings [sic] of millionaires on the hunt.'[65] At the first annual conference in 1901, a resolution was forwarded by the Independent Labour Party

> That, inasmuch as modern Imperialism with its attendant militarism is a reversion to one of the worst phases of barbarism, is inimical to social reform and disastrous to trade and commerce, a fruitful cause of war, destructive of freedom, fraught with menace to representative institutions at home and abroad, and must end in the destruction of democracy, this Congress desires most earnestly to impress upon the working class the urgent need there is for combating this dangerous and barbaric development in all its manifestations.[66]

Thus, imperialism was seen as a danger to democracy within Britain as well as leading to war between states.

Influenced by the experience of the Boer War, J. A. Hobson, a radical Liberal economist who later joined the Labour Party, wrote what was to become a major text, *Imperialism: A Study*, which appeared in 1902. He argued that imperialism was not caused by selfish individuals, or by capitalists seeking raw materials or markets, but that it was economically determined by under-consumption. Hobson's theory of under-consumption argued that capitalists had to invest profits abroad, to export capital, and that this caused imperialism. 'The economic root of Imperialism is the desire of strong organized industrial and financial interests to secure and develop at the public expense and by the public force private markets for their surplus goods and their surplus capital. War, militarism, and a "spirited foreign policy" are the necessary means to this end.'[67] Furthermore, 'Imperialism makes for war and for militarism, and has brought a great and limitless increase of expenditure of national resources upon armaments. It has impaired the independence of every nation which has yielded to its false glamour.'[68] Indeed, according to Hobson, 'Imperialism is a depraved choice of national life, imposed by self-seeking interests which appeal to the lusts of quantitative acquisitiveness and of forceful domination surviving in a nation from early centuries of animal struggle for existence.'[69] Not only did he provide an economic explanation for foreign policy, but he also provided an explanation for the relationship between the working class and imperialism. Imperialism not only benefited financial and industrial interests, but also appealed to those classes of workers in trades particularly dependent on government employment or contracts, such as shipbuilding, car and aeroplane manufacturing, and the arms trade.[70] However, in terms of Hobson's methodology, Taylor notes that 'Hobson put the growth of external investments in one column of the figures, the increase of colonial territories in another; and, since they were both going up, argued that the caused the other. The conclusion may have been faulty. Nevertheless its political influence was enormous.' It provided an explanation for international relations and the causes of war for both Labour and the radical Liberals, lending them 'a common ideology and rhetoric',[71] as well as impacting on the Marxist understanding of international conflict through the subsequent study by Lenin.

Lenin used Hobson's work as the basis for his study of imperialism, first published in 1917, which became the starting point for any Marxists' understanding of international relations. Lenin noted that in Britain, the 'tendency of imperialism to divide the workers, to encourage opportunism among them and to cause temporary decay in the working class movement', had revealed itself in the middle of the nineteenth century, earlier than in other countries, because of its vast colonial possessions and its monopolist position in the world market.[72] For Lenin, imperialism was the monopoly stage of capitalism, where the export of finance capital (the combination of bank and industrial capital) led to the formation of international capitalist monopolies which had divided the world among themselves.[73] The territorial division of the whole world among the greatest capitalist power was now completed, and this lead to tension and conflict between them. This viewpoint strongly reflected the Marxist reaction to the First World War, which had been seen as a conflict between competing imperialist powers. The more underlying influence of this economic perspective of imperialism, international relations and conflict, however, was the perspective that politics and economics were intimately linked and that it was not possible to separate out the two. This tied in with Norman Angell's work, *The Great Illusion*, though this claimed to destroy the economic argument for war. He explained that the motivation for the international rivalry in armaments was due to the view that military and political power gave a nation commercial advantage, and that it was to a state's economic advantage to subjugate a weaker state. This, Angell argued, was an optical illusion, for it is an impossibility for one nation to enrich itself by subjugating another.[74] While war was entered into for economic reasons, the victor was left the poorer, and so war was economically futile.[75] Modernisation was leading to the disappearance of state rivalry, but 'so long as nations believe that in some way the military and political subjugation of others will bring with it a tangible material advantage to the conqueror, we all do, in fact, stand in danger from such aggression.' The real guarantee of the good behaviour of one state to another 'is the elaborate interdependence which, not only in the economic sense, but in every sense, makes an unwarrantable aggression of one State upon another react upon the interests of the aggressor.'[76]

H. N. Brailsford's *The War of Steel and Gold* applied Hobson's 1902 theory of imperialism, that is, the search for profitable investment overseas, to the European powers. He critiqued the current faith in a balance of power, for 'The balance is a metaphor of venerable hypocrisy which serves only to disguise the perennial struggle for power and predominance. When a statesman talks of a balance, he means a balance favourable to himself.' He argued that the leaders of finance capitalism controlled the policy of their respective states, and that 'It is an economic motive which underlies the struggle for a balance of power.'[77] The doctrine of continuity in foreign policy in Britain meant that there was little chance of change, and 'whichever party is in power, the Foreign Secretary will always be an Imperialist.' However, he thought that war between the European powers was

unlikely, as 'In Europe, the epoch of conquest is over, and ... the frontiers of our modern national states are finally drawn.'[78] This book was
published in May 1914, and so he was proved wrong on this point, but
it was sufficiently popular that a second edition was printed in
December 1914 and a third in June 1915, in which he argued that the
Great War demonstrated that the system of alliances had to be replaced
with an international organisation, and laid out a 'rough tentative
sketch' of the constitution of a League of Peace, 'which might direct
its united forces against any Power which breaks the harmony of
Europe.'[79]

This chapter has demonstrated the impact that the different influences on the Labour Party had on its developing foreign policy. The
ILP, the trade union movement, the SDF and various Marxist groups,
the Fabian Society and the radical Liberals, each had their own particular influence over the way that foreign policy and international affairs
was thought about. Each had their own particular analytical framework
for understanding relations between states, and each their own way of
responding to concrete situations. These different influences provided
a rich source for ideas on international politics, but also produced
impulses towards Labour's appropriate response to particular foreign
policy issues that were sometimes antithetical to each other. This
demonstrates the problems of attempting to generalise about the
nature of Labour's foreign policy from its very beginnings in 1900,
while also explaining in part the depth of some of the intra-party
conflict on international affairs. These conflicts are examined in more
depth in the following chapters, starting with an assessment of
Labour's response to the First World War.

Notes

1 James Jupp, *The Radical Left in Britain, 1931–1941* (London: Frank
   Cass, 1982), p. 18.
2 For general information on the international trade union movement, see
   Gary Busch, *The Political Role of International Trade Unions* (London:
   Macmillan, 1983); Robert Cox, 'Labour and transnational relations',
   special issue of *International Organization*, 25:3 (1971), 554–84; Lewis
   Lorwin, *The International Labor Movement: History, Policies, Outlook*
   (New York: Harper, 1953); John Windmuller, *American Labor and the
   International Labor Movement, 1940–1953* (Ithaca, NY: Cornell
   University Press, 1954), and Windmuller, *The International Trade
   Union Movement* (Deventer: Kluwer, 1980).
3 In 1945, the AFL was the larger of the two trade union national centres

in the US, the other being the more recently established Congress of Industrial Organizations (CIO). These were rivals until the mid-1950s when they merged. See, for example, Windmuller, *The International Trade Union Movement*.

4 J. Ramsay MacDonald, *The History of the ILP* (London: ILP, 1921), pp. 5 and 6, held in the University of Leeds Library, Brotherton Collection, Mattison, LAB.

5 Jupp, *The Radical Left in Britain*, p. 17.

6 An excellent overview of the ILP is provided in Robert Dowse, *Left in the Centre: The Independent Labour Party 1893–1940* (London: Longmans, 1966).

7 A. J. P. Taylor, *The Trouble Makers: Dissent Over Foreign Policy 1792–1939* (London: Hamish Hamilton, 1957), p. 104.

8 J. Ramsay MacDonald, *Labour and the Empire* (London: George Allen, 1907). See David Marquand, *Ramsay MacDonald* (London: Jonathan Cape, 1977), pp. 76–8 and 100.

9 V. I. Lenin, *British Labour and British Imperialism: A Compilation of Writings by Lenin on Britain* (London: Lawrence and Wishart, 1969), p. 52.

10 Kenneth O. Morgan, *Keir Hardie: Radical and Socialist* (London: Weidenfeld and Nicolson, 1975), p. 195. For MacDonald's views on the Empire, see Bernard Porter, *Critics of Empire: British Radical Attitudes to Colonialism in Africa 1895–1914* (London: Macmillan, 1968).

11 F. W. S. Craig, ed. and comp., *British General Election Manifestos 1900–1974* (London: Macmillan, rev. and enlarged edn, 1975), p. 31.

12 David Marquand, *Ramsay MacDonald* (London: Jonathan Cape, 1977) p. 57.

13 At the 1896 London Congress, Hardie and Tom Mann voted in favour of seating the anarchist delegations, MacDonald voted against, having 'a deep loathing for anarchism as a political movement', Marquand, *Ramsay MacDonald*, p. 60.

14 Marquand, *Ramsay MacDonald*, p. 165. There is correspondence regarding MacDonald's protests over the King's visit to the Tsar of Russia in *Labour Leader* in the Public Records Office, Kew, Ramsay MacDonald Papers, 30/69/1417, folios 16–22.

15 *House of Commons Debates* (hereafter *H.C. Deb.*), 4th series, vol. 190, col. 253, 4 June 1908.

16 *Labour Party Annual Conference Report* (hereafter *LPACR*), 1912, p. 98.

17 Lorwin, *The International Labour Movement*, p. 21.

18 Marquand, *Ramsay MacDonald*, pp. 164–5; Morgan, Keir Hardie, pp. 181–2. See also Stefan Berger, *The British Labour Party and the German Social Democrats* (Oxford: Oxford University Press, 1994).

19 For a history of the Fabian Society, see books listed below, and Edward Reynolds Pease, *The History of the Fabian Society* (London: Fabian Society, 1916); G. D. H. Cole, *Fabian Socialism* (London: George Allen and Unwin, 1943).

20 Alan McBriar, *Fabian Socialism and English Politics, 1884–1918* (Cambridge: Cambridge University Press, 1962), p. 21.

21 Margaret Cole, *The Story of Fabian Socialism* (London: Heinemann, 1961), pp. 27–30.

22 G. Bernard Shaw, *et al.*, *Fabian Essays in Socialism* (London: Walter Scott, 1889), pp. 34–5.

23 Geoffrey Foote, *The Labour Party's Political Thought* (New York: St Martin's Press, 3rd edn, 1997), p. 26.

24 Cole, *Story of Fabian Socialism*, p. 85.

25 G. Bernard Shaw, ed., *Fabianism and the Empire: A Manifesto by the Fabian Society* (London: Fabian Society, 1900), pp. 3 and 44–6, held in the University of Leeds Library, Brotherton Collection, Mattison, FAB.

26 McBriar, *Fabian Socialism and English Politics*, p. 127.

27 Foote, *The Labour Party's Political Thought*, p. 31.

28 *New Statesman*, 2 August 1913, p. 525, cited in *ibid*.

29 See Partha Sarathi Gupta, 'Imperialism and the Labour government', in Jay Winter, ed., *The Working Class in Modern British History* (Cambridge: Cambridge University Press, 1983), p. 123; Kenneth O. Morgan, *Labour in Power 1945–1951* (Oxford: Oxford University Press, 1985), pp. 189 and 205.

30 Foote, *The Labour Party's Political Thought*, p. 20. See also Stanley Pierson, *Marxism and the Origins of British Socialism: The Struggle for a New Consciousness* (Ithaca: Cornell University Press, 1973), for information on this.

31 Dowse, *Left in the Centre*, p. 2.

32 See H. M. Hyndman, *The Record of an Adventurous Life* (London: Macmillan, 1911); and *Further Reminiscences* (London: Macmillan, 1912).

33 Chushichi Tsuzuki, *H. M. Hyndman and British Socialism*, edited by Henry Pelling (Oxford: Oxford University Press, 1961), p. 40.

34 For example, *The Bankruptcy of India* (London: Swann Sonnenschein, 1886); *The Unrest in India: Verbatim Report of the Speech delivered on 12th May 1907* (London: Twentieth Century Press, 1907); *The Emancipation of India* (London: Twentieth Century Press, 1911).

35 On the creation of the British Socialist Party, see Tsuzuki, *H. M. Hyndman and British Socialism*, pp. 173–8.

36 Frank Bealey, ed., *The Social and Political Thought of the British Labour Party* (London: Weidenfeld and Nicolson, 1970), p. 4.

37 On the influx of radical Liberals to the Labour Party, see Catherine Ann Cline, *Recruits to Labour. The British Labour Party, 1914–1931* (Syracuse, NY: Syracuse University Press, 1963).

38 Taylor, *The Trouble Makers*, pp. 33 and 90.

39 The decision to establish the UDC was taken at a dinner party. See Marquand, *Ramsay MacDonald*, p. 171. See also Marvin Swartz, *The Union of Democratic Control in British Politics During the First World War* (Oxford: Clarendon Press, 1971). Morel became the Secretary of the UDC.

40 Taylor, *The Trouble Makers*, p. 120.

41 Cited in *ibid*.

42 Henry Winkler, 'The emergence of a Labor foreign policy in Great Britain, 1918–1929', *Journal of Modern History*, 28:3 (1956), 249.

43 British Library of Political and Economic Science, London School of Economics, E. D. Morel papers, F8/112/57, letter from Morel to Count Max Montgelas, 24 May 1921.

44 *H.C. Deb.*, 5th series, vol. 88, cols 1727–30, 21 December 1916.

45 Taylor, *The Trouble Makers*, p. 145.

46 Norman Angell, *Foreign Policy and our Daily Bread* (London: Collins, 1925), p. 157.

47 *Report of the First Annual Conference of the Labour Representation Committee*, 1901, pp. 13 and 20.

48 William Stewart, *J. Keir Hardie: A Biography* (London: Cassell, 1921), p. 151.

49 Morgan, *Keir Hardie*, p. 104.

50 *Ibid.*

51 For accounts of this, see Cole, *Story of Fabian Socialism*, pp. 98–101; McBriar, *Fabian Socialism and English Politics*, pp. 120–5; Marquand, *Ramsay MacDonald*, p. 66.

52 Bealey, *Social and Political Thought of the British Labour Party*, p. 11.

53 *Report of the First Annual Conference of the Labour Representation Committee*, 1901, p. 20.

54 Morgan, *Keir Hardie*, p. 105.

55 Taylor, *The Trouble Makers*, p. 107.

56 *Ibid.*, p. 109.

57 The 1900 Labour manifesto called for the 'Abolition of the Standing Army, and the Establishment of a Citizen Force. The People to decide on Peace and War.' The 1906 general election manifesto stated that 'Wars are fought to make the rich richer; and school children are still neglected.' Both manifestos were extremely short, consisting of a list of points. See Craig, *British General Election Manifestos 1900–1974*, pp. 3–4 and 9–10. See also Iain Dale, ed., *Labour Party General Election Manifestos* (London: Routledge, 2000).

58 *LPACR*, 1912, p. 10; *LPACR*, 1913, p. 20.

59 *LPACR*, 1912, p. 101.

60 *LPACR*, 1913, pp. 123–4. They also said that, 'War with all its horrors is always inimical to the interests of the working class, and is always in these days undertaken for the benefit of the financial and propertied classes.' The Boer War was given as a recent example of this.

61 Bealey, *Social and Political Thought of the British Labour Party*, p. 11.

62 Clement Attlee, *The Labour Party in Perspective* (London: Victor Gollancz, 1937), p. 200.

63 *LPACR*, 1912, pp. 98–9.

64 *Ibid.*, p. 100.

65 Marquand, *Ramsay MacDonald*, p. 65, citing *ILP News* (January 1898).

66 *Report of the First Annual Conference of the Labour Representation Committee*, 1901, p. 20.

67 J. A. Hobson, *Imperialism: A Study* (London: George Allen and Unwin, 3rd rev. and reset edn, 1938), p. 106.

68 *Ibid.*, p. 138.

69 *Ibid.*, p. 368.

70 *Ibid.*, pp. 48–9.

71 Morgan, *Keir Hardie*, p. 108.
72 V. I. Lenin, *Imperialism, the Highest Stage of Capitalism: A Popular Outline* (New York: International Publishers, revised translation, 1939), pp. 106–7.
73 *Ibid.*, pp. 88–9.
74 Norman Angell, *The Great Illusion: A Study of the Relation of Military Power in Nations to their Economic and Social Advantage* (London: Heinemann, 3rd edn, 1912), p. xi.
75 Norman Angell, *Foreign Policy and our Daily Bread* (London: Collins, 1925), p. 12.
76 Angell, *The Great Illusion*, pp. viii, 277 and p. 252.
77 H. N. Brailsford, *The War of Steel and Gold: A Study of the Armed Peace* (London: Bell and Sons, 3rd edn, 1915), pp. 28 and 46. The first edition had been published in May 1914.
78 *Ibid.*, pp. 35 and 132.
79 *Ibid.*, p. 319.

Chapter 3

Labour and the First World War

The Labour Party grew only moderately in parliamentary strength following its 1906 election success of thirty seats, gaining forty seats in the election of January 1910, and forty-two seats in the election the following December.[1] However, the labour movement in general was growing significantly in terms of its economic, social and political impact, with trade union membership increasing from just under two million in 1900 to over four million in 1914, at a time of rising union militancy. Major strike waves broke out in 1908 and from 1910 through to 1914, when the number of working days lost rose from an average of two-to-three thousand days a year to ten thousand days a year, and hit a peak of nearly forty-one thousand days a year in 1913.[2] Domestic discontent over trade union rights, social conditions, women's suffrage and Home Rule for Ireland coincided with rising international tension.[3] The European states became increasingly competitive over access to markets, with Germany and Italy in particular seeking to build up their own empires. Alliance diplomacy became increasingly volatile, and crises broke out in the Balkans in 1908–9 when Austria-Hungary annexed the provinces of Bosnia-Herzegovina; and between French and German interests in Morocco in 1906 and 1911. The arms race between Britain and Germany escalated, as Germany appeared to be directly preparing to challenge Britain's naval supremacy.[4] However, despite these tensions, the outbreak of war in Europe came as a great shock to most of Britain.[5] In the spring of 1914 the Cabinet had been focusing its attention on the issue of Home Rule for Ireland, to the extent that a permanent under-secretary at the Foreign Office noted in May that 'I have not seen such calm waters' in foreign affairs.[6]

The crisis that led to the outbreak of war in 1914 occurred when

Archduke Franz Ferdinand, the heir to the throne of Austria-Hungary, was assassinated by a group of Serb and Croat nationalists during a visit to Sarajevo on 28 June 1914. To summarise events very briefly, on 23 July Austria-Hungary presented Serbia with an ultimatum to be met within forty-eight hours. This included the suppression of any anti-Austrian propaganda in Serbia, and Austrian participation in the Serbian investigation into the assassination. Serbia, which was suffering from domestic political problems at the time, raised objections to this last demand. Germany pressured Austria-Hungary into declaring war on Serbia on 28 July, with both thinking that if they were united, Russia, the Serbs' ally, would not get involved. Austria-Hungary subsequently began mobilising its armed forces. However, Russia supported Serbia and felt that if it got its ally, France, to stand firm, Germany and Austria-Hungary would back off. Unfortunately, nobody backed off, and all the states involved began mobilising their troops. Britain, which had signed alliances with France and Russia, was under increasing pressure to announce its support for them, but, with divisions in the Cabinet over what course of action to take, the government was trying to avoid any public commitment to intervene. This situation changed somewhat when Germany demanded the right to move its troops through Belgium in order to launch a pre-emptive strike on France. Belgium had been guaranteed neutrality through an 1839 treaty by the main European powers, and Britain was one of the guarantors. The violation of Belgium's neutrality, along with Britain's treaty with France, the fear that the European balance of power would be undermined in Germany's favour and a wider concern that if Britain remained aloof from a European-wide conflict its independence and its powerful role in the world would be undermined, led the British Cabinet members to reluctantly agree on 2 August 1914 that if Germany violated France, it would intervene. Germany declared war against Russia on 1 August and against France on 3 August. Britain declared war against Germany on 4 August. Germany started moving its troops through Belgium, and on 6 August the British government decided to send an expeditionary force to France. On 12 August Britain declared war against Austria-Hungary.[7] The First World War, or 'Great War' as it was known at the time, had begun, which was to have far-reaching impact on British politics in numerous ways. It led to the introduction of conscription for the first time in 1916, due to the need to expand Britain's relatively small land army; the introduction of government control over parts of the economy vital to the war effort, including mining, which involved far greater consultation with trade union representatives than before; government control of the railways and shipping; government intervention in the supply and pricing of food; and the diversion of production to armaments. British defence expenditure rose from £91 million in 1913 to £1,956 million in 1918, by which time it accounted for 80 per cent of total government expenditure.[8] Under Lloyd George's Ministry of Munitions, production of guns, for example, rose from 91 thousand in 1914 to over 8 million in 1918, and production of machine guns rose from just 300 in 1914 to 120,900 in 1918.[9]

In addition to the First World War and its aftermath, this time period was extremely influential in the development of the Labour Party's foreign policy because of events in Russia. The revolution in Russia in 1917 was to have a resounding impact on Labour, in terms of temporarily raising hopes for a future based on international socialist solidarity, while quickly undermining this through the provision of a competing socialist world-view, foreign policy and international movement to that provided by the Labour Party.

Labour and the war

The outbreak of the First World War tested the Labour Party's attitudes to foreign policy and defence as no previous event had. In particular, it revealed the problems of forming a party out of an alliance of left-wing groups. Until 1914, the Labour Party had proclaimed itself as largely anti-war, and some of it leading members from the ILP held pacifist views. The annual conference had regularly passed resolutions condemning militarism and war, and in 1912 had passed a resolution calling for an investigation into the extent to which a general strike in countries about to engage in war would be effective in preventing the outbreak of hostilities.[10] The 1913 conference passed a resolution that called upon the wives and mothers of the working class to assist in defeating militarism and war 'by teaching their children the meaning of the international solidarity of the workers'.[11] At the following year's conference another successful resolution called upon the conference to resist conscription, increased expenditure on armaments, and for the TUC 'to consider joint action of the workers against war in this and other countries; and further urges the people to use their political power to democratise foreign policy and to replace our present system of armed peace by an alliance between all the workers of the world'.[12] Tom Fox, the conference chairman said that 'The Labour

Party is here to denounce war and war-mongering in any disguise, to warn and to arm our fellow workers of all nations against the common foe.'[13]

In the run-up to the declaration of war, the Labour Party continued to pass resolutions denouncing war and urging arbitration. On 2 August, Keir Hardie and Arthur Henderson took part in a mass anti-war demonstration in Trafalgar Square. On 3 August, Foreign Secretary Sir Edward Grey announced to the House of Commons that Britain was committed to supporting the French, and that 'it is clear that peace of Europe cannot be preserved.' Ramsay MacDonald, leader of the PLP, responded by stating the somewhat ambivalent view that the Labour Party was against war, but if it were announced, would not take action against it. 'We will offer him ourselves if the country is in danger. But he has not persuaded me it is.' Indeed, MacDonald argued that the British ought to have remained neutral.[14] The following day the Liberal government announced that Britain was at war with Germany. In response, on 5 August the Labour Party's NEC passed a resolution by eight votes to four that the war was the result of 'Foreign Ministers pursuing diplomatic polices for the purposes of maintaining a balance of power', condemned Sir Edward Grey for committing 'without the knowledge of our people the honour of the country to supporting France in the event of any war', and declared 'That the Labour Movement reiterates the fact that it has opposed the policy which has produced the war, and that its duty is now to secure peace at the earliest possible moment'.[15] However, that same day the PLP decided to support the government's request for war credits of one hundred million pounds, which was, in effect, a reversal of the party's existing policy. Ramsay MacDonald resigned as leader of the Labour Party in protest at this particular decision, but more generally over the PLP's view that it should support the war, and Arthur Henderson replaced him.

Once war broke out, it was supported by large sections of the working class, and trade unions agreed to suspend protective practices in order to increase war production, with areas such as mining and the railways coming under semi-government control for the duration. The Labour Party produced a manifesto in October 1914, *The British Labour Party and the War*. This stated that while the party had always stood for peace, the German military-caste were 'determined on war if the rest of Europe could not be cowed into submission.' It explained that the party had agreed to support the government's recruitment campaign due to a 'fervent desire to save Great Britain and Europe from the evils that would follow the triumph of military despotism'.[16] While before the outbreak of war the party had vehemently denounced militarism and continued to vote against increased military expenditure, once Britain had declared war, the party did not publicly speak against the war as such, or threaten the war effort in any way. It said that following the declaration of war, 'the opinion of the majority of the Party, after several meetings to consider the situation, crystallised into a conviction that under the circumstances it was impossible for this country to have remained neutral.'[17] In May 1915, Asquith decided that the war could not be prosecuted successfully without bringing other parties into the government. Asquith lacked popularity within his own party, with many Liberals having been bitterly opposed to Britain entering into war, and had been criticised more generally over his prosecution of the war, in particular over the shortage of munitions. He subsequently invited the Conservatives and the Labour Party to join him in a coalition government. This 'caused much searching of hearts', but the party decided to accept the invitation, and Arthur Henderson, now also a prominent member of the Fabian Society, was made president of the Board of Education and a member of the Cabinet. Henderson became the only Labour Cabinet minister in this coalition government, while the Conservatives were given nine ministerial posts, and the Liberals retained thirteen. Henderson himself was concerned about his position, seeing his post at the Board of Education as an office 'for which he did not feel fit'. He also feared that the government would use him to put across to the Labour Party and trade unions 'measures which were certain to arouse resentment, and that the effect might be to antagonise Labour from the war effort instead of strengthening its participation.'[18] This duly occurred when Asquith formally proposed in December 1915 a Military Service Bill to introduce conscription. Conscription was highly controversial within the Liberal Party as well as Labour, and Sir John Simon, the Liberal Home Secretary, resigned in protest. Henderson also offered his resignation from the Cabinet, but Asquith persuaded the PLP that he should remain in the government.[19] At the January 1916 annual conference the party voted by 1,796,000 to 219,000 votes against conscription 'in any form, as it is against the spirit of British democracy', and furthermore supported a resolution declaring the conference's opposition to the government's Military Service Bill by 1,716,000 votes to 360,000.[20] The TUC had passed resolutions against conscription in 1913 and 1915.[21] However, Labour's opposition to conscription then crumbled, and it voted to support temporary compulsory military service in April 1916.[22] Not only this, but the PLP and the NEC also agreed that the Labour Party organisation would join forces in a campaign to enlist military recruits, and that the party Head Office would be placed at the disposal of the recruitment campaign.[23]

The January 1916 Labour Party annual conference had actually seen a turning point in the party's position and reaction to the war. It moved publicly from grudging to outspoken support for Britain's position during the debate on a resolution championing the government and denouncing German militarism. The resolution stated that,

> [Conference] considers the present action of Great Britain and its Government fully justified in the present war, expresses its horror at the atrocities committed by Germany and her ally by the callous and brutal murder of non-combatants, including women and children, and hereby pledges the Conference to assist the Government as far as possible in the successful prosecution of the War.[24]

The mover, James Sexton of the Dock Labourers, noted that this resolution 'was practically word for word in substance and in fact' the same as the one passed by the TUC in September 1915, and declared that 'He was for this War and for all the risks associated with it, for the alternative was worse than any risk ... If Germany won, nothing else in God's world would matter!' Another trade unionist posed the question of when there were trade union members fighting in the services, how could any trade unionists tell his members that he had voted against the war? The resolution was controversial, and Ramsay MacDonald spoke against it. He also called for toleration, with a plea not to let differences of opinion over the war become 'reasons for permanent dispute in their midst', but with little real effect. He was opposed by the speaker for the NEC, who asked the conference, 'Who has the right to speak on behalf of the Labour Movement? Was it the small coterie of the Independent Labour Party or the great Trade Unions of the country who ... carried the same resolution with but two or three dissentients [sic] in that very city four months ago?' After an extensive and emotional debate, the resolution was passed by 1,502,000 votes to 602,000.[25]

Thus, the First World War led to a widening gulf within the Labour Party between two competing perspectives. The majority supported the war once it was underway, and also supported the coalition government. Some of the working class actually prospered under the war due to the boom created by weapons production, ensuring employment and good wages. The minority still supported the pre-war policy of international solidarity, and put this before what they saw as national self-interest. G. D. H. Cole noted that in Britain, as in other countries,

> [T]here were really two anti-war oppositions, the one, headed internationally by Lenin, revolutionary and entirely unconcerned with the merits of the case advanced by any capitalist government, and the other either out-and-out pacifist or working for peace by negotiation, but opposed to any attempt to invoke revolutionary violence as a means of ending the war by international working-class revolution.[26]

The ILP, led by Ramsay MacDonald, formed the centre of the opposition to British foreign policy and the war, and was criticised by the Labour Party and the TUC for doing so.[27] It was argued that, had events been left to the ILP, 'the Germans would be here now.'[28] While there was no great public schism between the two parties, the ILP lost much of its influence within the Labour Party during the war. When Keir Hardie died in 1915, at the resulting by-election in Merthyr the ILP candidate was defeated by the trade union candidate standing for the Labour Party who stood on a platform of support for the war. At the 1916 Labour Party annual conference, a resolution proposed by the ILP criticising British foreign policy, which before the war would have been uncontroversial, was defeated.[29]

The Fabians were more divided over the stance to take in response to the war. Following their brief interest in foreign affairs caused by the Boer War, they had returned to their domestic focus, and had said little on international relations. Upon the outbreak of the First World War, they held a discussion on the attitude to take to the war, which demonstrated divisions between the 'old guard' Fabians such as the Webbs who, like the Labour Party, supported the war, and the newer generation of Fabians who supported the ILP's opposition to the war.[30] However, in the end, Edward Pease, Secretary of the Fabian Society, noted that 'In accordance with the rule which forbids it to speak, unless it has something of value to say, the Society has made no pronouncement and adopted no policy' on the First World War.[31] This was in much the same way as it had made no pronouncement and adopted no policy on the Boer War. The main Marxist organisation, the British Socialist Party was split over the issue of the First World War. In 1916 Hyndman's more nationalistic faction withdrew from the British Socialist Party to form the National Socialist Party, where Hyndman campaigned for a more vigorous prosecution of the war abroad, while at the same time arguing for better conditions for the working class at home, and working on plans for the nationalisation of the railways and greater government control of industry.[32] The remainder of the British Socialist Party opposed the war, with some of its members being imprisoned for their political activities and for objecting to military service. In its Huddersfield branch alone, at one point twenty-five members were imprisoned.[33]

While the importance of the ILP and the other opponents of the war declined at this time, paradoxically the UDC gradually increased in importance. Morel, the Honorary Secretary and Treasurer of the UDC, proclaimed that the organisation 'has one supreme end and aim'. This 'is to create a public opinion in Great Britain, and eventually throughout the world, which will compel the so-called civilised and the so-called Christian Governments of Europe to settle their differences in future by some other means than the massacre and mutilation of multitudes of human beings.'[34] In its first pamphlet, *The Morrow of War*, the UDC said that it was set up to secure a new course of policy that would prevent the peril of war befalling the British empire again. It believed that 'First, it is imperative that the war, once begun, should be prosecuted to a victory for our country. Secondly, it is equally imperative, while we carry on the war, to prepare for peace.'[35] The UDC was formally constituted at an inaugural meeting on 17 November 1914. At this meeting four 'cardinal points' were adopted. These were, first, that no province was to be transferred from one country to another without the consent of the population. Second, no treaty or agreement was to be entered into by the government without the consent of Parliament. 'Adequate machinery for ensuring democratic control of foreign policy shall be created.' Third, British foreign policy was to aim not at maintaining a balance of power but at concerted action between the powers to set up an international council with machinery for securing an abiding peace. Fourth, Britain should propose, as part of any peace settlement, a drastic disarmament agreement between the powers, the general nationalisation of armaments industries, and controls over the export of armaments between states.[36]

The UDC and the ILP co-operated in their anti-war activities, and in this way the ILP in general, and Ramsay MacDonald in particular as a leading member of both groups, were to have an indirect impact on Labour's thinking about war and peace. While there was sometimes friction between the two groups, both came under virulent, and occasionally violent, criticism for their stance on the First World War.[37] Marquand notes that 'the very fact that both groups were swimming against one of the strongest and fiercest tides of opinion in recent British history created in both an exalted, almost religious, atmosphere of dedication and solidarity – the solidarity of persecution.'[38]

The UDC blamed the outbreak of the Great War on balance-of-power politics, secret diplomacy, the arms race between states, and the arms trade.[39] They were not pacifists as such, though they abhorred war. While condemning war in general, and blaming the First World War on all the participants rather than seeing it as a simple fight between good and evil, the UDC believed that Britain must win the war.[40] They were critical of the Foreign Office, believing that it had become 'avowedly and frankly autocratic.'[41] They saw the war as the failure of diplomacy, and 'Instead of taking advantage of the marked growth in the pacific inclinations of the peoples of the world', statesmen 'have insisted on encouraging between the Governments of Europe the most deadly and determined competition in preparation for war that the world has ever known.'[42] Thus, in the future, foreign policy should not be left in the hands of the professional diplomats and statesmen. Rather, there should be some form of popular control over foreign policy. As it was not in the interests of the public to go to war, they would resist aggression. Public opinion, if allowed to play a role in international affairs, would act to prevent war. The UDC believed in a rational, evolutionary view of the world, that modern, civilised, educated people, if only made aware of the facts, would choose peace not war, and so it was possible to get rid of war by willing it so and simply creating the necessary international machinery for conciliation and peace.

The machinery for peace was to be through a League of Nations. The suspicion and fear caused by exclusive alliances could be done away with by extending national law to the international arena and creating a League of Peace, 'which should undertake, in the event of a dispute, to offer mediation'. If one or both sides then resisted mediation, the League would throw its weight against the greatest aggressor though a system of collective security. 'If a sufficient number of nations entered into such a League, they could make aggressive war obviously doomed to failure, and could thereby secure the cessation of war.'[43] Richard Crossman described the League as an attempt 'to apply the principles of Lockeian liberalism to the building of a machinery of international order'.[44]

With hindsight it is possible to criticise the UDC for being unduly optimistic about the potential nature of international relations and the role that public opinion could play, as E. H. Carr scathingly did in

1939 when he compared the 'utopian' view of international politics as propounded by groups such as the UDC with what he described as the 'realist' perspective, which emphasised the over-riding importance of power in international politics and the competitive nature of relations between states in their pursuit of national power.[45] However, at the time, the views of the UDC anticipated and helped shape the general consensus about the ability of the League of Nations and open covenants to prevent war in the 1920s and 1930s. Indeed, the UDC developed ideas about foreign policy which have remained with the Labour Party, such as the need for the control of the arms industry, and the importance of the role of public opinion, particularly in preventing aggression between states.

One consequence of the First World War was that it recast divisions within the various groupings of the Labour Party, with the ILP declining in importance in particular. Another was that it led to Labour MPs, most notably Arthur Henderson, entering government for the first time. The coalition government that Asquith had formed in May 1915 was faltering, and on 5 December 1916 he resigned rather than accept demands from his ministerial colleagues that he establish a war committee led by Lloyd George to co-ordinate Britain's war effort.[46] Lloyd George replaced him as Prime Minister on 6 December, forming a new coalition government. Lloyd George held a meeting with members of the Labour Party the following day at which he offered places in a coalition government. Beatrice Webb noted in her diary that 'The pro-war Labour members drank in his sweet words; the pacifists maintained a stony silence whilst Sidney [Webb] and one or two of the waverers asked questions to which Lloyd George gave non-committal answers.' However, she did feel that this signified defeat for the pacifist wing of the party, as 'From the narrow standpoint of the pacifist movement, as a sect, the inclusion of pro-war Labour members in the Lloyd George Government may be a fortunate circumstance – a discredit to their warlike opinions.'[47] Conference had in fact voted overwhelmingly, by 1,674,000 votes to 269,000, to support entry into the Cabinet in 1916, and supported it retrospectively in 1917.[48] Henderson duly became a member of the inner War Cabinet, John Hodge became the newly created Minister of Labour, with four others in more minor posts.[49] However, during 1917 the atmosphere changed, as the United States joined the Allies, and Russia defected after the October Revolution.[50] Tensions quickly developed within the Labour Party over whether to stay in the war government or not, especially over the issue of British relations with Russia.

The 1917 Russian Revolution

Events in Russia caused another rethink in foreign policy, and a *volte-face* back to the anti-war and internationalist sentiments of the pre-war years. For example, in January 1917, the Labour Party had rejected an invitation to attend an international socialist conference in Stockholm on war aims and peace plans, but accepted it, after much prevarication, once Russia had indicated its willingness to take part following the revolution of February 1917.[51] 'Joy – an admixture of relief and pleasure – was the characteristic British reaction' to this revolution in Russia, and this was not confined to the Labour Party.[52] In the House of Commons, Chancellor of the Exchequer Bonar Law moved the government's statement of congratulation, saying that, 'This House sends to the Duma its fraternal greetings and tenders to the Russian people its heartiest congratulations upon the establishment among them of free institutions', though he could not resist tendering his compassion for the deposed Tsar.[53] Nye Bevan later described the emotional and psychological impact of the revolution thus:

> I remember so well what happened when the Russian revolution occurred. I remember the miners, when they heard that the Czarist tyranny had been overthrown, rushing to meet each other in the streets with tears streaming down their cheeks, shaking hands and saying: 'At last it has happened.' Let us remember in 1951 that the revolution of 1917 came to the working class of Great Britain, not as social disaster, but as one of the most emancipating events in the history of mankind. Let us also remember that the Soviet revolution would not have been so distorted, would not have ended in a tyranny, would not have resulted in a dictatorship, would not now be threatening the peace of mankind, had it not been for the behaviour of Churchill, and the Tories at that time.[54]

In response to the Russian Revolution of February 1917, the United Socialist Council, made up of the various British socialist organisations that had temporarily joined forces in 1916, organised the Leeds Convention of June 1917. This was described by Ralph Miliband as 'perhaps the most remarkable gathering of the period', for it brought together both the revolutionaries and constitutionalists on the left.[55] Graubard is less positive with his description that, 'The Leeds Convention stands out as one of the great anomalies in British Labour experience', for leaders such as Ramsay MacDonald and Philip Snowden, who had always argued that it was necessary to work inside the parliamentary system, agreed to a resolution creating extra-parliamentary workers' councils. 'The most generous interpretation would be that they were themselves swept along by the emotion of the mass. The least generous would be that they knew that nothing would come of the whole effort and simply enjoyed the platform provided them.'[56]

There were 1,150 delegates present at the Leeds Convention, including Ernest Bevin, Ramsay MacDonald, Philip Snowden, Tom Mann, Ben Tillet, Bertrand Russell and Sylvia Pankhurst. Four resolutions were passed by the convention. First, one proposed by Ramsay MacDonald was simply that the convention 'hails the Russian Revolution. With gratitude and admiration it congratulates the Russian people upon a Revolution which has overthrown a tyranny.' The second resolution supported the declaration on foreign policy and war aims of the Russian Provisional Government, and the third called for a charter of civil liberties establishing complete political rights for all. The fourth, and most controversial, called for the establishment of workers' and soldiers' councils in Britain 'for initiating and co-ordinating working class activity', which some interpreted to mean extra-constitutional and revolutionary activity. A message was also sent to the Russian Workers' Councils that the convention 'has today endorsed Russia's declaration of foreign policy and war aims, and has pledged itself to work through its newly constituted Workmen's and Soldiers' Council for an immediate democratic peace'.[57] The conference is significant for it united both constitutionalists and revolutionaries, and 'Reacting to the mood of their audience, mild trade unionists talked like Bolsheviks and for a few hours, within a crowded hall, a socialist revolution in Britain seemed a viable proposition.'[58] White, however, has argued that the Leeds Convention 'is better understood in a pacifist than in a revolutionary perspective', and reflected an opposition to the continuation of the First World War in the pursuit of total victory.[59]

The euphoria was short-lived. The Leeds conference was described by the Labour Party as being 'unrepresentative', and it stated that any members of the party present were there as individuals, and not as representatives of the party.[60] Not unsurprisingly, the appeal to establish British workers' soviets was not carried through. However, the first major problem that the Russian Revolution caused for the Labour Party was created by Russia's request for British involvement in a meeting of the International Socialist Congress, made up of all Socialist and Labour Parties, including Germany, to be held in Stockholm to discuss war aims. This caused tensions within the movement. The party's NEC rejected an invitation in May 1917 to send a delegation to the Stockholm conference,[61] but then voted in favour of attendance at the special Labour Party conference of August 1917 following a plea from Arthur Henderson. Henderson had just returned from an official visit to Russia, sent by an alarmed British government as 'its most conciliatory representative' to St Petersburg to find out 'what might be the result of the changes'.[62] He told the Labour Party conference that the Stockholm meeting would be held with or without British involvement, and 'it would be highly inadvisable and perhaps dangerous for the Russian representatives to meet representatives from enemy and neutral countries alone'. As long as Russia agreed that the conference would be for consultative purposes rather than being oblig- atory and binding, then the Labour Party should attend.[63] However, the British government had announced that it would refuse passports to delegates, and debate still raged within the Labour movement on whether minority groups, such as the ILP and the British Socialist Party, should be represented at Stockholm. Another vote on whether Britain should attend the Stockholm conference was held. This resulted in a tiny majority of 1,234,000 to 1,231,000, but in the end there was no British delegation.[64] Henderson, who supported Stockholm and all that it stood for in terms of securing international socialist co-operation in pursuit of peace, resigned from the Cabinet on 11 August following the 'doormat incident', when Lloyd George kept him waiting for an hour outside the doors of a Cabinet meeting while his Cabinet colleagues discussed his recent activities in promoting the Stockholm conference.[65] This did not result in Labour itself with- drawing from the coalition government, for Henderson was replaced in the inner War Cabinet by G. N. Barnes. This incident demonstrated the conflicting tensions within the party between socialist solidarity and national concerns, with a tenacious feeling against any negotia- tions with socialists from enemy countries, and was prescient of the troubles to come over the establishment of a post-war Socialist International.

These events also had an enduring impact on the Labour Party in that Henderson, slightly bruised from his experience of government, then devoted himself to reorganising the Labour Party's structure, drawing up the new constitution that was approved in 1918.[66] He was determined to change the party from a collection of affiliated organisations on the left to an organised, national, centralised but broad-based and moderate socialist party that was resistant to the extra-parliamentary and revolutionary left, for his trip to Russia had convinced him of the need to prevent extremists from taking control of the party.[67] He was also determined to create an organisation that would be able to exert more influence in parliamentary politics, following what he perceived as the coalition government's shoddy treatment of the labour movement. Labour's international committee, the Advisory Committee on International Questions, was set up as part of the major reorganisation of its machinery for the handling of foreign policy. This body had responsibility for making recommendations to the Executive and the Parliamentary Party on foreign policy. Allied intervention in Russia was the first important issue that the committee discussed. At its first meeting of 30 May 1918, Sidney Webb was appointed chairmen, and Leonard Woolf secretary. Members included H. N. Brailsford, G. D. H. Cole, Arnold Toynbee and, from July, Ramsay MacDonald.[68]

If the Russian Revolution of February 1917 had created a complex situation for the Labour Party to respond to, the October Revolution, which saw the more militant Bolsheviks oust the Mensheviks, compounded this. At this time there was no Communist Party in Britain, only the British form of Marxism propounded by the British Socialist Party and Hyndman's newly formed National Socialist Party. However, 'Bolshevik Russia was already becoming a focus of loyalty for the extreme left in all countries – and at the same time, or course, a focus of opposition for the right, whose friends among the Russian Socialists had been driven from power and in many cases were fleeing into exile.'[69] Many on the left were dismayed by the violence surrounding the second revolution, and 'The direct and muscular Marxism of the Bolsheviks was alien to the Fabian gradualists of the Labour Party and the socialist pacifists who led the ILP.'[70] Events in Russia radicalised the Labour Party, in that it provided a socialist 'utopia' for those on the far left to look to, work with and emulate, and, it is argued, major revolutions 'exert a demonstration effect' to those in other countries who also seek to overthrow the state.[71] The establishment of the Bolshevik regime also provided a communist foe for those on the centre and centre-right of the labour movement to be fearful of, thus deepening existing divisions between the revolutionary and the parliamentary left. As Skocpol points out, revolutions 'also affect those in other countries who oppose revolutionary ideals but are compelled to respond to the challenges or threats posed by the enhanced national power that has been generated' by a revolution.[72]

This tension was given an added dimension when the British Socialist Party, along with some smaller parties, formed the Communist Party of Great Britain (CPGB) on 1 August 1920. The instructions from Moscow were for the CPGB to affiliate to the

Labour Party and convert the bulk of the party to the communist cause. The CPGB's requests for affiliation were turned down in 1921 and 1922, and at the 1925 Labour Party annual conference a constitutional resolution proscribing all dealings with the CPGB was passed.[73] In March 1919, the first meeting of the Third International (also called the Comintern or Communist International), was held in Moscow, which proclaimed the arrival of world revolution. Part of its role was to bolster communist parties around the world, which were to be loyal to Moscow, follow Comintern policy and submit to its authority. However, while Moscow supported the fledgling CPGB, financially and otherwise, it also undermined its legitimacy on the left through the insistence that it be loyal to Moscow above all else. As Jupp notes, the establishment of the Comintern gave the leaders of the Labour Party the opportunity to exclude from its membership Marxists who wished to join it. This in turn 'hastened the process by which the Labour Party developed into a unitary political party in alliance with the trade unions and with a commitment to parliamentary socialism'. Indeed, before the Bolshevik revolution, the issue of whether Marxists belonged within the Labour Party, was a matter for individuals.[74] After, it became an issue of party unity and control.

Another attempt to affiliate to the Labour Party was made in 1935, as part of the campaign for a 'United Front' against fascism, which led the party leadership to delineate the difference between it and the Communists in its statement 'British Labour and Communism'. This stated that for nearly twenty years the Communist Party had sought to subvert the British labour movement, and 'Throughout the whole period the British Labour Movement has been subjected to one long stream of invective and vilification by the Communist Press subsidised by Russian money.' The sympathetic interest that British labour had shown in the Soviet Union 'has been qualified by growing resentment against Russian effort through the Communist International to establish and finance revolutionary Communist Parties in other countries with the object of destroying existing democratic industrial and political Labour Movements, and of bringing about the overthrow of the existing social system by violence.'[75]

The second 1917 revolution also had a particular impact on Labour's thinking on foreign policy in that it provided a major issue of contention between Labour and its Liberal and Conservative opponents. British foreign policy towards Russia following the October Revolution was based on non-recognition of the Soviet

Union, and limited intervention. The Labour Party bitterly opposed this, seeing it as the cause for bad relations between the Soviet Union and Europe, for 'By maintaining troops against Russia, the Allied Governments violate in their most flagrant manner the right of the Russian people to [govern] themselves … They are thereby multiplying the reasons for civil war in Russia.'[76] The Labour Party launched a manifesto in January 1920 that called for the 'Complete raising of the Blockade and a complete peace with Russia.' It also called for full recognition of the Soviet government, while pointing out that 'Such a formal recognition of a Government would no more imply moral approval of it than did our formal recognition of the Tsar's Government.'[77] One of the main actions of the first Labour government of 1924 was to recognise the Soviet Union. However, Labour was never fully comfortable with the Soviet Union, and large sections of the party quickly came to see it as a source of conflict in foreign policy, as will be demonstrated in the following chapters.

The Internationals, the post-war settlement and establishment of the League of Nations

One major consequence of the outbreak of the First World War was that it demonstrated the problems of transcending national loyalties in order to reach the goal of international socialist solidarity, and this was illustrated most clearly by the collapse of the Second International, the main international socialist body at that time. The Second International had had an impact on the development of Labour's foreign policy in its early years, providing a forum for British socialists to meet with their overseas counterparts, and an opportunity to focus on international issues. The split between parliamentary and revolutionary socialists within the Second International had become institutionalised when it moved to exclude anarchists and anti-parliamentarians from its meetings, but one remaining notable division was over the issue of whether to hold a general strike in the face of war. Within the British contingent, Keir Hardie and the ILP tended to support a general strike, while most Fabian socialists and some of the other members of the Labour Party did not. However, Keir Hardie and Arthur Henderson had proposed a resolution supporting the calling of a general strike to be used, if political action had failed, to prevent the outbreak of war. All the members of the Second International had been invited to comment on this resolution, and at an extraordinary Congress of the Second International held at Basle in 1912 the resolution had been passed.[78] This meant that at the outbreak of the First World War, the policy of the Second International was to call for a general strike in response to the threat of war. However, while the Second International held a series of rallies across Europe in the summer of 1914, with Hardie leading an anti-war demonstration in London on 2 August, its plans for mass popular resistance in the face of war came to little, and it disintegrated into different camps.[79]

Despite the collapse of the Second International, the Labour Party still kept in close contact with some of its European counterparts. Issues that united the British and European socialist parties were a belief that labour should have a role in the drawing up of the post-war settlement; that there should be some form of international socialist body to replace the Second International; and that socialist parties should campaign for the establishment of an international body to arbitrate between states and so prevent war. A conference was held by the Socialist Parties of the Allied Nations in London in February 1915, where it was agreed that,

> On the conclusion of the war the working classes of all the industrial countries must unite in the [Socialist] International in order to suppress secret diplomacy, put an end to the interests of militarism and those of the armament makers and establish some international authority to settle points of difference among the nations by compulsory conciliation and arbitration, and to compel all nations to maintain peace.[80]

The aim of internationalism and the commitment to an international federation of nations was then formally incorporated into the Labour Party's constitution, which was adopted in February 1918. This committed the party

> To co-operate with the Labour and Socialist organisations in other countries and to assist in organising a Federation of Nations for the maintenance of freedom and peace, for the establishment of suitable machinery for the adjustment and settlement of international disputes by conciliation or judicial arbitration and for such other international legislation as may be practicable.[81]

The commitment to international socialist co-operation, to the establishment of an international body for the socialist parties and to the establishment of an international body to act as a federation of nations, was clear. At a joint TUC and Labour Party conference on post-war aims on 28 December 1917, a resolution calling for a League of Nations was accepted.

The Labour Party took part in two Inter-Allied Conferences of Labour and Socialist Parties, held in London in February and in September 1918. The second of these passed resolutions strongly supporting the establishment of a League of Nations and welcomed the fourteen points laid down by President Wilson. Following a speech by Kerensky, a moderate socialist who had been the Russian Prime Minister from July 1917 until he was ousted by the October Revolution, a resolution was passed that said that 'the present effort of the Allied Governments to assist the Russian people must be influenced only by a genuine desire to preserve liberty and democracy in an ordered and durable world peace in which the beneficent fruits of the Revolution shall be permanently secure.'[82] It denounced the Versailles Treaty for its harsh treatment of Germany, in particular the 'War Guilt' clause.[83] This stated that 'Germany accepts the responsibility of Germany and her allies for causing all the loss and damage to the Allied governments and their nationals imposed on them by the aggression of Germany and her allies.'[84] Following this, an international labour and socialist conference was held in Berne in January 1919, at which steps were taken to reconstitute the Second International, which also became known as the Berne International. Resolutions were passed that welcomed German involvement in the conference, and said that this 'has convinced the Conference that, from now onward, the united working classes of the whole world will prove the most powerful guarantee for the suppression of all militarism and of every attempt to destroy international democracy.'[85] Despite the First World War providing evidence to the contrary, the Labour Party still expressed the belief that international socialist solidarity was possible.[86]

Another socialist international, the 'Two-and-a-Half' International, was established shortly afterwards, which aimed to unite the new Second International with the recently established Third (Communist) International. This body only existed for a short time, merging with the Second International in May 1923 at a conference in Hamburg to form the new Labour and Socialist International (LSI). This conference declared the post-war situation to be an 'imperialist peace'. It argued that: 'The imperialist war had for its objectives the conquest of the world's wealth and ended in the destruction of this wealth.' However, 'The Peace Treaties violate all economic principles; ... They have brought to the defeated nations insecurity and the menace of continuous violent oppression.' Therefore 'Labour opposes to the policy of imperialism its policy of peace', and 'One of the most important tasks of the workers of all countries is to watch over the foreign policy of their Governments.'[87] The Labour and Socialist International continued in existence up to the Second World War, with its headquarters initially in London, and then in Zurich. Arthur Henderson was its president until 1929. The LSI continued the work of the Second International, focusing on the gradual improvement of international relations and of working-class conditions by Parliamentary and trade union efforts.[88] However, the prospects for international socialist co-operation deteriorated through the rivalry of the LSI and the Third International, with the Third International instructed to wage a war on centrists, revisionists and social democrats, while the LSI sought to protect itself from dangerous revolutionaries.

The Labour Party's international role expanded in the immediate post-war years, with a greater influence within the Socialist International than before, partly as a result of the decline in the role of the German socialists within the International. The party also had a greater confidence in its right to have a role at the international level. This was largely evinced through its lobbying on the post-war international settlement, and on its stringent critique of the Versailles Treaty. A. J. P. Taylor has suggested that the Versailles settlement was condemned by the party before it was even made.[89] Winkler has argued that the immediate reaction to the peace settlement 'was bitter, and it was virtually unanimous'. Official party statements denounced the unilateral disarmament of Germany, and warned that the burden of reparations might ruin Germany and therefore endanger the entire European economy. They also made it clear that 'the party considered France – strong, armed, and in their view aggressive – a much greater danger to European stability than was Germany.'[90] Certainly MacDonald argued that the Versailles Treaty would result in 'unsettlement and war' and referred to the Paris peace negotiations as 'a heartless farce sinking into a melancholy tragedy'.[91] However, Labour's major contribution to the post-war settlement was over its drive to create a League of Nations, which was founded at the Paris Peace Conference on 24 April 1919.

Winkler also highlights that the Labour Party criticised the League of Nations once it was established. 'As for the League of Nations, Labor, whose agitation and enthusiasm had helped to make it possible, was profoundly disappointed. It was disappointed with the league's membership, its structure, and its proposed functions.'[92] This is too strong an interpretation, for Labour's attitude towards the League was more complex than this suggests. The party welcomed the League, and argued that it was better fitted than its political opponents to make a success of the League. The party felt a sense of pride in the lobbying role it had played in the League's creation. However, the party had major reservations about it as it was constituted. It regretted that it was a league of governments, and not an assembly of delegates chosen from national parliaments, that is, elected representatives. Labour had wanted a League that was 'so strong in its representative character and so dignified by its powers and respect that questions of national defence sink into the background of solved problems'.[93] In 1919 the Labour Party and TUC held a special congress to discuss the Covenant of the League of Nations. While it welcomed the League, the congress drew up a list of twenty-two proposals for amendments to the Covenant. These included the proposal that the League be under the control of a body of elected delegates, and not the Executive Council; that all countries, including Russia and Germany, be invited to join the League, as long as they agree to abide by its rules and decisions; and that the manufacture of armaments be under the direct control of the League.[94] The Labour Party was afraid that the League and the peace settlement were designed to shore up balance-of-power politics. It was argued that 'Each successive Peace Treaty, and almost every decision of the Supreme Council, has been conceived in a spirit of imperialism and national aggrandisement utterly inconsistent with the professed aims with which the country waged war', whereas the League of Nations had so far 'been quietly strangled by the victorious Powers almost at the moment of its birth'.[95] By excluding certain countries, and failing to address the issue of militarism and the causes of war, it was feared that the League would be undermined in its ability to carry out its role. Despite this, the League still provided the Labour Party with hope for the future, and was seen as the mechanism through which international disputes could be settled though conciliation and arbitration, and as the key to maintaining international peace.

As a consequence of the First World War and the resulting deliberations over the establishment of a League of Nations, some on the left, and in particular the UDC, began to wonder whether nationalism, rather than capitalism, was at the heart of militarism and war. The doctrine 'that peace could result only from national self-determination, had left is followers in disarray. It had caused chaos at the Paris peace conference, and it was increasingly clear that this mode of thought lent itself far more readily to right-wing authoritarianism ... than it did to any form of parliamentary democracy.'[96] Norman Angell pointed out that 'Governments formed by Socialist, Labour or Pacifist parties continue in some measure the policies of their bourgeois and Imperialist predecessors.' As he explained, the problem of the 'disorderly' state in the international system 'is not created by Capitalism, nor would it be solved by Socialism. It is the product not of Capitalism but Nationalism. And Socialist States which were also Nationalist would have even more cause for quarrel than States which permit individuals to form economic organizations which are often in fact international, which function in large degree irrespective of national barriers.'[97] The irony of the situation was that the ILP had declined in its importance within the Labour Party due to its opposition to the party's position on the war, and had also declined in its international role as the Labour Party increased in its. However, the UDC, which had shared some of the ILP's opposition to the war and included ILP members, in particular Ramsay MacDonald, gradually built up influence on the left so that when the war was over they became a guiding force for the Labour Party on foreign policy. Many of Labour's ideas on a League of Nations, on the importance of self-determination, on the dangers of the Versailles Treaty, originally came from the UDC. 'By 1918 UDC policy had virtually become Labour Party policy – the anti-war ILP-ers had joined the UDC and the anti-war Liberals had joined the Labour Party. Both groups together dominated the new Labour Party Advisory Committee on International Questions.'[98] This Committee 'was of the utmost importance' during the 1920s.[99] Despite the divisions and contentions caused by the First World War, not only within the Labour Party but within international socialism as a whole, by the early 1920s the internationalist, anti-war section of the party held sway, with a resolution agreeing to 'oppose any War … whatever the ostensible object of the war' being passed at the 1922 annual conference.[100] Their views were to remain dominant until the late 1930s.

In conclusion, the first major test of Labour's developing world-view was over the response to the outbreak of the First World War. This undermined certain meta-principles of Labour's ideology, namely an optimistic view of human nature, and a belief in progress and in international socialist solidarity, while at the same time providing evidence of the disastrous effects of militarism, secret diplomacy and imperialism, which Labour had been agitating against. Internationally, the First World War demonstrated that socialist parties had not yet found a way to overcome their national loyalties, nor achieved international socialist solidarity, with the collapse of the Second International following the outbreak of war in 1914. At home, the war led to bitter divisions within the Labour Party over foreign and defence policy. The majority of the party supported the war and the coalition government and put national interest before class interest. The minority of the party still supported the pre-war policy of international solidarity, and put this before national self-interest. However, out of this conflict developed an increased desire for a new approach to world affairs, strongly influenced by the work of the Union of Democratic Control, based on a League of Nations which would settle international disputes through conciliation and arbitration, and a renewed optimism in internationalism. This was to be severely tested by Labour's first experiences in government, which are analysed in the next chapter.

Notes

1 David Butler and Gareth Butler, *British Political Facts 1900–1985* (Basingstoke: Macmillan, 6th edn, 1986), p. 224.
2 *Ibid.*, p. 372.
3 See George Dangerfield, *The Strange Death of Liberal England* (London: Constable and Co., 1936), for a classic account of the domestic troubles.
4 See Paul Kennedy, *The Rise and Fall of British Naval Mastery* (London: Allen Lane, 1976), chs 8 and 9, and Kennedy, *The Rise of Anglo-German Antagonism 1860–1914* (London: Macmillan, 1980).
5 See Margaret Cole, *The Story of Fabian Socialism* (London: Heinemann, 1961), pp. 161–2, for an account of how unexpected the war was to the bulk of the population.
6 Zara Steiner, *The Foreign Office and Foreign Policy, 1898–1914* (Cambridge: Cambridge University Press, 1969), p. 153, citing letter from Arthur Nicholson, Public Record Office, FO 800/374, 4 May 1914.
7 This sequence of events is based on James Joll, *The Origins of the First World War* (London: Longman, 1984), ch. 2. For more information on the outbreak of the war, see B. H. Liddell Hart, *A History of the World War 1914–1918* (London: Faber and Faber, 1934), ch. 1; Zara Steiner, *Britain and the Origins of the First World War* (London: Macmillan, 1977). Michael Gordon, 'Domestic conflict and the origins of the First World War: the British and German cases', *Journal of Modern History*, 46:2 (1974), 191–226 provides an interesting perspective on the causes of the war, as does Steven Miller, Sean Lynn-Jones and Stephen Van Evera, eds, *Military Strategy and the Origins of the First World War* (Princeton: Princeton University Press, 1985).
8 Paul Kennedy, *The Rise and Fall of the Great Powers: Economic Change and Military Conflict from 1500 to 2000* (London: Fontana Press, 1989), p. 344.

9   Gerd Hardach, *The First World War 1914–1918*, translated by Peter and Betty Ross (London: Allen Lane, 1977), p. 87.

10 *Labour Party Annual Conference Report* (hereafter *LPACR*), 1912, p. 101

11 *LPACR*, 1913, p. 111.

12 *LPACR*, 1914, p. 121.

13 *Ibid.*, p. 93.

14 *House of Commons Debates* (hereafter *H.C. Deb.*), fifth series, vol. 65, cols 1809, 1830–1, 3 August 1914.

15 Manchester, Museum of Labour History, Labour Party archive, NEC minutes, 5 August 1914, pp. 86–7.

16 David Marquand, *Ramsay MacDonald* (London: Jonahan Cape, 1977), p. 176; G. D. H. Cole, *A History of the Labour Party from 1914* (London: Routledge, 1948), p. 21.

17 *LPACR*, 1916, p. 51.

18 Cole, *History of the Labour Party from 1914*, p. 25.

19 Roy Jenkins, *Asquith* (London: Papermac/Macmillan edn, 1986), pp. 389–90.

20 LPACR, *1916*, pp. 116–24. See also *LPACR*, 1912, pp. 99–100.

21 *Trades Union Congress Annual Report* (hereafter *TUCAR*) 1913, pp. 337–9; TUCAR, 1915, pp. 79–91. There was no annual congress in 1914.

22 See *LPACR*, 1917, p. 4.

23 *LPACR*, 1916, p. 5.

24 *Ibid.*, p. 100.

25 *Ibid.*, pp. 103 and 105.

26 Cole, *History of the Labour Party*, pp. 29–30.

27 See *LPACR*, 1916, p. 102; *TUCAR*, 1915, p. 328.

28 *LPACR*, 1916, p. 102.

29 *Ibid.*, pp. 132–3.

30 Alan McBrier, *Fabian Socialism and English Politics, 1884–1918* (Cambridge: Cambridge University Press, 1962), has an account of this discussion, held at Essex Hall, pp. 139–41. For information on the division of the Fabian Society between the 'old guard' of the Webbs and their followers, and the 'new guard' of Guild Socialist rebels, see Cole, *Story of Fabian Socialism*, pp. 143–58.

31 Edward Reynolds Pease, *The History of the Fabian Society* (London: Fabian Society, 1916), p. 234.

32 Chushichi Tsuzuki, *H. M. Hyndman and British Socialism*, edited by Henry Pelling (Oxford: Oxford University Press, 1961), p. 231.

33 *Ibid.*, p. 235.

34 E. D. Morel, *War and Diplomacy* (London: UDC, pamphlet no. 11, 1915), p. 2. The contents of this pamphlet were originally given as a speech on May 15 at a public meeting called by the Society of Friends at Devonshire House, London. This and subsequent UDC pamphlets are held at the University of Leeds Library, Brotherton Collection, Mattison, UNI.

35 Union of Democratic Control, *The Morrow of War* (London: UDC, pamphlet no. 1, 1914), p. 1.

36 *Ibid.*, pp. 1–2.
37 See Marvin Swartz, *The Union of Democratic Control in British Politics during the First World War* (Oxford: Clarendon Press, 1971), ch. 6; Marquand, *Ramsay MacDonald*, pp. 184–93. See also Sally Harris, *Out of Control: British Foreign Policy and the Union of Democratic Control 1914–1918* (Hull: University of Hull Press, 1996).
38 Marquand, *Ramsay MacDonald*, p. 184.
39 UDC, *The Morrow of War*, p. 9.
40 H. N. Brailsford, *The Origins of the Great War* (London: UDC, pamphlet no. 4, 1914), p. 18.
41 UDC, *The Morrow of War*, p. 4.
42 Arthur Ponsonby, *Parliament and Foreign Policy* (London: UDC, pamphlet no. 5, 1914), p. 1.
43 Bertrand Russell, *War, the Offspring of Fear* (London: UDC, pamphlet no. 3, 1914), p. 12.
44 R. H. S. Crossman, 'British political thought in the European Tradition', in J. P. Mayer *et al.*, *Political Thought: The European Tradition* (London: Dent, 1939), p. 202. He adds that this 'has failed as decisively as the Conservative struggle to return to pre-War "normalcy".'
45 E. H. Carr, *The Twenty Years' Crisis, 1919–1939* (London: Papermac/ Macmillan, 2nd edn, 1981).
46 See Jenkins, *Asquith*, chs 16 and 17.
47 Beatrice Webb, *Beatrice Webb's Diaries, 1912–1924*, vol. 1, edited by Margaret Cole (London: Longmans, 1952), pp. 72–3.
48 *LPACR*, 1916, pp. 124-5; *LPACR*, 1917, p. 98.
49 Cole, *A History of the Labour Party*, p. 31.
50 Frank Bealey, ed., *The Social and Political Thought of the British Labour Party* (London: Weidenfeld and Nicolson, 1970), pp. 12–13.
51 See Cole, *A History of the Labour Party*, pp. 33–8. *LPACR*, 1917, and *LPACR*, of January 1918. There were two Labour Party Conferences in 1918, one at the end of January, and one in June.
52 Stephen Richards Graubard, *British Labour and the Russian Revolution, 1917–1924* (Cambridge, Mass: Harvard University Press, 1956), p. 17.
53 *H.C. Deb.*, series 5, vol. 91, 22 March 1917, cols 2085–6.
54 *LPACR*, 1951, p. 121.
55 Ralph Miliband, *Parliamentary Socialism: A Study in the Politics of Labour* (London: Allen and Unwin, 1961), pp. 55, 56–7.
56 Graubard, *British Labour and the Russian Revolution*, pp. 39–40.
57 *British Labour and the Russian Revolution. The Leeds Convention*, A Report from the Daily Herald, with an introduction by Ken Coates (London: Bertrand Russell Peace Foundation/Spokesman, no date), pp. 21, 29–32, and 35.
58 Bill Jones, *The Russia Complex. The British Labour Party and the Soviet Union* (Manchester: Manchester University Press, 1977), p. 3.
59 Stephen White, 'Soviets in Britain: the Leeds Convention of 1917', *International Review of Social History*, 19:2 (1974), 166.
60 *LPACR*, 1922, p. 80.
61 *LPACR*, January 1918, p. 3.

62   Andrew Williams, *Labour and Russia: The Attitude of the Labour Party to the USSR, 1924–34* (Manchester: Manchester University Press, 1989), p. 7.

63   Reprinted in *LPACR*, January 1918, pp. 47–51.

64   *LPACR*, January 1918, p. 5.

65   For further information on the Stockholm conference, see Hildamarie Meynell, 'The Stockholm Conference of 1917', *International Review of Social History*, 5 (1960), 1–25 and 202–25.

66   The new constitution included the celebrated 'Clause Four', committing the party to the common ownership of the means of production.

67   Museum of Labour History, Labour Party archive, HEN/1/31, letter to G. H. Roberts, 21 June 1917, and HEN14/3. See also J. M. Winter, 'Arthur Henderson, the Russian Revolution and the reconstruction of the Labour Party', *The Historical Journal*, 15:4 (1972), 733–73.

68   Museum of Labour History, Labour Party archive, Advisory Committee on International Questions, Minutes, 30 May 1918, and 14 June 1918.

69   Cole, *A History of the Labour Party*, p. 41.

70   Jones, *The Russia Complex*, p. 4.

71   Elbaki Hermassi, 'Towards a comparative study of revolutions', *Comparative Studies in Society and History*, 18:2 (1976), 214.

72   Theda Skocpol, *States and Social Revolutions: A Comparative Analysis of France, Russia and China* (Cambridge: Cambridge University Press, 1979), p. 4.

73   *LPACR*, 1922, pp. 74–83; *LPACR*, 1925, pp. 38, 181–9. An application by the CPGB to affiliate to the Labour Party was also rejected in 1936, see *LPACR*, 1936, pp. 50–1, 296–300.

74   James Jupp, *The Radical Left in Britain, 1931–1941* (London: Frank Cass, 1982), pp. 18–19.

75   *LPACR*, 1936, 'British Labour and Communism', pp. 296–7.

76   *LPACR*, 1919, Special resolution on 'Intervention in Russia', p. 225.

77   Labour Party, *Labour's Russian Policy: Peace with Soviet Russia* (London: Labour Party, 1920), p. 3, held in the University of Leeds Library, Brotherton Collection, Mattison, LAB.

78   *LPACR*, 1913, appendix v, pp. 123–7.

79   For information on the Internationals, see Julius Braunthal, *History of the International, vol. 1, 1864–1914*, translated by Henry Collins and Kenneth Mitchell (London: Thomas Nelson, 1966); Braunthal, *History of the International, vol. 2, 1914–1943*, translated by John Clark (London: Thomas Nelson, 1967); G. D. H. Cole, *A History of Socialist Thought, vol. 3, parts 1 and 2, The Second International, 1889–1914* (London: Macmillan, 1956); James Joll, *The Second International, 1889–1914* (London Boston: Routledge and K. Paul, rev. and extended edn, 1974).

80   *LPACR*, 1916, p. 32.

81   See *LPACR*, 1918, p. 141. This part of the constitution remained unaltered until 1953 when the language was updated. See *LPACR*, 1953, p. 217.

82   *LPACR*, 1919, pp. 3–10.

83   *Ibid.*, pp. 216 and 142.

84 Cited in Joll, *Origins of the First World War*, p.1.

85 *LPACR*, 1919, p. 196.

86 See *LPACR*, 1919, appendix 8, 'International Labour and Socialist Conference, Berne, 26 January to 10 February 1919, text of resolutions, p. 196.

87 *LPACR*, 1923, pp. 11–12.

88 G. D. H. Cole, *A History of Socialist Thought, vol. 4, part 2, Communism and Social Democracy 1914–1931* (London: Macmillan, 1958), p. 688.

89 Taylor, *The Trouble Makers*, p. 158.

90 Henry Winkler, 'The emergence of a Labor foreign policy in Great Britain, 1918–1929', *Journal of Modern History*, 28:3 (1956), 248.

91 J. Ramsay MacDonald, *A Policy for the Labour Party* (London: Leonard Parsons, 1920), pp. 132 and 134.

92 Henry Winkler, *The League of Nations Movement in Great Britain, 1914–1919* (New Brunswick, N.J: Rutgers University, 1952), pp. 167–8.

93 MacDonald, *A Policy for the Labour Party*, pp. 131, 161 and 172.

94 *LPACR*, 1919, pp. 23–4.

95 Chairman's address, *LPACR*, 1920, p. 112.

96 Michael Howard, *War and the Liberal Conscience* (London: Temple Smith, 1978), p. 95.

97 Norman Angell, *The Unseen Assassins* (London: Hamilton, 1932), pp. 201–2.

98 Bealey, *The Social and Political Thought of the British Labour Party*, p. 18.

99 Winkler, 'The emergence of a Labor foreign policy', p. 248.

100 *LPACR*, 1922, p. 200.

Chapter 4

The Labour minority governments

The Labour Party saw an improvement in its electoral fortunes in the immediate post-war period. At the 1918 election Labour gained 22 per cent of the vote, a tremendous increase from 7 per cent at the last election held in 1910.[1] During the war both the trade union and the Labour Party membership had doubled, and working-class militancy had increased in the first few years of peace.[2] With the concomitant increase in class-consciousness, the working class now identified far more strongly with the Labour Party than the Liberals and the Liberal Party was split between the followers of Lloyd George and Asquith. The Labour Party became the official opposition in 1922, out-stripping the Liberals in the election of that year. They formed minority governments in 1924 and 1929–31, but were unable to gain a majority of seats. Rather surprisingly, it is in the area of foreign policy that Labour is seen as having had the most success in these two early experiences in government, even though foreign policy is subject to more external restraints than other policy areas.[3] The Labour Party and minority Labour governments had considerable impact on Britain's stance on open diplomacy, internationalism, the arms trade, and the League of Nations. From the early 1920s to the late 1930s, the internationalist, anti-war section of the party, strongly influenced by the UDC, dominated Labour Party thinking on international affairs. While this wing of the party had initially been highly critical of the League of Nations, they came to see it as the avenue through which peace could be maintained.

Despite, or possibly because of, the trauma of the First World War, the post-war years saw a period of remarkable optimism about the ability to banish war and conflict through the rational application of international law and the operation of the League of Nations. The ideas of the UDC, developed through their publications during the war, coincided with liberal internationalist views propounded by President Woodrow Wilson. In particular, they were similar to, and preceded, the Fourteen Points of the peace programme Wilson outlined in his address to Congress on 8 January 1918, and took with him to the Versailles Conference in December. These included 'Open covenants of peace, openly arrived at', with no secret agreements; freedom of the seas; the removal of economic barriers to trade; the reduction of national armaments to the lowest level consistent with domestic safety; a free hearing of all colonial claims to self-determination; the restoration of occupied territories; and the formation of a general association of nations 'for the purpose of affording mutual guarantees of political independence and territorial integrity to great and small states alike.'[4] In terms of national self-determination, the Labour Party's 1918 general election manifesto said that Labour would 'extend to all subject peoples the right of self-determination within the British Commonwealth of Free Nations' and called for 'freedom' for Ireland and India.[5] This was repeated in its 1922 general election manifesto, which also advocated support for the new constitution of the Irish Free State.[6] In terms of open covenants, the Labour Party's perspective was that public opinion would ensure that open agreements conformed to the highest morality and public opinion would prevent the outbreak of war, for a League of Nations could rely on public opinion rather than the use of force or economic sanctions to ensure compliance within itself. For those on the political left, having found a way of resolving conflict between states, it was also necessary to deal with the domestic causes of state aggression. Central to this was dealing with and regulating the arms industry, with foreign policy radicals believing that 'if there were no armaments, there would be no war'.[7] The obvious conclusion was to cut down and abolish armaments. At this time there seemed no reason not to, as there was no obvious aggressor in the world. As Ben Pimlott explains: 'The lack of an identifiable foreign danger focussed attention on the danger within: the threat presented by the capitalist system, by arms dealers and manufacturers, by imperialist competition, above all by the inertia or hypocrisy of governments in their relations with neighbours.'[8] What developed within the Labour Party was the closest they had had to date to a comprehensive and widely accepted viewpoint on foreign policy. Windrich has argued that Labour followed a 'socialist' foreign policy in the post-war years;[9] Winkler that the party developed a 'League of Nations' policy.[10] Certainly these years were marked by a fair degree of agreement within the different wings of the party on the basis of a British foreign policy, despite the widespread and enduring differences between the various groups and factions of the party and the mutual suspicion between the trade unionists and the intellectuals. Both pacifists and non-pacifists could agree on the need to remove aggression and conflict from the international system through the League of Nations. While those who had fought most to get such a body as the League established were the most critical of it once it was created, there was a general belief in its ability to maintain peace. This agreement continued until the mid-1930s, when the horrors of the Spanish Civil War broke down the consensus on the ability to maintain peace through non-intervention and the ability of the League of Nations system to regulate and control conflict.

Labour in government, 1924

The election of November 1922 saw a marked improvement in the standing of the Labour Party, with 142 MPs elected. The Liberals were still divided, with the Independent Liberals gaining fifty-four seats and the National Liberals sixty-two.[11] This meant that for the first time Labour was the second most powerful party in Britain and could sit on the opposition front bench. Ramsay MacDonald, who had lost his seat at the 1918 election as a result of his anti-war record, was returned to Parliament, as were Philip Snowden and George Lansbury. E. D. Morel of the UDC was elected to Parliament for the first time, as were Sidney Webb, Clement Attlee, Herbert Morrison and Emanuel Shinwell. A number of former Liberal MPs were returned as Labour Party ones, including Arthur Ponsonby and Charles Trevelyan, founding members of the UDC. Arthur Henderson, the most senior Labour MP at the time, lost his seat. Ramsay MacDonald was elected chairman of the PLP, making him leader of the party. This was somewhat remarkable given his rift with the party over the First World War, and while he had been busy in the international labour movement since the end of the war, the loss of his parliamentary seat in 1918 had meant that he had continued to have a low profile within the party during the intervening years. Bonar Law led the Conservative government until May 1923 when, due to his ill health, Stanley Baldwin replaced him as Prime Minister. Foreign affairs took up much parliamentary time, with the crisis over Germany's reparation payments and France's occupation of the Ruhr. Marquand notes how 'Foreign crises usually strengthen the Government of the day. This one brought greater benefits to the Opposition. MacDonald knew more about foreign affairs than Bonar Law or Baldwin, and spoke on them with greater authority.'[12] MacDonald linked the economic conditions at home with the crisis abroad, arguing that 'the unemployment problem at home could not be resolved until Europe had been pacified and the reparations issue resolved.'[13] The 1922 Labour Party manifesto had called for revisions of the Peace Treaties, with German reparations being brought within Germany's capacity to pay, an all-inclusive League of Nations 'with power to deal with international disputes by methods of judicial arbitration and conciliation', and arms limitations. Labour's 1923 manifesto expressed similar sentiments, calling for 'a policy of International Co-operation through a strengthened and enlarged League of Nations; the settlement of disputes by conciliation and judicial arbitration' and the revision of the Versailles Treaty, especially regarding German reparations.[14] Sidney Webb argued in his speech to the 1923 annual conference that the peace treaties had failed because they ignored both economics and morality, and called for a foreign policy based 'not on what we presume to think our rights, but on what we can discern to be in the common interests of the world' and on how 'we can best serve humanity as a whole'.[15]

The general election of 6 December 1923 resulted in the Conservatives winning 258 seats, with Labour on 191 and the Liberals 159.[16] The Conservatives under Baldwin tried to establish a government, but the Liberals, united again under Asquith, made it clear that they would support a minority Labour government rather than a minority Conservative one. There was fevered speculation about which party would form a government. Following the King's Speech on 15 January laying out the Conservatives' legislative programme, the Liberals voted with the Labour amendment to it. This meant that the Conservative government was beaten, and the King called upon MacDonald to form a minority Labour government. On 22 January 1924 Ramsay MacDonald visited the King and became, with the support of the Liberals, the head of the first-ever Labour government.[17] He not only became Prime Minister, but also appointed himself as Foreign Secretary, arguing that the position needed a powerful figure. Arthur Ponsonby, who had earlier worked as a diplomat in the Foreign Office, became MacDonald's parliamentary secretary at the Foreign Office. Attlee was made the Under-Secretary for War under Stephen Walsh 'who, though he had no experience of military matters, was an excellent chief and very popular with the Army.'[18]

MacDonald faced a number of problems in forming a government as a result of Labour's unexpected victory. First, the Labour Party was used to making decisions through committees and conferences, and this 'was not easy to reconcile with the constitutional necessity of entrusting power to one man – MacDonald himself – to form a government'.[19] This problem was overcome by Sidney Webb persuading the various committees of the labour movement that MacDonald should have an entirely free hand in appointing his Cabinet.[20] Second, neither MacDonald nor his colleagues had any real experience of government, with MacDonald never having held even the most junior of ministerial posts. Arthur Henderson was the politician with the most experience of government, having been in the War Cabinet, but he had lost his seat and MacDonald did not choose to find a way of bringing him into the government.[21] This lack of experience certainly put the Labour government at a disadvantage. MacDonald attempted to overcome this problem by appointing some Cabinet members from outside the Labour Party; most notably Lord Haldane, the former Liberal War Minister, became Lord Chancellor, and Lord Chelmsford, a Conservative peer, became First Lord of the Admiralty.[22] Third, there was also a lack of experience and of ministerial talent amongst the Labour MPs in general. MacDonald wrote to Henderson that 'we are terribly short of men' to put in the ministries, and 'We shall have to put into some of the offices men who are not only untried, but whose capacity to face the permanent officials is very doubtful.' However, he felt it was important to have someone good working at Eccleston Square, the Labour Party headquarters, for 'I may be wrong, but, for the life of me, I cannot see this Parliament lasting any time.'[23] Fourth, Labour did not have a clear policy programme to draw upon, as, according to Attlee, 'I do not think that MacDonald had envisaged having to take office, and the Party programme, except on foreign affairs, was very much a minority document. It gave no clear lead on priorities.' Furthermore, 'The position of a minority Government is always difficult. There were those in our ranks who thought that we should have declined the responsibility.'[24] While sections of the press and the political elite were horrified at the prospect of a Labour government, the Labour Party itself was amazed and somewhat overawed. Only a few years ago they had been a minor party, trailing far behind the Liberals, with no expectation of assuming power. Sidney Webb noted that 'The sudden responsibility of so sudden and unexpected an assumption of office gave the Party a shock which sobered even the wildest of shouters.'[25]

In addition to all these problems, the ability of the Labour government to affect change in either foreign or domestic policy was minimal given that it relied on the Liberals for support in the House of Commons to push its legislation through. Despite, or possibly because of this, foreign affairs was seen as this historic government's major area of success during its brief period in office. Rather than seeing a conflict between domestic and international priorities, to MacDonald and the rest of the Cabinet 'it seemed obvious that Britain's domestic problems were the product of a much larger international crisis, which could only be solved by international agreement.'[26] In electoral terms, success with foreign policy was important for the Labour government, as it provided an opportunity for Labour to demonstrate that it was capable of representing the nation, and not just class interests.

The Labour government had four areas of foreign policy for which it is remembered. First, its achievement in dealing with the main problem at the heart of European security, namely Franco-German relations. In opposition, Labour had been united in its condemnation of the Versailles Treaty, and its election manifesto had called for its revision, particularly with regard to German reparations. The Labour Party tended to see France, rather than Germany, as the expansionist power de-stabilising Europe and many, including MacDonald, had been opposed to reparations of any sort. However, on assuming office, MacDonald went out of his way to court the French, breaking with diplomatic tradition by writing personally to the French Prime Minister, and supported the American plan drawn by the Dawes Committee for improving the system of German reparations.[27] During July 1924 MacDonald chaired a conference in London consisting of government delegations from France, Germany, the USA and Britain, where his informal and friendly diplomatic approach were much praised, and eased the way to reaching agreement on the Dawes Plan.[28] Successful agreement was reached on the French evacuation of the Ruhr, on the easing of the system of reparations, which had previously been seen by many as intractable problems, and the conference saw the Germans being dealt with as equals for the first time since the war. Lyman calls this achievement 'the high point of MacDonald's career'.[29] Pelling has argued that 'It was no small success to have brought the French and Germans back into almost friendly negotiation, and to have found a temporary solution of the reparations question.'[30] The Labour Party was delighted that MacDonald 'had exploded the myth that foreign affairs were a secret science, the last mystery of state,

which only members of the traditional ruling classes could master'.
However, many also saw the Dawes Plan as betrayal of their earlier
policy on reparations. Morel argued in the House of Commons that it
'is not going to solve the problem of reparations', that it would bring
about the ruination of German industry, that it was viewed with
'profound apprehension' by Labour back-benchers, and that,

> [T]he only serious justification for accepting the Dawes Report would be
> if that Report puts an end to the latent state of war which has existed in
> Europe ever since Allied statesmanship admitted the principle ... that it
> was tolerable that there should be an invasion of German soil, an abroga-
> tion of German civil law, and an elimination of German sovereignty, in
> order to force payment of reparations.[31]

The TUC accepted the Dawes Plan but was critical of it, and during
the presidential address at the 1924 annual conference it was pointed
out that it was the German worker who would have to make sacrifices
as a result of the Dawes Plan.[32] One of the complaints was that
MacDonald had changed Labour's policy on reparations on his own,
without referring it back to the party, which was against the democratic
and consensual ethos of the party.

Second, the Labour government fulfilled its manifesto pledge to
end secret diplomatic agreements by announcing that it would inau-
gurate a new practice of laying all treaties with other nations on the
table of the House of Commons for a period of twenty-one days, after
which the treaty would be ratified. This, MacDonald argued, would
strengthen the control of Parliament over the conclusion of international treaties and agreements, allow discussion of them, and 'By this
means secret Treaties and secret clauses of Treaties will be rendered
impossible.'[33] As far as the Labour Party was concerned, it was felt
'With pride and appreciation that the nine months of the British
Labour Government was an expression of a new spirit in diplomacy
and the beginning of a policy for Great Britain of the promotion of
peace and reconciliation among the peoples.'[34] The lack of parliamentary control over foreign policy and diplomacy had been one of the
Labour Party's main criticisms while it was in opposition. However,
MacDonald's own approach was actually quite secretive: as both Prime
Minister and Foreign Secretary he had a very unusual amount of
control over the development of Labour's foreign policy. He did not
refer many foreign policy questions to the Cabinet, nor discuss them
with his ministerial colleagues.[35] 'This tendency towards tight personal
control contrasts unfavourably with MacDonald's own insistent

demand in his opposition days for the "democratic control of foreign policy".[36] Indeed, the 'relative freedom of action in foreign affairs gave the Labour Government its greatest opportunity for accomplishment'.[37]

One of MacDonald's decisions that was very unpopular amongst many sections of the Labour Party was his agreement to build five replacement Navy cruisers, for which he was criticised in the House of Commons for not adhering to the principles of disarmament to which he had pledged the government. MacDonald argued that construction would keep 4,750 dockyard workers from losing their jobs, an issue that has always proved problematic vis-à-vis the arguments for disarmament, and that the decision was not against disarmament as such as they were replacement ships, not new ones. He said that the way to disarmament was not to allow the Navy 'to disappear by wastage from the bottom', for 'what a magnificent conception of pacifist principles are held by hon. Members who think the best way to do that is to allow your ships to fall to pieces!'[38] MacDonald did, however, go against the advice of the Admiralty and the Foreign Office by rejecting the proposal to build a new naval base at Singapore, fearing that there would be no hope of reaching an international agreement on disarmament if Britain went ahead with this project.[39]

The third main foreign policy issue was Britain's attitude towards the League of Nations and the form that its collective security was to take. The Labour government rejected the draft Treaty of Mutual Assistance, which had been put forward at the fourth session of the Assembly of the League of Nations in September 1923. This treaty was based on a system of collective assistance, including military, of all of the members of the League for any of their number who was the object of a war of aggression, combined with a reduction in national armaments commensurate with the security furnished by the Treaty of Mutual Assistance. MacDonald argued that 'the guarantee afforded by the draft Treaty is so precarious that no responsible Government will feel justified in consenting to any material reduction of its armaments in return.' This undermined the whole objective of the Treaty, which furthermore would 'involve an increase rather than a decrease in British armaments'.[40] Britain was only one of several countries that rejected the draft Treaty, and in its place the Geneva Protocol for the Pacific Settlement of International Disputes was drawn up. This placed more emphasis on the settlement of international disputes by conciliation and arbitration before they led to war. This was supported by both the Labour government and the Labour Party.[41] The Labour Party

passed a resolution on 17 March 1925 that stated 'That this Party
holds that this Country should do everything in its power to obtain the
acceptance of the principles of the Protocol and the holding of the
Disarmament Conference. It stands by the Protocol on the ground
that it furnishes the only practical plan at present for obtaining disarmament, and substituting arbitration for war as the method of settling
disputes.'[42] The rhetoric of the Geneva Protocol was more in line with
both Labour Party and radical liberal thought on international affairs.
However, while the emphasis of the Treaty and the Protocol were
different, the Geneva Protocol depended ultimately on the sanction of
the use of force, and was therefore not so dissimilar to the Mutual
Security Pact, or even to the covenant of the League of Nations. Article
16 of the covenant stated that should any member of the League resort
to war, it shall be deemed to have committed an act of war against all
other Members of the League, and all financial, commercial and diplomatic relations will be broken off. 'It shall be the duty of the Council
in such case to recommend to the several Governments concerned
what effective military, naval or air force the Members of the League
shall severally contribute to the armed forces to be used to protect the
convents of the League.'[43]

MacDonald played a leading role at the Assembly of the League of
Nations in September 1924 in getting the Geneva Protocol accepted
by the delegations to it, and in the League recommending that the
governments of the member states accept the Protocol.[44] However,
MacDonald and the Cabinet then prevaricated over the Geneva
Protocol, arguing that they needed more time to discuss the implications of any of the Protocols drawn up at Geneva before the government agreed to it.[45] Before further negotiations could take place,
Labour was replaced by a Conservative government, which in turn
refused to sign the Protocol. MacDonald then railed against the
Conservative government for not signing the Geneva Protocol, for
'The Protocol ... brings into diplomacy a new moral obligation ... it
supplants a system of force by one of justice'. The Protocol would
involve 'powers of enforcement', that is, sanctions, but these would
only need to be used once or twice before 'it will become impossible
for a nation to defy it – impossible, not owing to the menace of force,
but to habit and other psychological and moral reasons. The nations
will simply accept it.' 'The new order of the Protocol will be its own
sanction,' and 'The era of peace will have come at last.'[46] Overall,
MacDonald was fairly ambivalent towards the League of Nations;
he was not convinced that collective security would work, preferring

disarmament instead, but argued that the League needed to be strengthened and made more representative by admitting Germany and the Soviet Union to its ranks, and convincing the USA to join without having 'to go cap in hand to America to beg her to come in'.[47]

The fourth area of foreign policy for which the Labour government is remembered was its action in granting *de jure* recognition to the Soviet Union. It did this on 1 February 1924, just over a week after gaining office. 'In recognizing the Soviets the Government had laid its hands on the most explosive issue in British politics ... For many Labourites, friendship with Russia was the one foreign policy issue that really mattered; for many of their opponents, to make overtures to the Soviets was to embrace Evil itself.'[48] However, while the Labour government was keen to establish diplomatic and economic ties with the Soviet Union, the Labour movement continued to fight communism and communists within their own ranks and within the international labour movement, seeing a re-invigorated Labour and Socialist International as a bulwark against an expansionist Third International.

As part of the recognition process, MacDonald invited the Soviets to London to a conference to discuss the proposed recognition treaty, which included negotiation for a loan to Russia, compensation for British creditors who had suffered losses during and since the Russian Revolution, and the basis for Anglo-Russian trade. These negotiations opened on 14 April, and dragged on for four months with little progress, but with much criticism and tension. Two treaties were eventually signed, the Commercial Treaty, which laid out conditions for trade, and the General Treaty, which pronounced that there would be a later treaty to outline the settlement of all claims for compensation, and which made a British loan to the Soviet Union conditional upon this settlement.[49] Attlee notes that 'The Labour Government made earnest attempt to arrive at an agreement with the U.S.S.R., Ponsonby, the Under-Secretary of State for Foreign Affairs, showing great patience. The position was not made more easy by the activities of the British Communist Party.'[50] While recognition was in keeping with its policy of international solidarity and was seen by many on the left as a policy success, it led to domestic political problems, feeding the accusations of being 'soft' on communism that arose out of the Zinoviev letter and the Campbell case and which contributed to the general election defeat in October.[51] J. R. Campbell, the acting editor of a Communist paper, *Workers Weekly*, and a leading member of the British Communist Party, was arrested under the Incitement to Mutiny Act on a charge of attempting to 'seduce' members of the armed forces from their loyalty to the King, following the publication of an article calling on the armed forces not merely to refuse to go war, but to join forces with the workers to smash capitalism. The prosecution was dropped by the Labour government, but it was 'alleged that the prosecution was stopped for political reasons', and Asquith, the Liberal leader, proposed a Motion that an inquiry into the government's role be held.[52] This Motion was passed, producing a difficult position for the government, and MacDonald decided to dissolve the Labour government. During the election campaign, the *Daily Mail* produced a copy of a letter that the Foreign Office had obtained, which had allegedly been written by Zinoviev, the Secretary of the Third International, to the British Communist Party. This urged them to do everything possible to assist the ratification of the two Russian Treaties.[53] The Conservative opposition and most of the press presented this as evidence that the Labour Party was much the same as the Communist Party, even through the letter was thought to have been a forgery. The government was unsure of how to deal with the situation, and it has been argued that both the Zinoviev letter and the Campbell case were mishandled by MacDonald, 'who might have made them both recoil effectively upon the Conservatives'.[54] The result was that although the Labour Party increased its vote by over a million at the election of 29 October 1924, they lost forty seats. The Liberals also fared badly, with only forty MPs being returned. On 4 November the Conservatives formed a government with Stanley Baldwin as Prime Minister. Labour had been in power for only nine months.

Following its loss of power, the Labour Party's foreign policy was based on a return to its pre-government position of support for disarmament. Labour back-benchers in particular, and the wider Labour movement in general, took the opportunity to exert their influence over policy after having had to restrict their comments during Labour's period in office. MacDonald also seemed keen to assert his disarmament credentials more forcefully. The party attended the League of Nations conference on the regulation of the international traffic in arms and ammunition in May 1925, and generally showed a more positive stance towards the League than previously. Despite Labour's efforts to pressurise the British government into supporting the Arms Traffic Convention proposed by the conference, it only did so after gaining an amendment which excluded from the agreement 'ships of all kinds' and their armaments, including ships, aeroplanes and submarines.[55] This of course benefited the British arms industry. The party flirted with the idea of supporting moves to outlaw war, and discussed with seriousness the proposal being put forward in the USA by Senators Borah and Capper outlawing war. There were conflicting views on whether the 'outlawry of war' coincided or conflicted with Labour Party policy. The Party supported the idea in the abstract, but not the US Senators' proposal as it included scrapping the League of Nations and instead relying on alliances between individual states. Leonard Woolf, for example, was very critical of the Senators' proposals.[56] The Labour Party International Department Advisory Committee produced a number of memos outlining its position. The Locarno Pact was criticised, and Norman Angell raged against the Conservative government's failure to sign an arbitration treaty.[57] The Labour Party repeatedly voted against the government's defence estimates, its position being that the party 'whether in power or in opposition, supports *some* expenditure on Armaments', but that the party 'believes that the present expenditure could be drastically reduced'. The party line was that,

> Support of some expenditure on armaments is based on the assumption that the Covenant of the League [of Nations] is taken seriously. The plea that our forces are used only to maintain peace, if not hypocritical, means that we repudiate the use of force to press purely British claims ... Our policy is the maintenance of peace: the pre-war policy was the pursuit of national advantage.[58]

The party's attitude towards the nature of the armed forces was that a national military capability was only acceptable to the extent that it formed part of an international military force that could be for international intervention, under the control of the League of Nations, in the last resort.

Labour Party rhetoric also took a more Marxist turn, and at the 1926 Labour Party Conference a resolution was passed supporting the concept of a general strike against war.[59] This came only five months after the British general strike had collapsed, partly, it was argued, through lack of support from the TUC and Labour Party leadership, causing massive disappointment and acrimony on the political left. Anti-war statements were supported in the international labour and socialist arena, and by the Parliamentary Labour Party in the House of Commons. Hugh Dalton, for instance, made many speeches in favour of disarmament in the-mid 1920s.[60] However, following a trip to Poland in 1926, where Dalton became aware of Polish fears of Germany, he became 'determined' to 'rewrite the Foreign Policy of the

Labour Party', and to shift it away from the current anti-French, pro-German stance.[61] Dalton published his views in *Towards the Peace of Nations* in 1928, in which he called for a strong League of Nations to police the world.[62] Dalton actually defended the Versailles settlement, and argued against frontier changes. He also argued in favour of an international air force under the control of the Council of the League of Nations, to replace national air forces.[63] Dalton was not in the majority, and for much of the 1930s the official Labour Party foreign policy was to oppose rearmament and to believe in the ability of the League of Nations to deter aggression.

The 1929–31 government

The next general election was held in on 30 May 1929, when the Conservatives fared badly, dropping from 419 seats to 260. Labour won the election with 288 seats, which was nearly double their achievement at the last election, but the result did not give them an overall majority.[64] With the support of the Liberal Party, they formed a minority government with Ramsay MacDonald as Prime Minister. This time the formation of MacDonald's Cabinet was acrimonious. He reluctantly appointed Arthur Henderson as Foreign Secretary upon Henderson's insistence that he would not accept the more junior post originally offered to him, which served to exacerbate existing tensions between the two men.[65] Philip Snowden became Chancellor of the Exchequer, 'one of the few Cabinet ministers to be given office without dissent'.[66] This was a key post, for the government was soon faced with a mounting economic crisis.

The Wall Street crash of October and November 1929 had a dramatic effect on the British economy, as it was caught in what MacDonald described as the 'economic blizzard' from America. There was a sharp decline in world trade and a collapse in world commodity prices, which greatly affected Britain's exports at a time when the government had been pinning its hopes on a trade revival to deal with existing economic problems. Britain's balance of payments worsened, and there was declining confidence in sterling. Unemployment rose rapidly from 1.164 million in June 1929 to 2.5 million in December 1930.[67] The rate of unemployment rose from 9.9 per cent in September 1929 to 22.4 per cent in September 1931.[68] The 'Great Depression', as it subsequently became known, was 'the most important event of the inter-war years. It killed the bright hopes of the nineteen-twenties. It brought ruin and poverty to millions and wreaked havoc with their political faiths.'[69]

The government was faced with a limited range of options: to come off the Gold Standard and devalue the pound in order to increase British exports, while adopting protectionist policies to decrease imports; or to cut government expenditure while raising taxation; or to try to reverse the recession by expanding the economy through public works and increasing the purchasing power of the workers. Snowden was firmly committed to the idea of free trade, and would not countenance the introduction of tariffs in imports or the rejection of the gold standard. Indeed, Attlee's view was that Snowden 'clung obstinately to the Gold Standard, while he had a fanatical devotion to Free Trade'.[70] Snowden's perspective did reflect the economic orthodoxy of the day, namely that devaluation would lead to financial disaster and to retaliatory measures by other countries, but, 'Lacking vision, Snowden had no alternative strategy to offer.'[71] Therefore, his response to the economic crisis and mounting unemployment was to increase taxation and reduce expenditure. Particularly controversial was his plan to cut unemployment pay. This was against Labour's previous commitment to treat the unemployed humanely and its 1929 election manifesto pledge to provide more generous maintenance for the unemployed, and was met with fierce resistance by his Cabinet colleagues. Sir Oswald Mosley, who held the ministerial post of the Chancellor of the Duchy of Lancaster with special responsibility for unemployment, proposed a very different policy to deal with both the general economic crisis and the high levels of unemployment, in what was called the 'Mosley Memorandum'. He advocated import controls combined with the expansion of public works, along with a complete overhaul of the way that unemployment was dealt with within the government administration. His proposals gained some support inside and outside of the government, but were rejected by the Cabinet, and he resigned from the government in May 1930.[72] At the 1930 Labour Party annual conference there was a resolution calling for an NEC report on Mosley's Memorandum, which was only very narrowly defeated. However, his popularity within the party had increased greatly, and he received a huge ovation from the floor for his speech, and was elected to the NEC for the third time.[73]

In terms of foreign policy, Labour's election manifesto had proclaimed that 'Peace is one of the greatest issues of the Election.' It stated that the Labour Party 'stands for arbitration and disarmament', and that it would press 'for the speedy completion of the Disarmament

Treaty and the convocation of a General Disarmament Conference'. It said that Labour would re-establish diplomatic and commercial relations with Russia, which had been terminated by the Conservative government, and would 'give the fullest and most cordial support' to the League of Nations and the International Labour Office.[74] This it did, and the 1929–31 Labour government pursued what Henry Winkler has called a 'League of Nations' policy.[75] This was based on 'the limitation of national armaments, the eradication of outstanding grievances, particularly in Europe, the arbitration or other pacific settlement of international disputes, and the provision of pooled security against aggression.'[76] This was to be done through a strengthening of the League, and a small reduction in national defence expenditure. Whereas the 1924 government had agreed to military sanctions to maintain security, the 1929 government relied on the sanction of the law and disarmament. Both governments tended to see the British empire as a single unit when it came to foreign and security policy, and the colonies and the self-governing Dominions were expected to support unreservedly British initiatives at the League of Nations for disarmament and peace as part of imperial diplomatic unity.[77] The 1929 Labour government signed the Optional Cause of the Statute of the Permanent Court of International Justice. This provided for the settlement, through the Court, of disputes between nations, which had been argued for back at the 1926 Labour Party annual conference.[78] Other government actions included evacuating British troops from the Rhineland; re-establishing diplomatic and economic relations with Russia, which had been terminated by the Conservatives; and signing up to a revised version of the Young Plan, which reduced German reparations by 20 per cent, at the Hague Conference of August 1929. MacDonald visited the USA in October 1929, which was the first time that a British prime minister had done so. Following a ticker-tape parade in New York, he met with President Herbert Hoover in Washington D.C., and was then taken to the President's holiday retreat at Rapidan in the Blue Ridge Mountains. From there MacDonald went on to meet with Canadian Prime Minister Mackenzie King in Ottawa. According to Hugh Dalton, the Under-secretary of State for Foreign Affairs, this trip to the USA 'removed many misunderstandings'.[79] The trip was heralded as a success both in the media and by the leaders of all the British political parties.[80]

Labour's 1929 general election manifesto had made no mention of the British empire but MacDonald did take a keen personal interest in the development of self-government in India. He supported a policy of giving India Dominion status, which had been announced by the viceroy, Lord Irwin, in October 1929, and called a round-table conference to discuss India's future in 1930. This was at a time of mounting tension in India. At the end of 1929 the Indian National Congress called for complete independence from Britain, and in March 1930 Gandhi started his campaign of civil disobedience with his 200-mile march to the sea to collect salt in symbolic defiance of the British salt law, for which he was arrested. MacDonald hoped to diffuse the situation by offering concessions to the nationalist movement. However, at the same time, the findings of the Simon Commission, appointed by the Conservatives in 1927, were presented, which did not even mention the option of giving India Dominion status and self-government. The first round-table conference, convened in November 1930, was fractious, being marked by communal differences and mutual suspicion. However, it was agreed, subject to certain reservations, that India would become a self-governing federation.[81] When he presented the results of the conference to the House of Commons, MacDonald said that the purpose of the conference had been to demonstrate that Britain was 'honestly endeavouring to meet the legitimate expectations of India', for the only alternative to concessions to self-government was 'Repression and nothing but repression ... a kind of repression from which we shall get neither credit nor success. It is the repression of the masses of the people' and 'it will develop into the repression of the whole of the population'. He declared that 'If you are prepared to subdue by force not only the people but the spirit of the time – then refuse to allow us to proceed.'[82] It was the first occasion at which the British government had discussed constitutional reform with representatives of the colony concerned. Despite the problems and lack of real consensus, this first round-table conference did go some way to help prepare the ground for the 1935 Government of India Act, which gave the federal assemblies full responsibility for government, and for the independence of India in 1947.

In the Middle East, MacDonald continued existing policy during the second Labour minority government in much the same way as he had during the first, that is, to support what were seen as Britain's strategic defence interests. Iraq had become a British Mandate under the auspices of the League of Nations in 1920. The Labour government renegotiated the 1927 Treaty with Iraq, which had been unpopular in Iraq, but extended the lease of the British air force base at Basrah for twenty-five years as part of a limited military alliance.[83] Sidney Webb, Secretary of State for the Colonies and for the

Dominions, argued that a military alliance with Iraq was 'vitally necessary in order to secure Imperial interests ... there is no other means of
securing that unfettered use in all circumstances of our strategy air
route, of adequately safeguarding our position at the head of the
Persian Gulf'.[84] Security and defence interests were prioritised over any
Labour Party aspiration to reform Britain's imperial role. Henderson
sought, against the wishes of MacDonald, to improve Britain's relationship with Egypt in terms of making some marginal concessions
over the withdrawal of British troops from Cairo and Alexandria,
while continuing the policy of retaining British troops and bases in the
Suez Canal zone and refusing to accede to Egyptian claims on the Suez
Canal itself.[85]

MacDonald's personal interest and involvement in foreign affairs
meant that tension between MacDonald and Henderson remained
high. Henderson's standing internationally grew during his period in
office. He campaigned for the League of Nations to call a World
Disarmament Conference, which had been part of the Labour Party's
1929 manifesto. The League agreed to this, and invited Henderson to
be its president, but the conference was not convened until 2 February
1932, by which time the Labour government had been replaced by the
National government. However, in recognition of his role, in 1934
Arthur Henderson became the second Englishman ever to receive the
Nobel Peace Prize for his work on disarmament.

The 1929–31 government has been criticised for not achieving a
great deal in terms of foreign policy, and for being overly optimistic
about basing its policy on arbitration, international co-operation and
disarmament.[86] However, it was widely believed at the time that it was
possible to eliminate conflict through disarmament and through international legislation. These views were not confined to the left, but
were reflected in the proposed policies of all the parties. What is significant here is that the Labour Party had, by this time, accepted that it
had to work through the League of Nations, rather than railing against
it as it had after the First World War. Holding office in 1924 had
provided a change in expectations, resulting in an increased sense of
responsibility within the party, and a more realistic assessment of what
was achievable by the PLP. The party seems to have been unusually
pleased with the government's handling of foreign affairs, with little
in the way of criticism from the back-benchers or from the annual
conference. While the foreign policy achievements of the 1929–31
government were limited, this has to be seen within the context of the
mounting financial crisis in Europe. Germany was unable to pay its

reparations, and was facing financial collapse. MacDonald tried desperately in the summer of 1931 to secure a final settlement of the reparations problem, but France would not agree to a moratorium or a reduction of German reparations.[87]

Germany's plight impacted on Britain, there was a run on sterling, and in July 1931 Britain lost a quarter of its reserves. As the economic crisis worsened during 1931, Snowden continued to oppose the introduction of tariffs or devaluation, and supported cutting expenditure, including unemployment payments. This was against the advice of numerous committees and commissions, and against the wishes of the majority of his Cabinet colleagues. In August 1931 the crisis peaked, and Snowden proposed cutting some public sector pay, and cutting unemployment benefit by 10 per cent, along with an increase in taxation in order to have 'equality of sacrifice'. The Cabinet was asked to vote on 23 August for a 10 per cent cut in unemployment benefit, without having been informed by Snowden that the Treasury had decided that the taxation increases were impracticable and would have to be reduced. The TUC and parts of the Labour Party vehemently opposed the cuts, and the Cabinet was divided. As it was likely that ministers such as Arthur Henderson would resign if the proposals were forced through, the Cabinet agreed that it was impossible to continue. There had been some discussions within the Cabinet about the proposal for some kind of national government to deal with the economic crisis, and it was agreed that MacDonald should offer his government's resignation to the King, and recommend to him that he should meet the three party leaders. The King accepted the resignation of the Labour ministers, but not that of MacDonald, inviting him instead to form a temporary national government with Stanley Baldwin and Sir Herbert Samuel, made up of individuals rather than representing one party, to deal with the immediate economic situation.[88] On 21 September Britain was forced off the gold standard, and although this did not bring about the disasters that had been predicted earlier, the economic crisis continued. Against all previous announcements, the National government then determined that it should continue in power, and called a general election for 31 October 1931 in order to extend its mandate beyond dealing with the immediate economic crisis. Labour opposed the National government, and moved to the opposition benches.[89] On 1 October the Labour Party announced that supporters of the National government would immediately cease to belong to the party. This effectively expelled MacDonald from the Labour Party, and made formal the growing rift between him and the labour movement, for up until this point it seems that MacDonald had hoped to maintain the co-operation of the party and possibly bring in Labour politicians such as Henderson to any future government.

The 1931 defeat

Despite initial statements to the contrary, at the October 1931 general election Ramsay MacDonald, along with Philip Snowden, J. H. Thomas and Lord Sankey, ran as part of the National government coalition. This was elected with a massive landslide, gaining a total of 554 seats, 473 of which were Conservative, thirteen were National Labour, thirty-five National Liberal, and thirty-three Liberal. While the Conservatives won the bulk of the seats, Ramsay MacDonald remained Prime Minister until the following election of 1935, which was also won decisively by the National government. The Labour Party was dramatically defeated in 1931, and Labour dropped from having 288 MPs to only 52, with the Independent Liberals led by Lloyd George gaining four seats.[90] Apart from George Lansbury, all the ex-Cabinet ministers lost their seats, including Arthur Henderson who had taken over as party leader. Many of the younger generation of MPs, who later went on to take up the top posts in the Attlee government, including Hugh Dalton, Herbert Morrison, Emanuel Shinwell, and Philip Noel-Baker, also lost their seats. MacDonald's defection to the National government was blamed by the Labour Party for their defeat, and he and Snowden were picked out as being personally responsible for the inability of the Labour government to deal with the economic crisis. 'The shock [of the defection] to the Party was very great, especially to the loyal workers of the rank-and-file who had made great sacrifices for these men.'[91]

Subsequent to his defection to the National government, MacDonald was seen as a traitor to his class and to his party, who, it was argued, had either engineered the events of the previous few months so as to stay in power, or had been seduced by his high friends from the opposition. Marquand describes how,

> Old enemies rushed forward to testify to his defects; old supporters kept silent, or joined in the chorus of denunciation ... Little by little, the MacDonald of flesh and blood faded from the party's collective memory. In his place appeared a two-dimensional monster of vanity, snobbery and social cowardice, whose systematic flattery by the upper class adequately explained his own behaviour and his party's downfall.[92]

Even Philip Snowden, who had also defected to the National government, accused MacDonald of deliberately planning the establishment
of a National government in order to be able to remain in power with
his Liberal colleagues, while attributing his own actions to a sense of
duty, which were only undertaken with deep regret at being separated
from his Labour colleagues.[93] Nevertheless, Snowden managed to
overcome any remaining loyalty he might have felt towards his Labour
colleagues by describing the Labour Party's 1931 manifesto as 'the
most fantastic and impracticable document ever put before the electors'. Its economic policy was 'Bolshevism run mad'.[94]

The party itself moved to the left, and George Lansbury became
leader of the PLP, with Clement Attlee as his deputy. Apart from these
two, the only other Labour MP left of any repute was Stafford Cripps,
of whom Dalton said the disaster of the 1931 election produced 'an
adolescent Marxist miasma'.[95] The crisis of 1931 polarised the medley
of political standpoints within the labour movement. The collapse of
the party in Parliament produced a division between the few remaining MPs and the Labour Party officials and trade unionists at Transport
House, who viewed the MPs as left-wing, in particular on foreign
affairs and defence. It also reduced the influence of the PLP vis-à-vis
Transport House and the annual conference at a time when the trade
unions were taking an increased interest in the direction of the Labour
Party. The trade unions became increasingly outspoken, as their leadership developed new policies for the party, which then became part of
the Labour Party creed. Bevin and Citrine of the TUC were instrumental in getting the party to accept a Keynesian approach to the
country's economic problems, based on devaluation and maintaining
expenditure rather than the deflationary policies the party had previously backed. Both the PLP and the unions had moved to the left on
foreign policy, adopting a more pacifist stance than previously, but it
was largely the TUC who then shifted Labour Party policy away from
the pacifism that they had embraced to a policy based on rearmament
in the late 1930s.

The general atmosphere of betrayal, confusion, and loss of faith in
the leadership of the Labour Party was added to by breakaway
groups.[96] Oswald Mosley, who had not only been a minister in the
previous Labour government, but had also apparently been considered
for the post of Foreign Secretary,[97] established the British Union of
Fascists in 1932.[98] Attlee later said that 'This was at first not much
more than a "ginger" group which attracted such young men as
Aneurin Bevan, John Strachey and John Beckett', and that after a while

'Genuine socialists' left Mosley, while he and the residue became the British Union of Fascists.[99] However, this was an embarrassment to the Labour Party, and made Labour supporters uncomfortably aware of the dangers of fascism at home as well as abroad. Those on the far left tended to argue that Mosley's followers were the 'storm troops' of the National government.[100] Meanwhile, the Independent Labour Party disaffiliated in July 1932. Relations between the ILP and the Labour Party had seriously deteriorated during the 1929–31 government, and the ILP had been particularly critical over Labour's handling of the economic crisis. Attlee, who left the ILP just before this point, felt that 'a great loss to the Labour Movement' when the ILP broke away, but that 'The I.L.P. became more and more a narrow sect rather than a broadly based political party, and its influence steadily declined.'[101] The ILP then campaigned on a more militant and left-wing programme, but it lost many members following its purge of reformist branches and became increasingly isolated from the organised working class.[102] In turn, a group broke away from the ILP to form the Socialist League, with Sir Stafford Cripps as its leading figure. They, nominally, worked within the Labour Party.

This is the context within which the Labour Party's foreign policy was revised. The party had little input into international affairs, apart from Arthur Henderson acting as President and Chair of the World Disarmament Conference in Geneva in 1932. The 1931 Labour manifesto had proclaimed that on international affairs 'The Labour Party has always been in the van of the Movement for International Peace; and it is universally recognised that its record, as a Government, above all in solving disarmament by Arbitration, gave to Great Britain the moral leadership of the world.' It would put forward proposals for drastic cuts in armed forces and the expenditure on them at the forthcoming Disarmament Conference.[103] At the time of the invitation to chair the conference, Henderson had been Foreign Secretary. Now he had lost his seat and was not even an MP, he was being undermined by criticism from the British press and from abroad and was suffering from ill-health throughout the conference.[104] His authority at the conference 'became little more than nominal', and the much-hoped-for conference achieved very little. 'Thus by July 1932, after five months of laborious haggling, all that had been accomplished was a general resolution affirming a commitment to substantial reductions in weapons without stipulating precise limits. Even those delegates who accepted the resolution as a basis for future negotiation viewed it was an admission of failure.'[105] There had been no concrete commitment to disarm, merely for future discussions, which then dragged on unsuccessfully until 1935. The Labour Party blamed the National government for the failure of the Conference, and accused it of sabotaging disarmament.[106] Many in the Labour Party still believed in disarmament and pacifism, and in the leadership role that Britain could play. They also believed in working through the League of Nations. However, these views had shifted from the consensus of the 1920s, and, with its defeat and MacDonald's policy of gradualism and responsibility discredited, Labour moved into a period of greater radicalism in its views. Labour was highly critical of the existing system of international relations and the government's foreign policy, and increasingly embraced pacifism. These views were not tested by external events, but were shaped and honed by internal problems and attitudes. Partly they were a response to the ambiguities of policy left from the 1920s, which resurfaced following the doubts produced by Labour's 1931 defeat.

In conclusion, the inter-war period was significant for the Labour Party's foreign policy. The two minority governments of 1924 and 1929–31 were not seen as particularly successful in terms of domestic policy, but were seen to have had some success in international affairs. This demonstrated that Labour could be trusted to represent the nation and not just class interests, which was reassuring to the electorate. The activities of the minority Labour governments, and of the Labour Party when in opposition, had some considerable impact on British views of internationalism, collective security and the League of Nations. From the early 1920s to the late 1930s, the internationalist, anti-war section of the party, strongly influenced by the Union of Democratic Control, dominated Labour Party thinking on international affairs. While this wing of the party had initially been highly critical of the League of Nations, they came to see it as the institution through which peace could be maintained. Despite, or possibly because of, the trauma of the First World War, the post-war years saw a period of remarkable optimism about the ability to banish war and conflict through the rational application of international law and the operation of the League of Nations.

Notes

1 David Butler and Gareth Butler, *British Political Facts, 1900–1985* (London: Macmillan, 6th edn, 1986), p. 224.
2 See Henry Pelling, *A History of British Trade Unionism* (London: Macmillan, 1963), pp. 261–4.

3 David Carlton, *MacDonald versus Henderson: The Foreign Policy of the Second Labour Government* (London: Macmillan, 1970), p. 15, says 'little has yet been written on foreign policy, although this represented the least unsuccessful feature of the history of the second Labour Government.'

4 E. David Cronon, ed., *The Political Thought of Woodrow Wilson* (Indianapolis: Bobbs-Merrill, 1965), pp. 442–4.

5 F. W. S. Craig, ed. and comp., *British General Election Manifestos 1900–1974* (London: Macmillan, rev. and enlarged edn, 1975), p. 31.

6 *Ibid.*, p. 38. On Labour's attitudes towards Ireland, see Geoffrey Bell, *Troublesome Business: The Labour Party and the Irish Question* (London: Pluto Press, 1982).

7 A. J. P. Taylor, *The Trouble Makers: Dissent over Foreign Policy, 1792–1939* (London: Hamish Hamilton, 1957), p. 181.

8 Ben Pimlott, *Hugh Dalton* (London: Papermac/Macmillan, 1986), p. 183.

9 Elaine Windrich, *British Labour's Foreign Policy* (Stanford, CA: Stanford University Press, 1952), pp. 258–9.

10 Henry Winkler, 'The emergence of a Labor foreign policy in Great Britain, 1918–1929', *Journal of Modern History*, 28:3 (1956), 247–58.

11 Butler and Butler, *British Political Facts*, p. 224. The Liberals had split after Lloyd George supplanted Asquith as Prime Minister in 1916.

12 David Marquand, *Ramsay MacDonald* (London: Jonathan Cape, 1977), p. 292.

13 *Ibid.*, p. 295.

14 Craig, *British General Election Manifestos*, pp. 38 and 48.

15 Mark Thomas and Guy Lodge, eds, *Radicals and Reformers: A Century of Fabian Thought* (London: Fabian Society, 2000), p. 51.

16 Butler and Butler, *British Political Facts*, p. 225.

17 For general information on this Labour government, see Richard Lyman, *The First Labour Government, 1924* (London: Chapman Hall, 1957).

18 Clement Attlee, *As It Happened* (London: Odhams Press, 1956), p. 75.

19 Henry Pelling, 'Governing without power', *Political Quarterly*, 32:1 (1961), 47.

20 Sidney Webb, 'The first Labour government', *Political Quarterly*, 32:1 (1961), 8.

21 F. M. Leventhal, *Arthur Henderson* (Manchester: Manchester University Press, 1989), p.137; Webb, 'First Labour Government', p. 14.

22 Pelling, 'Governing without power', pp. 47–8.

23 Public Record Office, London (hereafter PRO), Ramsay MacDonald Papers, PRO 30/69/1169, MacDonald to Henderson, 22 December 1923.

24 Attlee, *As It Happened*, p. 75.

25 Webb, 'The first Labour government', p. 9.

26 Marquand, *Ramsay MacDonald*, p. 329.

27 See Lyman, *The First Labour Government*, ch. 10; and Arnold Toynbee, ed., *Survey of International Affairs, 1924* (Oxford: Oxford University Press, 1926) pp. 359–71.

28 Lyman, *The First Labour Government*, p. 163.

29 *Ibid.*, p. 164.

30 Pelling, 'Governing without power', p. 49.

31 *House of Commons Debates* (hereafter *H.C. Deb.*), fifth series, vol. 176, cols 133–44, 14 July 1924.

32 *Trades Union Congress Annual Report*, 1924, p. 69.

33 *H.C. Deb.*, vol. 171, cols 2001–3, 1 April 1924.

34 *Labour Party Annual Conference Report* (hereafter *LPACR*), 1925, p. 252.

35 Webb, 'The first Labour government', p. 20.

36 Pelling, 'Governing without power', p. 48.

37 Lyman, *The First Labour Government*, p. 157.

38 *H.C. Deb.*, vol. 169, cols 2127–33, 21 February 1924.

39 Marquand, *Ramsay MacDonald*, p. 315.

40 Cited in Toynbee, *Survey of International Affairs, 1924*, pp. 31–2; see also Norman Angell, *After All: The Autobiography of Norman Angell* (London: Hamish Hamilton, 1951), pp. 241–2; and *LPACR*, 1925, p. 94.

41 *LPACR*, 1925, pp. 61, 94, and 252.

42 *LPACR*, 1925, pp. 94, 252, and 342.

43 Article sixteen of the Covenant of the League of Nations, *LPACR*, 1935, p. 322.

44 See Toynbee, *Survey of International Affairs, 1924*, pp. 36–46; Marquand, *Ramsay MacDonald*, p. 512.

45 Marquand, *Ramsay MacDonald*, pp. 355–6.

46 J. Ramsay MacDonald, *Protocol or Pact: The Alternative to War* (London: Labour Party, 1925), p. 5.

47 *H.C. Deb.*, series 5, vol. 169, cols 772–3, 12 February 1924.

48 Lyman, *The First Labour Government*, p. 186.

49 See *ibid.*, ch. 11.

50 Attlee, *As It Happened*, p. 76.

51 See Stephan Richard Graubard, *British Labour and the Russian Revolution, 1917–1924* (Cambridge, Mass.: Harvard University Press, 1956), ch. 13, for details.

52 Attlee, *As It Happened*, p. 76.

53 A full and useful account of this incident, drawing on Foreign and Commonwealth Office and Secret Intelligence Service documents, has been produced by Gill Bennett at the FCO, *'A Most Extraordinary and Mysterious Business': The Zinoviev Letter of 1924* (London: FCO, 1999).

54 Pelling, 'Governing without power', p. 51; Attlee, *As It Happened*, p. 77.

55 Modern Records Centre, University of Warwick (hereafter MRC), TUC archive, MSS 292/906/1, P. Baker, 'Memorandum on the arms traffic and the private manufacture of arms', Labour Party and Trades Union Congress Joint International Department, no. 337, April 1925; League of Nations Arms Traffic Conference, Report to the Executive of the Labour Party by Charles Roden Buxton and Mary Carlin, May 1925.

56 MRC, TUC archive, MSS 292/906/7, Leonard Woolf, 'Outlawry of War', Labour Party International Department Advisory Committee on International Questions, no. 379A, December 1927.

57 MRC, TUC archive, MSS 292/906/1, Norman Angell, 'Memorandum on the reactionary attitude of the government in international affairs', TUC and Labour Party Joint International Department, Advisory Committee on International Affairs, No. 341, November 1925.
58 MRC, TUC archive, MSS 292/906/1, Labour Party International Department, Advisory Committee on International Questions, C. Delisle Burns, 'Note on the estimates for the armed forces', no. 367, May 1927.
59 *LPACR*, 1926, p. 256; 1927, p. 63.
60 For example, speeches in House of Commons, 11 March 1926, *H.C. Deb.*, vol. 192, cols 2729–2734, 11 March 1926; H.C. Deb., vol. 208, cols 1827–1840, 11 July 1927.
61 Hugh Dalton, *Call Back Yesterday: Memoirs 1887–1931*(London: Muller, 1953), p. 167. Also referred to in Pimlott, *Hugh Dalton*, p. 184.
62 Hugh Dalton, *Towards the Peace of Nations. A Study in International Politics* (London: Routledge, 1928).
63 Pimlott, *Hugh Dalton*, pp. 185–6.
64 The results were: Labour 288 seats, Conservatives 260 seats, Liberals 59 seats. Butler and Butler, *British Political Facts*, p. 225.
65 For alternative interpretations of this, see Carlton, *MacDonald versus Henderson*, pp. 15–17; Leventhal, *Arthur Henderson*, pp. 136–7; Marquand, *Ramsay MacDonald*, pp. 489–91.
66 Keith Laybourn, *Philip Snowden: A Biography, 1864–1937* (London: Temple Smith, 1988), p. 115.
67 Butler and Butler, *British Political Facts*, p. 372.
68 Percentages of insured persons, male and female, recorded as unemployed for Great Britain and Northern Ireland, *Twenty First Abstract of Labour Statistics of the United Kingdom, 1919–1933* (London: HMSO, 1934), p. 52.
69 Robert Skidelsky, *Politicians and the Slump: The Labour Government of 1929–1931* (London: Macmillan, 1967), p. 141.
70 Attlee, *As It Happened*, p. 88.
71 Laybourn, *Philip Snowden*, p. 119.
72 See Skidelsky, *Politicians and the Slump*, ch. 8.
73 Robert Skidelsky, *Oswald Mosley* (London: Papermac/Macmillan, 3rd edn, 1990), pp. 229–31. On Mosley also see: A. K. Chesterton, *Oswald Mosley: Portrait of a Leader* (London: Action Press, 1937); Sir Oswald Mosley, *My Life* (London: Nelson, 1968).
74 Craig, *British General Election Manifestos*, p. 83.
75 Winkler, 'The emergence of a Labor foreign policy', pp. 247–58.
76 *Ibid.*, p. 247.
77 Partha Sarathi Gupta, *Imperialism and the British Labour Movement, 1914–1964* (London: Macmillan, 1975), pp. 99–100, 162.
78 *LPACR*, 1926, p. 331.
79 British Library of Political and Economic Science, London School of Economics (hereafter BLPES), Dalton Papers, part 2A, section 1/1, 46–7, New Year's Eve message to constituents, 1929.
80 Marquand, *Ramsay MacDonald*, pp. 506–9.
81 *Ibid.*, pp. 581–2.

82 *H.C. Deb.*, vol. 247, cols 637–50, 26 January 1931.
83 Gupta, *Imperialism and the British Labour Movement*, p. 165.
84 *Ibid.*, citing PRO, Cab 24/212, Cabinet Paper 167 (30).
85 See Carlton, *MacDonald versus Henderson*, ch. 8; Gupta, *Imperialism and the British Labour Movement*, pp. 164–5.
86 Pimlott, *Hugh Dalton*, p. 187; Winkler, 'The emergence of a Labor foreign policy', p. 247.
87 See Edward Bennett, *Germany and the Diplomacy of the Financial Crisis* (Cambridge, Mass: Harvard University Press, 1962).
88 Interpretations of events do vary, but useful accounts include Laybourn, *Philip Snowden*, ch. 12; Skidelsky, *Politicians and the Slump*, ch. 13. Marquand, in *Ramsay MacDonald*, provides detailed information on these events, and as good an understanding of MacDonald's motives and mindset as is possible. See chs 25 and 26. Other accounts include: Reginald Bassett, *Nineteen Thirty-One: Political Crisis* (London: Macmillan, 1958); Humphry Berkeley, *The Myth that Will Not Die: The Formation of the National Government 1931* (London: Croom Helm, 1978); Vernon Bogdanor, '1931 revisited: the constitutional aspects', *Twentieth Century British History*, 2:1 (1991), 1–25; Harold Nicolson, *King George the Fifth: His Life and Reign* (London: Constable, 1952); David Wrench, 'The parties and the National government, August 1931–September 1932', *Journal of British Studies*, 23:2 (1984), 135–53.
89 *LPACR*, 1931, p. 6.
90 Thirty-three Liberal MPs also joined the government benches. Butler and Butler, *British Political Facts*, p. 225.
91 Attlee, *As It Happened*, p. 90.
92 Marquand, *Ramsay MacDonald*, pp. 678–9.
93 Philip Snowden, *An Autobiography, vol. 2* (London: Nicholson and Watson, 1934), pp. 954–8.
94 *Daily Telegraph*, 19 October 1931, cited in Laybourn, *Philip Snowden*, p. 144.
95 Hugh Dalton, *The Fateful Years: Memoirs 1931–1945* (London: Mueller, 1957), pp. 148–9, 41.
96 See James Jupp, *The Radical Left in Britain, 1931–1941* (London: Frank Cass, 1982), ch. 1.
97 According to Harold Laski, who wrote to his friend, Felix Frankfurter, that MacDonald had considered Mosley for the post of Foreign Secretary, reported in, Kingsley Martin, *Harold Laski (1893–1950): A Biographical Memoir* (London: Victor Gollancz, 1953), p. 76.
98 Accounts of the establishment of the BUF include: Colin Cross, *The Fascists in Britain* (London: Barrie and Rockliff, 1961); James Drennan (W. E. D. Allen), *B.U.F. – Oswald Mosley and British Fascism* (London: John Murray, 1934); Richard Thurlow, *Fascism in Britain: A History 1918–85* (Oxford: Blackwell, 1987).
99 Attlee, *As It Happened*, p. 89.
100 Skidelsky, *Oswald Mosley*, p. 552.
101 Attlee, *As It Happened*, p. 88.
102 See Robert Dowse, *Left in the Centre: The Independent Labour Party 1893–1940* (London: Longmans, 1966), chs 12 and 13.

103 Craig, *British General Election Manifestos*, p. 97.
104 Attlee, *As It Happened*, p. 95.
105 Leventhal, *Arthur Henderson*, pp. 203 and 205.
106 *LPACR*, 1935, p. 4; Labour Party, *The 'National' Government's Disarmament Record* (London: Labour Party, 1935).

Chapter 5

The Labour Party, pacifism and the Spanish Civil War

On 18 September 1931 Japan invaded China on the pretext that a Japanese railway in Manchuria had suffered from Chinese sabotage. Japanese troops over-ran Manchuria and set up a puppet state. China appealed to the League of Nations for assistance under Article 11 of the Covenant, and the League responded by asking Japan to evacuate the territory it had occupied. Japan, which had signed up to the Covenant of the League of Nations and the Briand-Kellogg Pact (thereby agreeing to respect the territorial integrity of other member states and never to use war as an instrument of policy), then used Shanghai as a base for further incursions into China.[1] Condemnation of Japan by the League was muted, as both public opinion and the Western governments tended to think that China was exaggerating the threat from Japan. There was little sympathy for China, which, it was felt, was unable to govern and bring order to Manchuria. It was also argued by many that intervention by the League would do more harm than good.[2] The Labour Party and the TUC issued a declaration on 'The Far Eastern Situation' on 23 February 1932, saying that it was clear that Japan was 'responsible for this state of war'. They recommended that the member states of the League of Nations consider recalling their ambassadors from Japan, but hoped that this would not be necessary, and 'hope and believe that a manifestation of world opinion that the war must cease will not go unheeded in Japan'. If, however, Japan continued in its course then it may be necessary for the British government to propose that the League consider financial and economic measures.[2] George Lansbury, who had become leader of the Labour Party following the 1931 election, felt that 'There need not be war. The European powers, with the USA, have only got to make it plain that they will boycott Japan unless it acts reasonably and Japan will give way.'[4] Stanley Baldwin, leader of the Conservative Party and a Cabinet minister in the National government, argued that military action was too dangerous to consider as there was no defence against air attack, and 'the bomber will always get through'.[5] Indeed, by this point, concern about the ability of air power to render nations vulnerable to attack increased the belief that war was to be avoided at all costs. Prime Minister Ramsay MacDonald, after some prevarication, rejected America's proposal that the two countries should make a joint protest against Japan's actions. 'The Admiralty had made it clear that Britain was in no condition to go to war with Japan', and that Britain's armed forces were not strong enough to be able to back up any threat with the use of force.[6] The outcome of the Manchurian crisis was that Japan ignored the statements by the League of Nations. This discredited the League somewhat, and started to undermine the belief in the system of collective security that had been developed with Covenant of the League of Nations and the Geneva Protocol, designed to prevent the use of force and the outbreak of war between member states. This was the context in which the Labour Party embraced the most pacifist stance of its history, just as the optimism of the 1920s was being replaced by the growing fear of fascism in the early 1930s.

Labour and pacifism

The Labour Party's official foreign policy after the defeat of 1931 was based on collective security through the League of Nations, with support for the Geneva Protocol and the ultimate use of sanctions, and this was the policy supported by the bulk of the labour movement. In addition to this, the party was committed to supporting any multilateral agreements that arose from the World Disarmament Conference, held in Geneva in February 1932. However, the Labour Party came very close to briefly embracing pacifism instead of collective security as its remaining leaders, Lansbury, Attlee, and Cripps, all rejected the existing system of international relations and advocated their own visions of Labour's foreign policy. Lansbury, who had very strong Christian as well as socialist and pacifist views, espoused a form of absolute pacifism, opposing the use of force on humanitarian grounds under any conditions. He advocated unilateral disarmament and the dismantling of the British empire. He argued that 'Our people must give up all right to hold any other country, must renounce all imperialism and stand unarmed before the world.' Britain 'will then become the strongest nation in the world fully armed by justice and love ... Socialism, which is religion, is the one road which will lead to salvation.'[7] A strong believer in the power of public opinion, he told Cripps that what they needed was a public campaign on peace and disarmament, for 'no nation can stand out against the public opinion of the world'.[8] Attlee espoused what could be described as national pacifism, rejecting national defence in favour of an international military or police force. He argued in the House of Commons that 'There is no effective defence against air attack', and so in these circumstances 'the pacifist is the realist'.[9] Attlee went further when he stated that Labour 'did not believe in national armaments; we could only agree to armaments if those armaments were part of a system of pooled security to be used on behalf of the League for keeping the peace of the world.' However, recent events had shown that today there was no system of pooled security, and that the League had failed.[10] His pessimistic viewpoint lead him to conclude that the League of Nations needed to be replaced by a new organisation, such as a world commonwealth, which could provide collective security through an international military force. Sir Stafford Cripps, who had moved sharply to the left following the collapse of the 1931 government, espoused a form of class pacifism – war was to be resisted on all counts, unless it was a class war, and he argued against the working class joining the military forces, as the only acceptable form of army was a 'citizens' army'. Cripps had 'an incorrigible obtuseness to the effect of his utterances',[11] and Dalton, who had a low opinion of Cripps generally, said that his 'oratorical ineptitudes' meant that 'Tory H.Q. regard him as their greatest electoral asset.'[12] For Cripps, war was the result of economic nationalism caused by developed capitalism. This was a return to the left-wing view of imperialism espoused before the outbreak of the First World War. He was scathing about the League of Nations, arguing that it had become 'nothing but the tool of the satiated imperialist powers', and argued against the use of sanctions by the League as a deterrent to aggression, calling it an 'International Burglars Union'.[13]

While support for the League of Nations and multilateral disarmament through the work of the Disarmament Conference remained official party policy, a pacifist position was strongly asserted at the 1933 annual conference. One resolution was passed which called for the 'total disarmament of all nations throughout the world and the creation of an International Police Force'.[14] Another resolution was carried unanimously, which asked the party 'To pledge itself to take no part in war', to consult with the trade union and co-operative movements with a view to deciding 'what steps, including a general strike, are to be taken to organise the opposition of the organised working-class movement in the event of war or threat of war', and for the national joint bodies to endeavour to secure international action by the workers on the same line.[15] This effectively raised the issue of a general strike in the event of war, a policy that had been previously rejected. Arthur Henderson spoke in favour of the resolution, saying 'It is a dedication, a solemn vow, pledging us to the works of Peace.' He welcomed 'this new spirit, this willingness to dare and to risk all things in the cause of peace.'[16] Hugh Dalton was uncomfortable with the resolution, later noting that 'The Conference was in no mood to reject it or allow it to be withdrawn.'[17] Thus, with 'more expediency than courage',[18] he accepted it on behalf of the NEC, saying, somewhat confusingly, 'the resolution does not carry us perhaps quite far enough', in that it did not endorse economic and financial sanctions as well.[19]

Thus, the overall picture of Labour's foreign policy at this point was rather confused. Official policy remained in support of the League of Nations and any agreements on national disarmament that came out of the Disarmament Conference. However, some sections of the party were committed to the policy of a general strike in the event of war; some to complete national disarmament and the establishment of an international military force; while Lansbury, the leader of the party, was advocating national and international disarmament and pacifism. It was in the sphere of foreign policy that the most serious differences appeared between the PLP, which contained some of the most outspoken advocates of pacifism, and the rest of the Labour movement. This confusion was addressed by the National Council of Labour, comprised of the PLP, the party's NEC and the General Council of the TUC, which produced a memorandum, 'War and Peace'. This rejected the use of a general strike, since 'The lack of an independent trade union movement in such countries as Germany, Italy, Austria, e.t.c., makes the calling of a general strike against their Governments an impossibility.' The document accepted 'national pacifism' (in terms of meaning no war between nations), and maintained that 'loyalty to the world community on the issue of peace overrides any national duty and notably our duty to the government in war. We are world citizens because of our country's membership of a world community.' The over-riding claims of world citizenship were arbitration, 'the duty to insist that our Government settle all its disputes by peaceful means and eschew force'; the use of sanctions as collective action against a peacebreaker; and resistance to war.[20] This document was approved by the 1934 annual conference by 1,519,000 votes to 673,000.

The next major statement on foreign policy appeared in Labour's 1935 general election manifesto. This reiterated that Labour sought the 'whole-hearted co-operative with the League of Nations' and 'stands firmly for the Collective Peace System'. It stated that Labour would 'maintain such defence forces as are necessary and consistent with our membership of the League', but it also appeased the pacifists in the party by stating that, 'Labour will propose to other nations the complete abolition of all national air forces, the effective international control of civil aviation and the creation of an international air police force; large reductions by international agreement in naval and military forces; and the abolition of the private manufacture of, and trade in, arms.'[21] These were precisely the policies that had been put forward at the World Disarmament Conference, but which had not been passed. By the time of the 1935 election, the conference had collapsed, with no major agreements having been reached. Whereas the experience of holding office in 1924 had produced a more realistic assessment of what could be achieved in the realm of foreign policy within the party, by the mid-1930s this had been replaced by the assumption that a future Labour government could automatically deliver on disarmament and world peace, in spite of evidence to the contrary. Indeed, it was felt that the second Labour minority government had given Britain 'the moral leadership of the World',[22] and Labour just had to wait until it was in power again in order to implement its disarmament policies. Labour was not alone, however, in supporting policies of disarmament, collective security through the League, and, it was hoped, world peace. Pacifist sentiment was not confined to the left in Britain, and the memory of the horror of the First World War was still potent enough to convince many of the need to avoid war at all costs. The Peace Society had gained greatly in popularity, and its meetings were well attended. There was still a surprisingly strong faith in the League of Nations amongst the general public, despite the failure of the League to deal with Japan. A 'Peace Ballot', a sort of referendum on support for the League of Nations, was organised in the summer of 1935 by the members of the League of Nations Union, at which nearly 11,500,000 voted. The overwhelming majority supported a League of Nations policy, based on disarmament by agreement among nations, the abolition of air-warfare, the abolition of private arms manufacturing and sales, and support for economic sanctions, and, in the last resort, military measures by the League against an aggressor.[23]

The collapse of the World Disarmament Conference and the government's gradual disclosure that Hitler, who had become Chancellor in 1933, was rearming Germany, provided an alarming background to the Labour Party's flirtation with pacifism. The party voted against the 1935 defence estimates, but in anticipation that Baldwin would further propose the enlargement of the air force because of the threat being posed by Hitler and German rearmament, the PLP, the NEC and the TUC's General Council decided to meet to discuss the issue of British defence policy on 22 May 1935. The TUC met prior to this meeting to determine their position. Its leader, Walter Citrine, mapped out the pacifist positions being held by the Labour Party. He was concerned that not only was there 'mental confusion' over the Labour Party's foreign policy, but that sections of the labour movement refused to accept it. He complained that 'Lansbury is absolutely pacifist – from purely Christian motives – and he thinks that this country should be without defence of any kind... . but it certainly isn't our policy.' He continued that there were others, such as Henderson, who believed in the collective peace system, such as placing forces at the disposal of the League of Nations, 'but really they are not living in worlds of reality at all. The collective peace system should be operated, but did anyone think it would have to be operated in the next few months?' Citrine said that Hugh Dalton had told him the day before that German aircraft could reach Prague in twelve minutes, while German trade unionists had secretly sent him details of the German air force, munitions factories and underground aero-dromes. He further noted that 'in every country with the exception of France where there is a division of opinion, the Socialists have supported their Governments in one way or another in increasing their defence.'[24] Ernest Bevin, the leader of the massive Transport and General Workers' Union, prevaricated, suggesting that the TUC should speak to the Prime Minister since it had 'a big part to play' but 'We don't know what has been going on'. The meeting was recon-vened the following day, with heightened tension, just hours before the joint meeting was to be held, and just after Hitler's speech to the Reichstag in which he outlined Germany's foreign policy. He had stated that Germany would not return to the League of Nations unless it was given equality of status with the other great powers, and that while Germany would agree to non-aggression pacts and the limitation of arms, it would only do so once it had gained parity with each of these states and, until then, would continue in its expansion of its navy and air force. Ernest Bevin was more outspoken than the day before, saying that Germany would not listen to reasoned debate, and that dealing with Hitler was like dealing with communists:

> Have you ever tried to settle within your own Movement with any of your people who follow the philosophy of Communism – whenever you get the type of mind who follows the dictatorship, you can never get a compromise or settlement or trust. And really there is no difference between the Russians, Fascists or Communists.[26]

One delegate argued that they should listen to Hitler, but he was in the minority. Others argued that 'Hitler means war', and that 'Hitler is merely playing for time ... But the more weakness we show the more danger of war.' Another referred to the fate of their friends in the German Social Democrats who had been imprisoned, tortured, and sometimes killed: 'Pacifism in the face of that is absolute cowardice.' He also argued that Labour was partly to blame for the situation, having been in government for two years only recently. However, others felt that they were being tricked into voting for the defence estimates, and that they should call a disarmament conference.[27]

The meeting adjourned with no clear decision, but the deliberative process that the TUC General Council went through tells us much about how the trade union leadership was feeling, and how it came to have such an impact on Labour's position on rearmament. Bevin and Citrine had been holding discussions with Hugh Dalton, and all three agreed that Labour's foreign policy, vacillating between various forms of pacifism and support for the League of Nations, was not tenable in the face of German rearmament and the threat posed by Hitler. Together this unlikely combination – the rumbustious Bevin and ascetic Citrine co-operated but disliked each other immensely, and neither had much time for Labour Party intellectuals such as Dalton – formed an alliance that managed dramatically to shift the Party's position on defence.[28] Together they urged the PLP to stop voting against the estimates. Dalton accused Attlee of wanting 'to sponge on the Red Army',[29] while Attlee argued that there was no point trying to match German rearmament, since 'equality and parity, in the present conditions of international anarchy, being but new names for the old balance of power and the old armaments race'.[30] In the end the PLP decided to vote against the defence estimates and rearmament, with the left-wing still reluctant to give arms to a government to which it was opposed, but the ground had been prepared for a shift of policy position, and for the undermining of Lansbury's position as party leader.

The widely anticipated Italian invasion of Abyssinia (Ethiopia) on 3 October 1935, and its forcible annexation of Abyssinia into its East African empire in 1936, reinforced the tension between the conflicting views on foreign policy. The Labour Party was now divided between those who believed in strong support for the League of Nations and the implementation of economic sanctions in response to the Italian attack; the pacifists, led by George Lansbury, who opposed economic sanctions in principle; and those further to the left, such as Cripps, who viewed the League of Nations and its sanctions as a sham, run in the interests of capitalism and imperialism. In the lead up to the 1935 annual conference, it became clear that Labour was facing a show-down; this was not only on the future direction of the party's foreign and defence policy, but also on its leadership.

The 1935 conference, as Ben Pimlott puts it, 'focussed on the ritual martyrdom of George Lansbury'.[31] At the centre of the conflict was the resolution that the NEC had drafted for submission to the conference to support sanctions by the League of Nations if, as it looked increasingly likely, Italy was to invade Abyssinia. However, it was more than just Lansbury the man who was being rejected, it was his view of international socialism based on pacifism, and his position on Britain's foreign policy and role in the world. Even most of the Labour-left had by this time come to the conclusion that the use of force could not be ruled out against fascist aggressors, and that unilateral disarmament would leave Britain exposed and vulnerable to attack. However, there was deep mistrust of the National government and concern that it might use rearmament for aggressive purposes. According to G. D. H. Cole, 'Most of the Left in the Labour movement did not share Lansbury's pacifist convictions. But they were moved, as he was, by deep mistrust of the Government, and were exceedingly reluctant to agree to a re-armament policy which they felt sure would be used not to support the League but to do without it and to betray it.'[32] Tension was further heightened by Stafford Cripps resigning from the NEC on the eve of the conference over his objections to the resolution. Moved by Hugh Dalton on 1 October, it called for the League of Nations to 'to use all the necessary measures provided by the Covenant to prevent Italy's unjust and rapacious attack upon the territory of a fellow member of the League'. Cripps opposed the resolution, and after a lengthy debate, Lansbury then laid out his position on foreign policy and how it differed from Labour's official policy. He spoke against rearmament and the use of force even by the League of Nations, for 'I personally cannot see the difference between mass murder organised by the League of Nations, or mass murder organised between individual states.' While 'it is difficult for me to stand here today and publicly repudiate a big fundamental piece of policy,' he said that 'I believe that force never has and never will bring permanent peace and permanent goodwill in the world.' He went on to proclaim that given the chance he would go to Geneva and tell them that Britain was finished with imperialism and that 'we would be willing to become disarmed unilaterally'. He declared that 'God intended us to live peaceably and quietly with one another. If some people do not allow us to do so, I am ready to stand as the early Christians did, and say, "This is our faith, this is where we stand, and, if necessary, this is where we will die".'[33] He was received sympathetically by many, with applause at the beginning of his speech, and was supported by some; it was even recommended that Abyssinians offer hospitality to the invaders and 'trust to the moral judgement and moral pressure of the whole world'. However, Lansbury was strongly opposed by the majority of the leading figures in the Labour movement, with Attlee defending the use of sanctions 'for insuring the rule of law', and Bevin deconstructing Lansbury's moral scruples. He stated: 'It is placing the Executive and the Movement in an absolutely wrong position to be taking your conscience round from body to body asking to be told what you ought to do with it.'[34] Bevin pointed out that the Labour Party and the TUC had already endorsed the principle of sanctions in the document *For Socialism and Peace*, which had been supported at the 1934 annual conference. Neither Lansbury nor anybody else had suggested putting unilateral disarmament into the policy document, and for Lansbury now to speak against that policy was a betrayal. The trade unions had been let down by certain members of the Labour Party, and he reminded conference that 'our predecessors formed this Party. It was not Keir Hardie who formed it, it grew out of the bowels of the Trades Union Congress.' Bevin went on that while trade unionists were loyal, party members such as Stafford Cripps and Lansbury stabbed the Labour movement in the back by complaining to the press and resigning over policies which they had been involved in developing. He finished by saying that those who could not endorse the party's support for the League of Nations should 'take their own course'.[35] This made Lansbury's position untenable, and he resigned from the leadership of the party. Attlee later said that 'This was a grief to all of us, for we had a great admiration and affection for him, but he was right in thinking that his position had become impossible.'[36]

The differences between viewpoints had led to the resignation of the Labour Party's leader. This was the second time that a leader had left over a policy difference with the party, Ramsay MacDonald's resignation in 1914 over the PLP's support for the war being the first. That both leaders resigned over foreign and security policy was remarkable. Lansbury's departure occurred only a month before a general election, held on 14 November 1935. Deputy leader Clement Attlee became temporary acting party leader during the election, which saw 154 Labour MPs elected. This was a very good result compared with the scant fifty-two seats won in 1931, but Labour had expected to win more.[37] There followed a leadership election, between Attlee, Morrison and Arthur Greenwood. At the first ballot, Attlee gained fifty-eight votes, Morrison forty-four and Greenwood thirty-three. At the second ballot, most of Greenwood's supporters switched to Attlee, who subsequently won. Attlee assured the PLP that he had been elected to the leadership for one session only, and if they wanted him to stand down after that he would.

Attlee was an unlikely leader, 'Quiet, unassuming and with the appearance of a suburban bank manager'.[38] One of his early decisions was to form a Defence Committee to meet and discuss defence problems, and he spoke in favour of the creation of a Ministry of Defence, for he was 'determined to take steps to create a better knowledge of defence problems in the Party'. Indeed, Attlee, when made Undersecretary of State for War in the 1929–31 Labour government, had set out to learn as much as he could about defence problems, 'for I realised that, whatever might be done in the field of disarmament, there was bound to be the need for an army for policing the widespread territories of the British Commonwealth and Empire'. Attlee wrote that 'It always appeared to me that some of my pacifist friends in their insistence on the wickedness of warfare seemed to think that an inefficient Army was less wicked than an efficient one, a point of view to which I was unable to subscribe.'[39] Attlee made Hugh Dalton the opposition spokesman on foreign affairs, a position Dalton used not only to criticise the government on its position of neutrality on Abyssinia, and urge a tougher policy, but to get the Labour Party to shift its policy away from pacifism. He was helped in this by trade union leaders Bevin and Citrine.

Troops in Rhineland and German rearmament

Early in 1936 another conflict arose with the entry of German troops into the Rhineland, which had been demilitarised in the Treaty of Versailles. This posed a problem for Labour in that while it condemned Nazism, it had repeatedly blamed the Versailles Treaty for German rearmament and militarism. The NEC had even said in its report for 1934–35 that with regard to 'the Nazi regime's open reversion to power politics and international anarchy' that 'The verdict of history will assign to the British "National" Government a not inconsiderable share of responsibility for the present Nazi menace, in so far as it has been created by external factors.'[40] Even non-pacifists such as Dalton supported the government's policy of asking for a formal condemnation by the League of Nations, rather than any other form of immediate action. It was felt that no physical resistance could be taken, for 'public opinion in this country would not support, and certainly the Labour Party would not support, the taking of military sanctions or even economic sanctions against Germany at this time in order to put German troops out of the German Rhineland.'[41] Dalton later admitted that he had been wrong on this, and that Hitler's reoccupation of the Rhineland, against the advice of even his own military advisors, had been the 'greatest bluff of his life.' In his diary Dalton noted that 'Hitler's rearmament races on. Few people in the Labour Party seem to know or care anything about it.' He then attempted to get the PLP to abandon its yearly practice of opposing the defence estimates, but it voted by 57 votes to 39 to continue its practice of voting against them.[42]

The National Council of Labour reacted more strongly to the invasion of the Rhineland than the Labour Party's NEC did alone. It denounced it as a violation of the Locarno Treaty, which Germany had signed, and as evidence of the 'clear determination of Nazi Germany to repudiate its obligations and take what it wants by force'.[43] However, it also urged that 'a sincere effort must be made to discover a basis of negotiations with Hitler'.[44] At the 1936 TUC conference, Bevin said that it was time to re-examine the labour movement's commitment to a League of Nations system of collective security. He argued that 'The question of collective security it in danger of becoming a shibboleth rather than a practical operative fact … We are not going to meet the Fascist menace by mass resolution. We are not going to meet it by pure pacifism.' If this meant 'uprooting some of our cherished ideals and facing the issue fairly in the light of the development of Fascism, we must do it for the Movement and for the sake of posterity'.[45] Bullock notes that Bevin's point 'was accepted without challenge with that practical common sense which distinguished the discussion of foreign affairs in the TUC from the debates at Labour Party conferences throughout the 1930s'.[46] This is perhaps a little unfair, for of course the trade unions and the TUC played a not-insignificant role in the debates at the Labour Party conferences themselves.

The confusion within the Labour Party over foreign policy and disarmament continued. On the eve of the Labour Party's 1936 annual conference, Stafford Cripps argued against those who recommended conditional support for rearmament. In one of his more astounding pronouncements in a speech in Leeds, he urged an end to recruitment to the armed forces, saying that it would not necessarily matter if Britain were conquered by Germany. 'British Fascism would be less brutal than German, but the world situation would be no better.'[47] If Britain were pushed into war, he hoped that the workers would revolt, which would result in the fall of the capitalist government.[48] At the conference, the party's NEC then forwarded a resolution which ran counter to the stronger tone of the National Council, declaring that 'The armed strength of the countries loyal to the League of Nations must be conditioned by the armed strength of the potential aggressors', but concluding that 'having regard to the deplorable record of the Government, the Labour Party declines to accept responsibility for a purely competitive policy.'[49] Proposed reluctantly by Dalton, this suggests that the trade union influence was taking the National Council towards a more militarised stance than the NEC was prepared for, though no one was actually clear whether the above resolution implied that Labour would vote against the government's defence estimates or not. Bevin revealed his annoyance at the situation, referring to a speech by Morrison in defence of the resolution as 'one of the worst pieces of tight-rope walking I had ever seen in this Conference'. As for Cripps' position, Bevin was scathing: 'I say this to Sir Stafford Cripps. If I am asked to face the question of arming this country, I am prepared to face it ... Which is the first institution that victorious Fascism wipes out? It is the trade union movement.' Bevin, unlike the other speakers, was unequivocal in his support for rearmament, and said it was time to 'tell our own people the truth' about the situation:

The International Movement are wondering what we are going to do in Britain. Czechoslovakia, one of the most glorious little democratic countries, hedged in all round, is in danger of being sacrificed tomorrow. They are our brothers ... You cannot save Czechoslovakia with speeches.

> We are not in office but I want to drive this Government to defend
> democracy against its will, if I can ... I want to say to Mussolini and Hitler
> ... 'If you are banking on being able to attack in the East or the West, and
> you are going to treat the British Socialist Movement as being weak and
> are going to rely on that at the critical moment, you are taking us too
> cheaply.'[50]

This comment on Czechoslovakia was made two years before Munich,
and as Bullock notes, 'Bevin, commonly regarded as an uneducated
man, never made the mistake of referring, as Chamberlain did in 1938,
to Czechoslovakia as "a far-away country" of whose people "we know
nothing".'[51] Bevin further argued that it had been the mentality of the
liberal pacifists that had led Britain into war in 1914, and that the
League of Nations could not be left to defend democracy because it
has been proved weak: 'The League of Nations is the first puny attempt
at world organisation.' Therefore he would vote for armaments to
defend democracy and our liberty, though we must 'strive with all our
might ... to build the great moral authority behind international law,
[so] that in the end law will triumph by consent instead of by force'.
For the time being, he was afraid that 'we may have to go through
force to liberty'. He finished by calling for clarification on what the
resolution really meant in terms of supporting or not supporting rearmament.[52] This was not provided, and despite Bevin's comments the
resolution was passed. Adding to the confusion was the developing
crisis in Spain.

The Spanish Civil War

A republican, socialist, anti-clerical, Popular Front government had
been voted into power by a narrow margin in Spain in February 1936.
On 18 July the monarchist, nationalist, General Franco led an army
coup to topple it; the result was a bitter and all-out civil war, which
continued until the defeat of the Popular Front government in 1939.
The British government, along with the major European states and
America, signed a non-intervention agreement, which included an
arms embargo, for fear that the conflict might spread across Europe.
Despite the non-intervention pact, the right-wing nationalist rebels
received considerable support from the fascist regimes of Germany
and Italy in the form of weapons and men. At least 40,000 Italian
troops and up to 15,000 Germany troops were sent to Spain.[53] The
Soviet Union sent arms to the left-wing Republican government, and

volunteers from across Europe – including Britain – arrived in Spain to support the Republican cause. Numbers are difficult to estimate, but perhaps up to 15,000 such volunteers formed what were called the International Brigades.[54]

The dilemma that the Labour Party faced over the Spanish Civil War reflected the wider debate on foreign and defence policy in the 1930s. The Labour Party was horrified by events in Spain, and now found that relying on the League of Nations to defend democracy against fascism did not produce the desired results. However, at this time intervention was equated with precipitating war, not preventing it, and the underlying fear was that intervention would be worse than futile as it cause the conflict to spread across Europe.[55] Thus, the Spanish Civil War highlighted the confusion and divisions within the labour movement on foreign policy. Labour's immediate response to the Spanish situation in July 1936 was to send a delegation to see Anthony Eden, Secretary of State for Foreign Affairs. A special meeting of the PLP, the General Council of the TUC, and the NEC of the Labour Party was then held on 28 August, at which a statement was drawn up stating the party's position on the situation, ready to be presented at the annual conference. This in effect argued that non-intervention was the preferable policy as it would reduce the danger of a general war in Europe; but that it should only be supported so long as it was being carried out by all sides and that there should be an immediate inquiry into alleged breaches of the arms embargo. While expressing 'regret that it should have been thought expedient, on the ground of the dangers of war inherent in this situation, to conclude agreements among the European Powers laying an embargo upon the supply of arms', it said that 'such agreements may, however, lessen international tension'. The 'utmost vigilance will be necessary to prevent these agreements being utilised to injure the Spanish Government'. The statement ended by calling for the labour move-ment to support the International Solidarity Fund for Spain, which was created to provide humanitarian assistance to the Spanish people.[56]

Not everybody in the Labour Party supported this policy. Morrison was 'strongly and unconditionally against non-interven-tion'.[57] Many regretted that the non-intervention pact had been signed, but since the pact was originated by Léon Blum, the leader of the French Socialist Party and Prime Minister at the head of the Popular Front government, they felt that they had to support it. Attlee noted in his memoirs that 'The French attitude hampered us in bring-ing pressure to bear on our own Government, while the efforts of the

Communists to exploit Spanish resistance for their own ends did harm to the cause of freedom.' But 'Enthusiasm for the Republic ran very high in all Left Wing circles in Britain'.[58] Hugh Dalton, George Hicks and William Gillies, the Secretary of the Labour Party's International Department, had been to see Blum in September 1936, and according to Dalton, Blum had 'insisted that the policy of non-intervention in Spain was *his* policy. It was he and not Eden, as some alleged, who had first proposed it. He was sure that this policy, if it was fully observed by all the European Governments, would help the Spanish Government forces much more than the free supply of arms to both sides.' Dalton noted that Blum's preference for a non-intervention pact was due to concern that, having just disarmed the groups of right-wing extremists in France who had opposed his Popular Front government, any French intervention on a large scale would result in rearming both left and right within France.[59]

At the 1936 TUC and Labour Party conferences, support for the non-intervention pact was presented as policy in the report of the National Council of Labour. This was accepted more readily at the TUC conference than the Labour one,[60] where Arthur Greenwood, the Deputy Leader of the Party, was jeered when he moved the resolution supporting the report.[61] He did not help himself by pointing out to the conference that 'We know perfectly well that it was within the rights of any Government to provide all the necessary military equipment for the assistance of a nation fighting an internal rebellion. Unfortunately, that line was not taken', and the non-intervention pact was signed instead. This was 'a very, very bad second best'. The alternative now was to allow the situation in Spain 'which has almost broken the hearts of many of us', to develop into a European-wide struggle. Asking 'Is this Conference prepared to have the battle between dictatorship and democracy fought over the bleeding body of Spain?'[62] Greenwood argued that the alternative to non-intervention was free trade in arms, which would result in the collapse of the Popular Front government in France, and a war involving all of Europe, which was not what the British public wanted.

The resolution was carried by 1,836,000 votes to 519,000, but under pressure from the floor, it was announced that Attlee and Greenwood would go that evening to London to discuss the situation in Spain with Neville Chamberlain, who was acting Prime Minister while Baldwin was away. Attlee returned and urged a speedy investigation into the alleged breaches of the non-intervention pact: Labour's position was that if it were found that countries had been flouting the

agreement, then the British and French governments, who had initi-
ated it, should at once restore to the Spanish government the right to
buy arms.[63]

It quickly became apparent that the non-intervention agreement
was being breached. Spain complained of this to the League of
Nations, and lobbied the international labour movement to rethink
their policy of support, however reluctant, of non-intervention. At the
request of the Spanish trade union centre, a meeting of the International Federation of Trade Unions, the Labour and Socialist
International and the International Trade Secretariat was held on
28 September to discuss the situation in Spain. British representatives
argued against changing the existing line, that is, observation of the
non-agreement pact, but agreed that the accusations that Germany
and Italy were breaking the arms embargo be investigated.[64] A month
later another meeting was held, and this time the representatives
agreed there was evidence that the agreement was being breached.
They agreed that,

> In view of the fact that the Non-intervention Agreement has not
> produced the results expected in the international sphere, because of the
> determination of the Fascist Powers to assist the rebels and of the impos-
> sibility of establishing really effective supervision, the two Internationals
> declare that it is the common duty of the Working class of all countries,
> organised politically and industrially, to secure by their influence upon
> public opinion and upon their respective Governments the conclusion of
> an international agreement – for which the French and British
> Governments should take the initiative – restoring complete commercial
> liberty to republican Spain.[65]

Members of the trade unions and socialist parties of the two internationals should also do all they could 'to prevent the despatch of
supplies to the Spanish rebels'.[66] The PLP and the Labour Party's
NEC, along with the TUC's General Council, subsequently unanimously adopted a declaration on Spain on 28 October 1936. This
stated 'that the right of the constitutionally elected Government of
Spain to secure, in accordance with the practice of international law,
the means necessary to uphold its authority and to enforce law and
order in Spanish territory must be re-established'.[67] After this the
Labour Party lobbied, without success, for the lifting of the non-intervention pact and the recognition of the Spanish Republican government's right to buy arms from abroad, arguing that non-intervention
had been shown to be one-sided and a sham.[68]

The Labour leadership was sympathetic to the republican cause in Spain, and had a hard time defending their initial support for non-intervention. However, it was felt by some that Spain was a distraction from the real danger of German rearmament. Buchanan argues that for the leadership of the labour movement, the Spanish Civil War was 'a faction fight in a backward and feudal society which could have little relevance to Britain and which distracted attention from the real threat of a resurgent Germany. Thus, the Civil War had merely exposed Spain as an innately violent and undemocratic society.'[69] Certainly Hugh Dalton's position was that 'I valued France above Spain, both as a civilised modern state, and as a friend and pledged ally of Britain. I was not an admirer of the Spanish approximation to democracy.' Labour 'knew very little of the Spanish Left-wing leaders ... And there were other elements in the Spanish Left, including Anarchists, who did not inspire much confidence.' Furthermore, he did not support "Arms for Spain" if this meant that Britain was to supply arms which otherwise could be used for rearmament against the German threat. Dalton points out, however, that 'My own personal view of the Spanish Civil War ... differed from that of most of my colleagues.'[70]

Spain was 'at once a test of conscience and a symbol of protest' which stirred the emotions of the younger generation on the left 'as no other event in the pre-war decade'.[71] However, it was difficult for pro-interventionists to counter the Labour leadership's arguments, given that it was French socialist Prime Minister Léon Blum who had originally proposed and supported the non-intervention policy. Furthermore, the Soviet Union, officially at least, also supported it. Hardest of all reasons to overcome, most of the Labour Party had spent the last few years supporting pacifism, and the years since the First World War fighting for disarmament, and so now had to undergo massive shifts both intellectually and emotionally when confronted with the failure of the non-intervention policy to alleviate the situation in Spain. A few on the left resolved the situation for themselves by joining the International Brigades and fighting for Spain, but, more generally, discontent was strongly expressed by the rank-and-file on Spain.

Numerous resolutions were sent in to the Labour Party and the TUC urging action to support Spain. One asked the National Council of Labour to organise meetings and demonstrations for Spain up and down the country, and urged 'the smashing of the non-intervention pact' and 'full support for the Spanish government' in its 'heroic fight against Fascism'.[72] The reply from Labour headquarters was that while the PLP had raised the issue of the government's attitude to Spain, 'It is quite clear, however, that there will be no withdrawal from the Non-Intervention Pact either by the British Government or the French Government. Nor is there the least possibility of Munitions being sent to Spain from the Armaments Manufacturers in the country.' Furthermore,

> The Radical element of the Blum Government is as strongly opposed to the supply of Munitions to the Spanish Government in accordance with Treaty obligations as is the British Government, and any attempt to test the issue in the French Chambre would bring down the Blum Government with the possibility of a strong turn to the right rather than the left.

The official response ended with 'These are the facts of the situation which the National Council of Labour has had to face from the very beginning, and no Resolutions passed by enthusiastic Demonstrations will alter them – tragic as the situation is.'[73] Of course, we do not know what would have happened in France, but with the only left-wing European government lobbying for the Non-Intervention Pact to continue, Labour was left with very little scope for action. Another resolution, from the Birmingham Labour Party, expressed its 'grave concern' at the government's proposal 'to prevent the enlistment of British volunteers for the International Column to fight in the case of international Democracy'. It also called for the Labour Party 'to demand the immediate withdrawal of the arms ban and expose the pro-Fascist policy of non-intervention'.[74] A resolution from the South Wales Regional Council of Labour stated that 'This Conference views with dismay the tragic results arising from the farcical policy of non-intervention in Spain … which deprives the Spanish people of the means of defending their lives and liberties, while other members of the so-called Non-Intervention Committee are openly and defiantly supplying all the armaments they require to [the] rebels'. It was there-fore the view of the Conference that 'the present is the supreme moment' for the British labour movement 'to take such action as will force the British Government to remove the embargo on the supply of arms to the Spanish Government'. The Conference declared that it was ready 'to take such action as may be necessary to prevent the supply of materials of all kinds to the aggressive Fascist Powers, to force the Government to reverse its pro-Fascist policy, and we ask the National Council of Labour to call an immediate National Conference to decide upon the necessary action to secure that result'. This resolution had actually been 'altered' from its original format, which had specifically said that the labour movement was ready to take such action, both 'industrially and politically', to stop the 'supply of materials to the Fascist Powers'.[75]

Support groups for Spain also sprang up. The Labour Spain Committee, which represented local and divisional labour parties but did not represent the official line of the Labour Party leadership, campaigned under the slogan 'Arms for Spain'. It urged others to 'demand that our Leaders shall at once prepare to use all the power of the Trades Union and Labour Movement to end the farce of the Non-Intervention Agreement, and to secure for the Spanish people their right to purchase the arms of which they stand in such desperate need'.[76] The IFTU and the Labour and Socialist International launched an 'Aid for Spain' campaign, which the Labour Party and TUC vigorously supported. More specifically, the Basque Children's Committee was set up to provide support for displaced Basque children. A camp for refugee children was set up in May 1937 at Eastleigh, which held 4,000 refugee children prior to their dispersal to homes around the country.[77]

The labour leadership did make some attempt to influence the government. Citrine had written to the Prime Minister on 31 January 1937 to express his horror at the massacres in Spain during aerial bombing campaigns. This action was approved by the National Council of Labour, who determined that the government 'be urged to press forward with its proposals for securing a speedy agreement to put an end to such bombing outrages'.[78] A deputation from the General Council of the TUC, headed by Ernest Bevin and Walter Citrine, went to see the Foreign Secretary, Anthony Eden, on 22 March 1937 to inform him of the resolution passed at the recent international conference in London. They expressed the grave anxiety felt in the Labour movement at the delay in the operation of effective control over the non-intervention agreement, and the reports of the continued landing of German troops in Spain. 'The deputation urged that decisive steps should be taken to establish an effective system of control and to secure the early withdrawal of the foreign troops from Spain.'[79]

The Labour Party established a Spain Campaign Committee, with William Gillies and Ellen Wilkinson as its secretaries. This organised and advertised demonstrations around the county, held meetings and allocated speakers from the Labour Party, and organised appeals for money through a 'Milk for Spain' fund. It was not so different from the unofficial campaign for Spain in its aims, informing party members that, 'We are not neutrals in this conflict', and that 'We shall demand

Freedom, Food and Justice for Democratic Spain and the ending of Fascist intervention.' It pointed out that 'Democratic Spain is not merely confronted with enemies within' for it was having to defend itself against 'the men and resources of Hitler and Mussolini. The war in Spain is an international war.' Hence, 'We demand unconditional freedom of commerce for the Spanish Government in the purchase or arms.' It also highlighted the plight of the refugees in Spain, with official estimates that there were now 800,000 refugees in Catalonia alone. There was a desperate need for food and supplies, but 'the most urgent necessity of the moment is for milk' for the children. Labour Party members were asked to distribute leaflets and posters and to help the 'Milk for Spain' fund by buying milk tokens from Co-operative Society stores.[80] The party also organised a 'Christmas Gifts for Spain' campaign which asked people to buy parcels of food, clothing and soap to send to Spain, and collected money through the International Solidarity Fund.[81] Publicity leaflets were produced such as *We Saw in Spain*, a collection of articles by Attlee, Ellen Wilkinson, Philip Noel-Baker and John Dugdale on their trip to Spain,[82] and *What Spanish Democracy is Fighting For*, published on the second anniversary of the start of the civil war.[83] These highlighted the suffering of the Spanish people, and graphically described the plight of the refugees. In this way, the Spanish Civil War had a radicalising effect on many in the Labour Party and the trade union movement, leading people to question their previous conviction in the moral superiority of disarmament, arbitration through the League of Nations, and non-intervention.

The acceptance of British rearmament

One major effect of the Spanish Civil War was that it undermined the popularity of pacifism on the left, destroying the Labour Party's stance on pacifism and non-intervention, and paving the way for its acceptance of rearmament and the use of force. In July 1937, after extensive lobbying by Hugh Dalton, the PLP agreed by forty-five votes to thirty-nine to refrain from its usual habit of voting against the army, navy and air force estimates in the House of Commons. Instead, they would abstain. This signalled an end to the party's automatic stance against rearmament. Dalton notes that whereas the previous year he had been unsuccessful in attempting this, 'In 1937, after twelve months of Spain, the Party's policy being "Arms for Spain", it became impossible, in the view of many of us, to justify a vote which, whatever pundits in Parliament procedure may pretend, means to the plain man "No Arms for Britain".[84] He asked his colleagues 'what possible answer had we got in the country to the accusations that we want Arms for Spain, but no arms for our country?' He argued that people were 'bewildered' by Labour's attitude on foreign policy and defence.[85] The decision to abstain was greeted with approval by the conservative press. According to the *Daily Telegraph*, 'Labour's decision ... is the first indication that the Socialists are realizing the nature of the world in which they live.'[86] *The Times* expressed the opinion that 'Mr. Dalton's action is of special importance and there is no doubt that he considerably enhanced his Parliamentary prestige by his victory yesterday.'[87]

The change of stance on the defence estimates also helped pave the way for the adoption at conference of a new statement on *International Policy and Defence*. This stated that 'A Labour Government will unhesitatingly maintain such armed forces as are necessary to defend our country and to fulfil our obligations as a member of the British Commonwealth and of the League of Nations.'[88] As Bullock notes, 'the debates at the two autumn conferences made clear what the resolution left unsaid, that acceptance of the report meant the abandonment of opposition to rearmament.'[89] At the 1937 TUC conference the report was adopted by a show of hands.[90] Bevin was chair at this conference, with Dalton present as Chairman of the National Executive. At the Labour Party conference the following month, Dalton was chair, and devoted much of his speech to foreign affairs and defence. Lansbury spoke against the statement on *International Policy and Defence*, proposing that it be remitted back to the NEC rather than accepted as policy. Philip Noel-Baker described the report as 'bold, courageous and opportune', minimised the shift in policy, and said that 'There is really only one point of substance on which we differ from Mr Lansbury. It is on the proper use of power.'

> He wants a League of Nations that acts by conciliation, and conciliation alone. He wants us unilaterally to disarm ... For ten years we had in Geneva a League of Nations whose members all believed that the new law of the Covenant would be observed ... [but since] 1931 ... we have had a League of Nations without sanctions, a League of Nations where, with one feeble, transient exception, aggressors have had nothing to fear but resolutions. What are the results? The long, cumulative martyrdom of Manchuria, which still goes on; the squalid degradation of Mussolini's triumph over black men whom he burned and bombed ... the fearful holocausts in Spain; a major war in China ... a Europe where two great Powers bombed and burned Guernica systematically to the ground ... an

> Assembly of the League of Nations so demoralised that last week it
> refused to help the Chinese wounded in order not to irritate Japan ...
> That is the result of Mr. Lansbury's policy. It is cause and effect. Italy
> attacked disarmed Abyssinia and disarmed Spain, and Japan attacked
> disarmed China, because there was no collective security to make them
> safe.[91]

After a long and heated debate, the statement on *International Policy
and Defence* was adopted by a massive margin of nearly 2 million votes,
as Lansbury's motion to reference it back was defeated by 2,169,000
to 262,000 votes.[92] Bullock notes the role of the Spanish Civil War in
prompting this change, that 'More than anything else it was the
Spanish Civil War which produced the swing in Labour opinion
between 1936 and 1937.'[93] Buchanan, somewhat surprisingly,
disagrees, arguing that 'the conversion to rearmament, while genuine,
was often incidental to labour's response to the Civil War'.[94] It seems
likely, however, that Spain did indeed provide the catalyst for the rejection of disarmament and non-intervention, but it did so within the
wider context of a build up of awareness that fascism and rearmament
in Europe were not being deterred by the League of Nations' policies
of conciliation and arbitration.

   The period after the Labour minority governments saw significant
transformations in Labour's foreign policy, with the optimism of the
1920s being replaced by the growing pessimism and fear of fascism in
the 1930s. The initial reaction to the perceived failures of the League
of Nations over its inability to prevent the use of force by Japan in
1931 and then by Italy in 1935 was, paradoxically, to increase support
for the League in the short-term, for there appeared to be no alternative to this policy. This period saw Labour's foreign policy shift from a
fairly anti-militaristic, and almost pacifist stance in 1933 to 1936, to
support for rearmament and a policy of strength in the face of the
threat posed by fascism. This was quite a remarkable shift in policy in
a short space of time, resulting in the resignation of George Lansbury
as party leader, and an increase in the influence of trades union movement over foreign policy through the work of the TUC on the
National Council of Labour. In particular, the Spanish Civil War burst
the bubble of popularity of pacifism on the left, destroying the Labour
Party's stance on pacifism and non-intervention, and paved the way for
its acceptance of intervention and the use of force and the role of
power in international affairs. It meant that when the Chamberlain
government was replaced in 1940, the Labour Party was ready to join
forces with Churchill in a coalition government to support Britain's

war effort. It also meant an end to the perception that the Labour Party stood for non-intervention and was against the use of force as a tool of foreign policy.

Notes

1 Ramsay Muir, *The Record of the National Government* (London: Allen and Unwin, 1936), pp. 172–3.
2 Christopher Thorne, *The Limits of Foreign Policy: The West, the League and the Far Eastern Crisis of 1931–1933* (London: Hamish Hamilton, 1972), pp. 135–40.
3 *Labour Party Annual Conference Report* (hereafter *LPACR*), 1932, p. 68, 'The Far Eastern Situation: British Labour's Declaration'.
4 *Daily Herald*, 2 February 1932.
5 *House of Commons Debates* (hereafter *H.C. Deb.*), fifth series, vol. 270, col. 632, 10 November 1932.
6 David Marquand, *Ramsay MacDonald* (London: Jonathan Cape, 1977), pp. 714–15.
7 Manchester, Museum of Labour History, Labour Party archive, letter from Lansbury to James Middleton, 8 September 1934.
8 British Library of Political and Economic Science, London School of Economics, Lansbury papers, vol. 15, Lansbury to Cripps, 1 January 1934.
9 *H.C. Deb.*, vol. 286, col. 2044, 8 March 1934.
10 *H.C. Deb.*, vol. 287, col. 466, 14 March 1934.
11 Peter Clarke, *The Cripps Version: The Life of Sir Stafford Cripps, 1889–1952* (London: Allen Lane/Penguin Press, 2002), p. 52.
12 Hugh Dalton, *The Political Diary of Hugh Dalton: 1918–40, 1945–60*, edited by Ben Pimlott (London: Jonathan Cape, 1986), p. 181.
13 *LPACR*, 1935, pp. 157–8.
14 *LPACR*, 1933, p. 192.
15 *Ibid.*, p. 186.
16 *Ibid.*, p. 189.
17 Hugh Dalton, *The Fateful Years: Memoirs 1931–1945* (London: Mueller, 1957), p. 45.
18 Ben Pimlott, *Hugh Dalton* (London: Papermac/Macmillan, 1986), p. 228.
19 *LPACR*, 1933, p. 188.
20 *LPACR*, 1934, p. 245.
21 Labour Party general election manifesto, 1935, in F. W. S. Craig, ed. and comp., *British General Election Manifestos 1900–1974* (London: Macmillan, rev. and enlarged edn, 1975), p. 108.
22 Speech by Sidney Webb to conference, *LPACR*, 1932, p. 321.
23 Muir, *The Record of the National Government*, p. 188.
24 Modern Records Centre, University of Warwick (hereafter MRC), Trades Union Congress (hereafter TUC) archive, MSS 292/906/8,

TUC General Council 15, 1934–1935, Minutes of Special Meeting of the General Council 21 May 1935.

25 *Keesing's Contemporary Archive, vol. 2, 1934–1937* (London: Keesing's, 1937), pp. 1658–9.

26 MRC, TUC archive, MSS 292/906/8, TUC General Council 15, 1934-1935, Minutes of special meeting of the General Council, 21 May 1935.

27 *Ibid.*

28 See Walter Citrine, *Two Careers: A Second Volume of Autobiography* (London: Hutchinson, 1967).

29 Dalton, *The Fateful Years*, p. 64; *LPACR*, 1935, p. 88.

30 *LPACR*, 1935, NEC statement, p. 5.

31 Pimlott, *Hugh Dalton*, p. 229.

32 G. D. H. Cole, *A History of the Labour Party from 1914* (London: Routledge, 1948), pp. 306–7.

33 *LPACR*, 1935, pp. 175–7.

34 Many reports have Bevin saying 'hawking' rather than 'taking', but the account in the Labour Party annual conference report has 'taking'. *LPACR*, 1935, p. 178.

35 *LPACR*, 1935, pp. 177–80.

36 Clement Attlee, *As It Happened* (London: Odhams Press, 1956), p. 97.

37 See, for instance, Dalton's view, in Pimlott, *Hugh Dalton*, p. 230.

38 A. J. Davies, *To Build a New Jerusalem: The British Labour Party from Keir Hardie to Tony Blair* (London: Abacus, 1996), pp. 210–11.

39 Attlee, *As It Happened*, pp. 115 and 117.

40 *LPACR*, 1935, p. 3.

41 *H.C. Deb.*, vol. 310, col. 1454, 26 March 1936.

42 Dalton, *The Fateful Years*, pp. 88 and 90. See *LPACR*, 1936, pp. 109–11 for a summary of its opposition to the estimates.

43 *LPACR*, 1936, p. 34; National Council of Labour, 'Labour and the Defence of Peace', May, 1936, p. 3.

44 'Labour and the Defence of Peace', p. 9.

45 *Trades Union Congress Annual Report* (hereafter *TUCAR*), 1936, p. 358.

46 Alan Bullock, *The Life and Times of Ernest Bevin, vol.1: Trade Union Leader 1881–1940* (London: Heinemann, 1960), p. 583.

47 Glasgow *Forward*, 3 October 1936, cited in Bullock, *Ernest Bevin, vol. 1*, p. 583.

48 Simon Burgess, *Stafford Cripps: A Political Life* (London: Victor Gollancz, 1999), pp. 104–5.

49 *LPACR*, 1936, pp. 182.

50 *Ibid.*, pp. 203–4.

51 Bullock, *Ernest Bevin, vol. I*, p. 585, note 1.

52 *LPACR*, 1936, pp. 202–4.

53 Alan James, *Peacekeeping in International Politics* (London: Macmillan for the International Institute for Strategic Studies, 1990), p. 80.

54 *Ibid.*

55 See, for instance, Citrine's comments at the 1936 TUC annual conference, *TUCAR*, 1936, p. 362.

56 *LPACR*, 1936, p. 29.

57 Dalton, *The Fateful Years*, p. 96.
58 Attlee, *As It Happened*, p. 111.
59 Dalton, *The Fateful Years*, pp. 95–6.
60 *TUCAR*, 1936, p. 362.
61 Dalton, *The Fateful Years*, p. 99.
62 *LPACR*, 1936, pp. 169 and 171.
63 *Ibid.*, p. 258.
64 Manchester, Labour Party archive, LP/SCW/5/1, report of meeting of IFTU, International Trade Secretariats and the Labour and Socialist International, Paris, 28 September 1936.
65 *LPACR*, 1937, p. 7.
66 Dalton, *The Fateful Years*, p. 105.
67 *LPACR*, 1937, p. 7.
68 See, for instance, Attlee's speech in the House of Commons on 16 March 1938, *H.C. Deb.*, vol. 333, cols 486–91.
69 Tom Buchanan, *The Spanish Civil War and the British Labour Movement* (Cambridge: Cambridge University Press, 1991), p. 30.
70 Dalton, *The Fateful Years*, p. 96–7.
71 Bullock, *Ernest Bevin, vol. 1*, p. 586.
72 Manchester, Labour Party archive, LP/SCW/1/5, Haywood of the Erdington Divisional Labour Party to Middleton, Secretary of the Labour Party, 16 November 1936.
73 Manchester, Labour Party archive, LP/SCW/1/6, Middleton, Secretary of the Labour Party, to Haywood, Erdington Divisional Labour Party, 18 November 1936.
74 Manchester, Labour Party archive, LP/SCW/1/10, Garnett, Secretary of Birmingham Borough Labour Party, to Middleton, Secretary of the Labour Party, 18 January 1937.
75 Manchester, Labour Party archive, LP/SCW/1/16i, Morris, South Wales Regional Council of Labour, to Middleton, Secretary of the Labour Party, 8 April 1938.
76 Manchester, Labour Party archive, LP/SCW/1/19, Arms for Spain.
77 Manchester, Labour Party archive, LP/SCW/14/3, 7, and 8–27.
78 Manchester, Labour Party archive, LP/SCW/1/4, National Council of Labour decisions, 4 February 1938.
79 Manchester, Labour Party archive, LP/SCW/3/8, *The Times*, 23 March 1937.
80 Manchester, Labour Party archive, LP/SCW/1/21, Middleton, for the Spain Campaign Committee, November 1937.
81 Manchester, Labour Party archive, LP/SCW/1/24, Christmas Gifts for Spain, December 1938.
82 Manchester, Labour Party archive, LP/SCW/1/30, We Saw in Spain, Labour Party, no date.
83 Manchester, Labour Party archive, LP/SCW/1/31, What Spanish Democracy is Fighting For, Labour Party, July 1938.
84 Dalton, *The Fateful Years*, p. 133.
85 *Ibid.*, pp. 133 and 134.
86 *Daily Telegraph*, 23 July 1937, cited in *Labour Research*, 26: 9 (September 1937), pp. 200–1.

87   *The Times*, 23 July 1937, cited in *ibid.*
88   *LPACR*, 1937, p. 4.
89   Bullock, *Ernest Bevin, vol. 1*, p. 593.
90   *TUCAR*, 1937, pp. 426.
91   *LPACR*, 1937, pp. 202–3.
92   *Ibid.*, p. 212. At this conference, the disaffiliation of the Socialist League
     was approved by 1,730,000 to 373,000, and the United Front Policy was
     again rejected, by 2,116,000 votes to 331,000.
93   Bullock, *Ernest Bevin, vol. 1*, p. 594.
94   Buchanan, *The Spanish Civil War and the British Labour Movement*, p. 4.

Chapter 6

Hitler, Munich
and the Second World War

By 1937 the Labour Party had accepted the need for rearmament in the face of the threat posed by Hitler and the growth of fascism in Europe, whereas the National government combined a policy of rearmament along with conciliation towards Hitler. Hitler's remilitarisation of the Rhineland in 1936, in defiance of the Treaty of Versailles, and his failure to meet Germany's reparations payments, had been met with little resistance or even criticism by the British government. By 1937 all the European powers were rearming, with only the United States holding back from the rapidly escalating arms race, as shown in Table 6.1. In simple numerical terms, aircraft production had risen in Germany from just 36 in 1932 to 5,606 in 1937, while in the UK it had risen from 445 aircraft in 1932 to only 2,153 in 1937.[1] Diplomacy became increasingly tense, and the League of Nations increasingly redundant.

The British government still went under the title of 'national', but consisted mostly of Conservatives, with only a handful of Liberal and National Labour ministers, notably Ramsay MacDonald until his retirement in May 1937. MacDonald's death in November of that year was scarcely acknowledged by the Labour Party, which had entered a period of relative unity in terms of its leadership and for whom the crisis of 1931 was now in the past. Stanley Baldwin retired from his post as Prime Minister in May 1937, and was replaced by the sixty-eight-year-old Neville Chamberlain, also a Conservative. Chamberlain was appalled at the prospect of war in Europe, and thought that the best way to avoid war was through concessions to Hitler and Mussolini. Overall, Chamberlain was 'Suspicious of the Soviet Union, disdainful of Roosevelt's "verbiage", impatient at what he felt France's confused diplomacy of intransigence and passivity, and regarding the

Table 6.1   *Defence expenditure totals and as a percentage of national income, 1937*

State	% of national income spent on defence	Defence expenditure $000,000
British empire	5.7	1,263
France	9.1	909
Germany	23.5	4,000
Italy	14.5	870
Japan	28.2	1,130
USA	1.5	992
USSR	26.4	5,026

Source: Figures taken from Quincy Wright, *A Study of War* (Chicago: University of Chicago Press, 2nd edn, 1965), appendix 12, table 60, p. 672.

League as totally ineffective, the prime minister embarked upon his own strategy to secure lasting peace by appeasement.'[2] Not all the National government agreed with Chamberlain's policy, and in February 1938 Anthony Eden resigned as Foreign Secretary after repeated disagreements with the Prime Minister over his conciliation towards Germany. Winston Churchill led the parliamentary opposition to appeasement outside of the government, and his visceral criticisms of Britain's failure to rearm quickly enough or to stand up to Hitler sounded less erratic and more prescient as time went on. These criticisms were echoed, though in slightly more muted tones, by the Labour Party. Labour seemed relatively isolated at this time, making little headway either in electoral or policy-making terms. However, the irony is that despite its isolation from power, it was the Labour Party that finally brought about the downfall of the Chamberlain government in 1940, and it was Labour's exclusion from government that meant that it was the only party that was free from the taint of appeasement once war broke out.

The Munich crisis

On 12 March 1938 Hitler marched his troops into Austria, annexing Austria to the German Reich, without arousing much protest from the British National government. In August Hitler threatened to send troops into Czechoslovakia to reclaim the German-speaking Sudetenland, which had been transferred to the Czechs as part of the

Versailles Treaty to act as a buffer zone against Germany. Negotiations with Hitler led to the signing of the Munich Agreement by Britain, Germany, Italy and France, which ceded the Sudetenland back to Germany on the condition that Hitler would not invade Czechoslovakia. The Soviet government had made known its willingness to combine with Britain and France to defend Czechoslovakia against German aggression, but the offer was ignored, and the Soviet Union and Czechoslovakia were both excluded from the negotiations at Munich.[3] Hitler was surprised by the easy success of his territorial claim to the Sudetenland, having expected his armed diplomacy to provoke a confrontation from Britain and France. Neville Chamberlain returned from Munich on 30 September to a rapturous welcome from the British public, declaring that his policy of appeasement had guaranteed 'peace with honour' and 'peace for our time'. The agreement reached at Munich by Britain, Germany, France and Italy was that Czechoslovakia would start to evacuate the Sudetenland on 1 October, on which date German troops would begin to occupy these territories, and that this process would be completed by 10 October.[4]

The Labour Party was less sanguine about the agreement reached at Munich than the National government. During the Czech crisis the National Council of Labour had stated that 'The British Government must leave no doubt in the mind of the German Government that they will unite with the French and Soviet Governments to resist any attack on Czechoslovakia.'[5] This position, based on the assumption of collective action, continued throughout the crisis. However, the possible military consequences if collective action short of the use of force were to fail were not explained by the Labour Party. Its position was in contrast to the Conservative-dominated National government, which did not even share the assumption of co-operation with France and the Soviet Union. Labour did not support the terms of the Munich agreement, seeing it as 'a shameful betrayal of a peaceful and democratic people', and urged Chamberlain to discuss the agreement in Parliament before signing proposals 'which contemplate the dismemberment of a sovereign State at the dictation of the ruler of Germany'.[6] During the three-day debate in the House of Commons on the situation in Europe and the Munich Agreement, Attlee argued that 'The events of these last few days constitute one of the greatest defeats this country and France have ever sustained. There can be no doubt that it is a tremendous victory for Herr Hitler.' Munich, he said, left him with the same emotions he had at the evacuation of Gallipoli, a mixture of humiliation, relief, and foreboding. He continued:

> We all feel relief that war has not come this time. Every one of us has been passing through days of anxiety; we cannot, however, feel that peace has been established but that we have nothing but an armistice in a state of war. We have been unable to go in for carefree rejoicing. We have felt that we are in the midst of a tragedy. We have felt humiliation. This has not been a victory for reason and humanity. It has been a victory for brute force.[7]

On 5 October the Chancellor of the Exchequer put forward a motion approving the government's foreign policy 'by which war was averted in the recent crisis and supports their efforts to secure a lasting peace'. Arthur Greenwood, the Deputy Leader of the Labour Party, put forward an amendment to this motion, stating that Parliament, 'while profoundly relieved that war has been averted for the time being, cannot approve a policy which has led to the sacrifice of Czechoslovakia under threat of armed force and to the humiliation of our country and its exposure to grave dangers'. He called instead for support for collective security through the League of Nations, and for the government to initiate 'a world conference to consider the removal of economic and political grievances which imperil peace'.[8] The House of Commons then passed the motion of confidence in the government's foreign policy by 366 votes to 144, and the Labour amendment was rejected by 369 votes to 150.[9] Nineteen Conservatives abstained from voting, including Winston Churchill, Anthony Eden, and Harold Macmillan.[10]

Only a very few in the Labour Party disagreed with the party's position in rejecting the Munich Agreement, most notably George Lansbury, who had urged further conciliation with Hitler. Philip Noel-Baker rather cruelly pointed out at the 1941 Labour Conference that 'The road to war, and I say it with all veneration, was paved with Lansbury's good intentions.'[11] Lansbury had caused consternation on the left when he took independent diplomatic action by visiting Hitler on 19 April 1937 in an attempt to negotiate personally with the German leader. Lansbury found that 'The whole talk was as satisfactory as those with Blum and Roosevelt. Hitler treated the interview very seriously. I think he really wants peace.' Lansbury felt 'The discussion was quite a triumph.'[12] He reported that Hitler '*will not* go to war unless pushed into it by others'.[13] The German Social Democrats protested to the Labour Party that they had been 'amazed to learn' that Lansbury had 'undertaken an independent diplomatic action with Hitler. This step shows neither willingness to help the German opposition in their bitter struggle, nor understanding for their point of view.' They further argued that Lansbury's meeting assisted the Nazis in their propaganda, and gave the impression that Hitler was willing to come to an understanding.[14]

After the immediate Munich crisis had passed, the Labour leadership was slightly more cautious in its support for collective action against the German menace. In its November pamphlet, *The Full Facts of the Czech Crisis*, the Labour Party's official line was that 'war was not the alternative' at the time of the Munich crisis.[15] However, still unhappy at the government's policy of appeasement towards Hitler, Hugh Dalton for the PLP proposed a motion of no confidence in the government's foreign policy on 19 December 1938. After a debate that went on until 11.00pm, the motion was defeated by 340 to 143 votes.[16] Rather confusingly, Labour continued to oppose conscription, while at the same time advocating action against Hitler. This exasperated the Conservative rebels, and occurred at a time when 'public opinion had been coming round to the idea that Labour, not the Tories, were the patriots'.[17] Labour voted against the National Service Bill in April 1939, which provided for compulsory military training of all men aged twenty to twenty-one years, with the National Council of Labour announcing its 'uncompromising opposition' to conscription in April 1939.[18] Attlee later told his biographer that 'the line he took against conscription in 1939 was a mistake', and that the Labour Party did not realise 'the 'extent to which its stand on conscription would be misinterpreted'. Apart from the 'various rational objections to conscription at the time', the 'real motive for resisting the idea was distrust of Chamberlain', who had previously assured the Labour Party that conscription would not be introduced in return for its support for the government's scheme for voluntary recruitment to the military.[19] Attlee had argued at the time that the Prime Minister was breaking the pledge he had given to the country that compulsory military service would not be introduced in peace-time; that this would add to 'the already widespread distrust of the Prime Minister'; and that rather than strengthening the armed forces, he would be 'sowing division in the ranks' and undermining the national effort.[20] The party's opposition to conscription was reaffirmed at the 1939 annual conference in May when a resolution proposed by the NEC was passed by 1,967,000 votes to 574,000.[21] In addition, this resolution, also released as a statement on *Labour and Defence*, called for the establishment of a Ministry of Supply, and urged the democratisation of the armed forces through reforms in conditions and in the appointment and promotion of officers.[22] At this conference the Labour Party also urged action to face the fascist menace, arguing that the military guarantees made to Poland, Turkey, Greece and Rumania, should be extended to the Soviet Union, as 'Moscow is a custodian of peace.'[23] Whereas the Labour Party had criticised Britain's bilateral alliances for being partly responsible for the First World War, it was now calling for a strengthening of such alliances, particularly an Anglo-Soviet pact.[24] The Soviet Union was seen as a vital ally in any fight against fascism.

On 18 April the Soviet Foreign Minister, Maxim Litvinov, had proposed an Anglo-Soviet pact, but Chamberlain had only very reluctantly and belatedly opened negotiations. These culminated in a British mission to Moscow in the middle of August, by which time Litvinov had been replaced by Molotov. While these discussions were adjourned, the German Foreign Minister, von Ribbentrop, arrived to discuss a rival German-Soviet pact. The signing of the non-aggression pact between the Soviet Union and Germany was announced on 23 August 1939, signalling a realignment of Soviet foreign policy. The Nazi-Soviet pact not only provided Hitler with an assurance of non-interference from the Soviet Union, and a pledge that neither party would attack the other or aid any other country or coalition that did so, but it also divided Poland and the Baltic states of Lithuania, Latvia and Estonia between Germany and the Soviet Union.

The Labour Party was shocked to find that the negotiations for the non-aggression pact had been 'proceeding secretly and concurrently' with the discussions between Britain, France and the Soviet Union on collective action against Germany.[25] This development destroyed not only Labour's foreign policy regarding German aggression, which was based on co-operation with France and the Soviet Union to deter Hitler, but also for some the faith that they had held in the Soviet Union. Coming after the purges and show trials of the 1930s, Stalin's willingness to collude with Hitler reinforced the view that Soviet communism had been corrupted. Walter Citrine told the TUC annual conference that the apologists for the Soviet Union have blinded themselves for years, while they 'have seen a dictatorship in Russia as severe and as cruel as anything that has happened in Germany'.[26] However, some on the left blamed the British and French governments' exclusion of the Soviet Union in the Munich discussions and their reluctance to enter into negotiations on multilateral treaties with the Soviets for this development to a greater or lesser extent. They argued that the Soviet Union feared that it would be 'double-crossed in the long-run' by Britain and France, and that it was merely remaining neutral in the same way that the USA had done during the early years of the First

World War.[27] Nevertheless, Stalin's rapprochement with Hitler gave the Labour Party greater opportunity to oppose requests from the British Communist Party for a united campaign and national front. This standpoint was reinforced when the Soviet Union invaded Poland's eastern territories on 17 September, and again when it invaded Finland on 30 November 1939. Dalton referred to this latter act as 'indefensible' in the House of Commons,[28] while the National Council of Labour issued a statement on 7 December declaring that the British labour movement 'views with profound horror and indignation' the Soviet government's 'unprovoked attack' upon Finland, and that 'Soviet Imperialism has thus revealed itself as using the same methods as the Nazi power against which the British Working-class is united in the War now raging.' In particular, the NEC said that British labour 'repudiate utterly' the claims of the Soviet government to be the 'leader of the World's Working-class Movement, guardian of the rights of peoples against their oppressors, interpreter of Socialist principles, and the custodian of International Peace'.[29] Following a request from the Finnish Labour Party, a delegation was sent to Finland, which reported back in March 1940 that the Finnish resistance could have continued the struggle against the Soviet forces for much longer had they received more assistance from Britain.[30] The Soviet invasions of Poland and Finland marked the 'severance of the umbilical cord of socialism' which had formerly connected the centre and the right of the Labour Party to the Soviet Union.[31] They also resulted in the utter isolation of those on the left who continued to express support for the Soviet Union.

Despite the setback of the Nazi-Soviet non-aggression pact, the National Council of Labour upheld its support in August 1939 for 'the obligations undertaken by Britain in defence of the independence of Poland shall be honoured to the full'.[32] On 25 August the National Council of Labour issued a message to the German people, that 'We have no wish to destroy the German people. We have been, we still are, your friends.' However, if Hitler attacked Poland, Britain would stand firmly by its pledge to Poland, despite the German pact with Moscow. It said that if war came, then Britain and France would command the seas, cutting off the supply of raw materials and foodstuffs to Germany, thus lowering the standard of living in Germany even further.[33] On 1 September Germany invaded Poland. On 2 September the PLP and the party's NEC agreed that Arthur Greenwood, acting party leader owing to Attlee's absence due to ill-health, should inform the Prime Minister that they were 'prepared to support the fulfilling of the Treaty with Poland'.[34] The party also voted in support of conscription by fifty-one to fifteen votes, a reversal of their earlier policy.[35] In the House of Commons that evening, there was as an 'eruption of revolt' at 'Chamberlain's apparent continued equivocation'.[36] When Arthur Greenwood rose to speak for the Labour Party, the anti-appeaser Conservative Leo Amery shouted 'Speak for England, Arthur!' Greenwood called on the government to end its vacillations 'at a time when Britain and all Britain stands for, and human civilization, are in peril', to honour its treaty obligations with Poland, and to declare 'It is either peace or war'.[37] The following morning at 9.00am, the British Ambassador in Berlin delivered an ultimatum to the German Foreign Minister, for Germany to withdraw its forces from Poland. This ultimatum expired at 11.00am, at which time Chamberlain announced in a broadcast to the nation that Britain was at war with Germany. In contrast to the outbreak of the First World War, the Labour Party, already appalled at the fascist triumphs in Spain as well as Austria and Czechoslovakia, whole-heartedly backed the use of force to counter German aggression. The TUC also supported the use of force, passing a declaration at the annual congress on 4 September in vivid language, stating that,

> Under its leadership of its Nazi Dictators, Germany has destroyed the Peace and order of the World. By an appalling act of injustice and ill will it has once more broken faith with the civilised nations and has deliberately provoked armed conflict in Europe to further its aims of domination and conquest ... No concessions that Poland could have made would have saved her people from the dismemberment that befell the brave Czech nation. Nor would compliance with these demands have satisfied the insane ambition of Germany's rulers. It would not have saved the Peace of Europe ... The defeat of ruthless aggression is essential if liberty and order are to be re-established in the World. Congress, with a united and resolute nation, enters the struggle with a clear conscience and steadfast purpose.[38]

The Labour Party embraced the war because it thought that there was no chance of a peaceful settlement with Hitler. Indeed, it was 'astonished' that anybody could expect compromise with dictators, and stated that 'We declare once more that we can have no part, directly or indirectly, in a policy of accommodation, and that the necessary prelude to a just Peace is total victory.'[39] However, the party presented its position in terms of support of international working-class solidarity, the sanctity of international law, and the expression of international morality, and said that the party 'regards victory as the only basis upon which the achievement of its ideals becomes possible'.[40] The party thus could present the war as compatible with earlier foreign policy statements. Attlee said at the 1940 annual conference that 'We have to preserve the hope of our movement. Whatever may be the conditions in capitalist democracies, there is always that hope, there is always that opportunity; but where Nazism reigns all hope is gone.'[41] In contrast, the ILP refused to support the government in its war against Germany. At its 1940 annual conference in March, it adopted a resolution describing the war as imperialist, and urged that it be brought to an end.[42] On 5 December 1940 the ILP tabled a motion in the House of Commons criticising the government for failing to organise a conference to negotiate peace. This gained only four votes, and was massively defeated.[43]

The Labour Party and the Second World War

While Labour experienced a sense of relief once war had broken out, believing the use of force to be the only deterrent to Nazi aggression, some sought to apportion blame for the war to the Conservatives. The argument was that since the Labour Party was not responsible for governing Britain, they were not to blame for the war. *Guilty Men*, written anonymously by Michael Foot and the journalists Frank Owen and Peter Howard over a four-day period in June 1940, produced an excoriating criticism of the government's policy of appeasement and its failure to rearm and to prepare for war. In particular, it accused Chamberlain and his colleagues of sending men into battle 'without a chance', when they were unprepared and did not possess the necessary weapons and equipment.[44] Attlee said at the 1941 Labour Party conference that, 'If our policy had been followed, you would never have had this war.'[45] Bevin, on the other hand, took a more magnanimous viewpoint about responsibility for pre-war policy:

> If anybody asks me who was responsible for the British policy leading up to the war, I will, as a Labour man myself, make a confession and say, 'All of us.' We refused absolutely to face the facts. When the issue came of arming or rearming millions of people in this country, people who have an inherent love of peace, we refused to face the real issue at a critical moment. But what is the good of blaming anybody?[46]

The party's NEC and the PLP had agreed not to join a coalition government headed by Chamberlain, despite several requests to do so, because they distrusted him and lacked confidence in his leadership. This prevented Labour from being associated with Chamberlain's failures, while at the same time depriving the Chamberlain government of the wider legitimacy it would have gained from the support of the main opposition party. Furthermore, Labour managed to support the war, but not the government, without appearing to be undermining the war effort, which leant credence to the developing perspective that Britain needed a broader coalition government that included all the political parties.

Labour's statements on the long-term aims of the war in the first few months of hostilities were often slightly nebulous, as were those of the government. On 16 November Attlee called on Chamberlain for discussions on the peace aims of Britain and the Commonwealth, for 'there is a demand in this country for a closer definition of peace aims' and 'The people of this country want to know for what we are fighting', and 'just what kind of world it is that the Government in their minds are contemplating when we have brought this war to an end'.[47] The Labour Party laid out its long-term plans in a statement on *Labour's War Aims* in February 1940. This statement was far-reaching and outlined an ambitious view for the future of international relations, as well as dealing with specific issues such as French and German security. It demanded that any 'Peace Settlement shall establish a new Association or Commonwealth of States, the collective authority of which must transcend, over a proper sphere, the sovereign rights of separate States.' In addition, 'Labour will be no party to imperialist exploitation, whether capitalist or other. Labour, therefore, demands that Colonial peoples everywhere should move forward as speedily as possible, towards self-government.' For these policies to be successful, a 'new world order' based on socialism and democracy must be founded, for 'Lasting Peace depends on social justice within States, no less than on political justice between States.'[48] This statement demonstrates how the Labour Party embraced the war as an opportunity to create a better international system in the long term, rather than just as a short-term calamity that needed to be dealt with.

After a period of 'phoney war', when the British population had to adapt to wartime privations while waiting for the war to happen, and to prepare for air attacks which did not occur, hostilities intensified.[49] Hitler successfully invaded the neutral state of Norway in February 1940 despite the presence of a powerful Royal Navy fleet. By 16 April German forces controlled much of southern Norway, and despite initial successes, British and French troops abandoned their positions in central Norway at the beginning of May. This military failure acted as a political catalyst in Britain, and during a dramatic and remarkable two-day Commons debate on the Norwegian campaign on 7 and 8 May, both Labour and a number of Conservatives called for Chamberlain to resign as Prime Minister. The Conservative Leo Amery, quoting Cromwell to Chamberlain, said 'You have sat too long here for any good you have been doing. Depart, I say, and let us have done with you. In the name of God, go.'[50] Attlee described Chamberlain's litany of failures over Czechoslovakia, Poland, and now Norway.[51] Lloyd George, in what was to be his last decisive intervention in the House of Commons, called on Chamberlain to 'sacrifice the seals of office' for he had been 'worsted' by Hitler in both peace and war, and 'there is nothing which can contribute more to victory in this war'.[52] On the recommendation of the Labour Party's NEC, the PLP agreed, though with some dissentients, to vote against the government's adjournment on the handling of the war.[53] This, in effect, meant a vote of censure on Chamberlain's leadership. Only 481 out of 615 MPs voted in the division of 8 May, giving a result of 281 votes to 200.[54] Forty-two Conservatives voted with Labour. While this still gave the National government a majority, it had been reduced to eighty-one, at a time when the government's formal majority was 220. Given the outcome of the division and the vehemence of the proceeding debate, Chamberlain realised he could not sustain the confidence of Parliament. This was to be the only occasion in the twentieth century when a majority government was forced out of office by a vote in the House of Commons.[55]

On 9 May Attlee and Greenwood visited Chamberlain, and he 'begged' them to join a coalition government under his premiership, to which Attlee replied that this was impossible and that the mood of the country required a new leader.[56] Attlee later wrote with characteristic understatement that he found 'It was not a pleasant task to tell a Prime Minister that he ought to go, but I had no option but to tell him the truth'.[57] Chamberlain also asked whether Labour would join a coalition government led by someone other than himself, to which Attlee replied that he would have to consult the party. The party was duly consulted the following day, which was the first day of the Labour Party annual conference at Bournemouth, when the NEC decided unanimously that Labour would serve under a new prime minister. This decision also had the approval of the General Council of the TUC. Attlee and Greenwood returned to London immediately, where they were asked to meet with Churchill. Discussions had been going on about the premiership between Chamberlain and Churchill and Lord Halifax, the two front-runners to succeed him, but Halifax had said that he felt that his position as a Peer, and thus a member of the House of Lords rather than the House of Commons, would make it very difficult for him to discharge the duties of Prime Minister.[58] This meant that the premiership went to Churchill. Churchill formed a coalition government on 10 May 1940, the day that Hitler invaded both Holland and Belgium. Labour had agreed to two seats out of five in the new War Cabinet, to be filled by Attlee and Greenwood, and one out of the three defence ministries, with A. V. Alexander replacing Churchill at the Admiralty. Attlee became Lord Privy Seal and Deputy Leader of the House of Commons, and Greenwood became Minister without Portfolio. Ernest Bevin, who had been elected MP for Wandsworth at a bye-election in 1940, became Minister of Labour and National Service on 3 October. Hugh Dalton headed the Ministry for Economic Warfare. Morrison became the Home Secretary. Stafford Cripps was appointed Ambassador to Moscow, which boosted his profile once the Soviet Union entered the war, and in March 1942 he headed a mission to India to secure its support for the war effort against Japan, and to reach agreement on its post-war constitutional settlement, in which he was unsuccessful.[59] In February 1942, Attlee was formally appointed as Deputy Prime Minister with responsibility for domestic policy.

Little has been written about how the Labour ministers got on with Churchill. It has been suggested that at one point Attlee had said that Labour would not serve under Churchill.[60] Others cast doubt on whether this happened. Harris says that Attlee in fact preferred Churchill to Halifax, and 'did not feel that the Labour Party's long-standing distrust of Churchill, mainly because of his behaviour during the General Strike, was a bar to serving under him in a wartime coalition'.[61] Given that Labour did join a Churchill government, this interpretation of events seems the more likely. Churchill says that it was Chamberlain who implied that the Labour Party would not serve under him, though this possibility did not seem to worry Churchill, who says that he still would have formed the strongest government possible if this had been the case.[62] On the whole, Attlee defended the actions of the coalition government, and called for national unity and support from the labour movement. This did provoke some criticism from within the party; for instance, on the eve of the June 1941 conference, Nye Bevan accused the Labour leadership of insisting upon regarding itself as a junior partner in the government.[63] Overall, however, this criticism was fairly muted. The issue that was to provoke the most criticism from within the Labour Party was over the opening of a Second Front.

On 22 June 1941, Hitler had invaded the Soviet Union, thus breaking the non-aggression pact. From this point onwards, the Soviet Union became an ally in the fight against Nazism, and Stalin called for the immediate opening of a second major front on the European mainland in order to divert pressure away from the Red Army, which was struggling in its fight against the invading German forces on Soviet territory. From this point onwards, a campaign was waged by the Soviet Today Society, a communist organisation, to lobby the British government to open a Second Front, and a series of 'spectacular' meetings were held all over the country.[64] Within the Labour Party, the Second Front campaign was led by Nye Bevan, who spoke on platforms with communist supporters, which was against Labour Party rules. However, Labour ministers within the coalition government 'were largely unsympathetic to left-wing demands for even more aid to Russia'.[65] During a debate in the House of Commons on the progress of the war, Labour back-benchers called for a Second Front and for Britain to provide maximum assistance to Russia, to which Attlee replied that 'There would be nothing more stupid ... than to make a futile and dangerous gesture for fear someone should think that you were not doing your best.' He went on that the government shared the public's concern that everything should be done to support Russia, and 'We shall give all we can to Russia, but, remember, it has to come out of our production, which is not yet adequate for all our own needs.'[66] To some extent the reluctance of Attlee and the other Labour ministers to get involved in the calls for a Second Front was because, publicly at least, they left strategic decisions to Churchill. Concern that the Soviet Union might try to extend its influence over Europe once Germany had been defeated may also have contributed to their reluctance to appease the calls for more assistance to Russia. Once the Soviet Union had entered the war on the side of the Allies, its popularity dramatically increased, which was also a cause for concern for the centre-right leadership of the Labour Party.

Despite the acquiescence over the issue of the Second Front, at this point the leadership of the Labour Party still argued that it had a distinct foreign policy from that of the previous National government or a future Conservative government. In particular, this was over their vision of the post-war world, of a 'new world order' based on 'socialism and democracy'.[67] The NEC said that, 'The Labour Party reaffirms its conviction that there is no road to enduring Peace save by the growing acceptance of Socialist principles. No peace, therefore, which does not aim at a Socialist reconstruction of international society can be accepted by the Labour Party as adequate.'[68] Within the Labour Party, 'the war was considered to have accelerated important changes that would ultimately rebound to Labour's advantage', as increased planning and state intervention became accepted by the population.[69] Indeed, Attlee made a point of asserting that 'the Labour Party was not only supporting the government of the day in the cause of security and justice but was in the war to fight for its own existence and its own vision of what society should be'.[70] This applied not only to Britain, but also to the international arena, where Attlee said that 'the world that must emerge from this war must be a world attuned to our ideals'.[71] In particular, it was argued that the post-war settlement needed to include international economic planning, for the world was 'a single economic unit'. This needed to be combined with the establishment of an international organisation 'possessing many powers hitherto exercised by a competing anarchy of national sovereignties'.[72] The party focused on outlining Labour's policies for after the war, setting up a committee to study the problems of post-war reconstruction on 6 August 1941, and drawing up Labour's blueprint for the post-war international order. In the spring of 1942, the NEC issued an interim report on *The Old World and the New Society*, which was discussed in regional conferences. This declared that the revolutionary impact of the war meant that the 'old world' of 1939 was dead, and its ideas were 'already obsolete'. In terms of international relations, national sovereignty would have to be given up, with a new, much stronger version of the League of Nations forming a superstructure through which a new World Society could be formed, founded upon democratic Socialist ideas.[73] At the 1942 annual conference, the NEC's resolution on the international situation gave far greater emphasis to collaboration with the Soviet Union, both 'in victory and peace'.[74]

At the 1943 annual conference delegates called for a more specific statement of post-war aims. Consequently the NEC appointed Hugh Dalton to prepare one. Dalton, who had been instrumental in shifting Labour to support rearmament, was determined to impress his personal views on the statement. He saw to it that he was named to prepare each revision of the document, though he was forced to accept substantial additional sections written by Harold Laski and Noel-Baker.[75] This document, *The International Post-War Settlement*, argued that,

[W]e must begin, without delay, to build a World Order, in which all
people unite to pursue their common interests. We are confident that the
vital interests of all nations are the same. They all need Peace; they all need
security and freedom; they all need a fair share in that abundance which
science has put it into our power to create.

The document also emphasised the need for 'the closest possible
Anglo-American-Russian co-operation'. However, it moved away from
traditional Labour Party policy in that it saw the basis of a future world
organisation as being a continuation of the relationship between these
three Great Powers, rather than some form of League of Nations.
Pacifism had been proved to be 'an unworkable basis of policy'.
Instead, 'Strength is essential to safety and, as we now know, there
are terrible risks in being weak. It is better to have too much armed
force than too little'. This was a rejection of Labour's policy for
much of the 1930s. Joint occupation of Germany was suggested as 'a
practical experiment in an international force'. It did sound a more
traditional note with its argument that 'The international political
organisation must establish the binding force of international law',
its call for a World Court of International Justice, and its call for
disarmament to be a major object of a future international political
organisation. The document also called for new forms of international
economic organisation, 'new international institutions and agreements
to plan relief and rehabilitation, to organise abundant world-wide
food supplies, to regulate international trading and transport and
monetary relationships'.[76] This document contained a clear and new
vision of Labour's foreign policy, and was actually very prescient
in many of its propositions, reflecting an understanding of the need
for a post-war international regime that provided for economic growth
as well as control of military aggression. This held echoes of the
American New Deal, though there does not seem to have been
much contact between the Labour Party and the American Democrats
at this point. For the Labour Party, these ideas came from a combination of its socialist faith in economic planning, transferred to the
international arena, the liberal doctrine of free trade as a tool for
preventing conflict, and its enduring belief in internationalism. The
document on the *International Post-War Settlement* was approved
at the 1944 annual conference by an overwhelming majority. However,
when Attlee moved the resolution supporting this document he
reassured the delegates at conference that the party still believed that
the foundations of international peace could be strengthened through
the spreading of socialist ideas and the application of socialist measures

in all parts of the world, along with the close association of socialist parties in all countries.[77]

One issue that the Labour Party failed to address in their policy statements on the nature of the post-war international settlement was that of decolonisation. At the 1942 annual conference a resolution was passed that called for the abolition of 'the status of Colony', and for all colonial states to be given independence.[78] This went further than previous Labour Party resolutions on colonial policy in that it proposed independence rather than self-governing Dominion status, and covered all of Britain's colonies. However, at the 1943 annual conference, the NEC then reverted to Labour's earlier policy position by stating that India should become a self-governing Dominion, and that the goal of the whole Commonwealth, in time, should be political self-government, while the 'Colonial Empire [should] now enter a period of unprecedented development and progress under the guidance of the Mother Country.'[79] Labour Party policy on colonial affairs at this point was underdeveloped and inconsistent. Indeed, the party's leadership had 'lapsed into near silence on colonial reform' since the fall of the second minority Labour government in 1931.[80] The Labour Party Advisory Committee on Imperial Questions had produced a number of reports, most notably its policy statement of 1933, and published a pamphlet in 1936 which focused on the fears of a rising inter-imperialist rivalry in Europe.[81] These had been largely ignored within the party. The lack of any coherent Labour Party policy on colonial affairs had begun to be addressed with the establishment in 1940 of the Fabian Colonial Bureau, but to a large extent this was subsumed during the war years by the focus on the post-war international system, rather than concern with ending British imperialism as such. However, the TUC had taken an increasing interest in colonial affairs, and had established its own Colonial Advisory Committee in 1937. Against a backdrop of repression following labour unrest in the West Indies, the TUC had lobbied the government to introduce legislation for the establishment of trade unions in the colonies, and to introduce reforms to improve working conditions and working-class living standards. The TUC also became increasingly involved in advising the Colonial Office on labour issues, and in setting up educational links with trade unionists in the colonies. Trade union leaders such as Citrine and Bevin saw the work of the TUC as largely supporting the work of the Colonial Office in terms of guiding colonial labour organisations away from militancy. Part of the aim was to prevent trade union movements in the colonies falling under the influence of communism, and to foster non-political 'responsible' trade unionism that focused on bargaining over working conditions rather than agitating for national independence. After lobbying by the Labour Party and the TUC, the Colonial Office established a Colonial Labour Advisory Committee in 1942, which included representatives from the TUC, and the first British trade unionists were sent to work as advisors on labour relations to the local administrations in the colonies. In this way, the TUC became part of the institutional structures for the oversight of colonial trade union movements.[82]

While they reassured the Labour Party of the continuation of the leadership's belief in international socialist solidarity, involvement in the wartime coalition was having a profound effect on Labour's leaders such as Attlee and Cripps. Their perspective was shifting away from their earlier support for a 'socialist' foreign policy, while the already more realist outlook of Bevin and Dalton was further consolidated. Bullock explains that 'By joining the coalition the Labour leaders had recognized that for them, as much as for Churchill and the Tories, there was an overriding national interest, a concept which many in the Labour Party had traditionally rejected, in theory at least, as incompatible with loyalty to internationalism and irreconcilable with the class war.'[83] This did not, however, mean that deciding on which strategy to pursue was unproblematic or without debate. There were huge arguments within the British coalition government, and between the British, the United States, the French and the Soviet Union, over strategy. Issues that were particularly contentious included whether to give priority to the Pacific War or to Europe; whether to pursue a Mediterranean strategy; and when to launch a Second Front. To a large extent, the Labour Party remained quiet on these issues, restricting their pronouncements on foreign policy to the outlining of their post-war aims, though the Second Front was a particular issue to many because of a sense of solidarity with the Soviet Union. At the wartime Labour Party annual conferences, the NEC put forward statements and reports outlining Labour's position on the war, which took the place of the usual resolutions on foreign and defence policy, thus limiting debate on the prosecution of the war.

However, behind the scenes, from 1943 onwards the Labour government ministers were actively involved in planning British post-war foreign policy. Attlee was particularly influential in discussions on the future of Germany and the post-war settlement. In 1943 Churchill made him chair of all the War Cabinet sub-committees dealing with British post-war international policy, namely the committee on armistice terms, which was replaced by the committee on armistice terms and civil administration, and the committee on the post-war settlement, which also included Bevin. Regarding suggestions for a joint Allied occupation of Germany, Attlee advocated extensive social, political and economic changes within Germany in order to reorient it, rather than just limiting the size of its army or prohibiting the production of aircraft, as had happened following the First World War.[84] More generally, he also advocated a much closer relationship with the USA as part of the post-war settlement, arguing that Britain would be unable to meet all its possible European and imperial commitments without military support from the USA, particularly within the context of an expansionist Soviet Union.

During the last few months of the war, Attlee and the Labour ministers became increasingly involved in the development of the post-war international settlement. For Labour Party members, their expectations of change in both British foreign policy and in international relations intensified as victory, and the prospect of a general election, approached. Denis Healey, then on the left of the Labour Party, told the annual conference which was held in May 1945, just before the election, that,

> The crucial principle of our own foreign policy should be to protect, assist, encourage and aid in every way the Socialist revolution wherever it appears ... If the Labour Movement in Europe finds it necessary to introduce a greater degree of police supervision and more immediate and drastic punishment for their opponents than we in this country would be prepared to tolerate, we must be prepared to understand their point of view.[85]

At this conference, Bevin tried to restrain such sentiments, by asking the party 'not to bury its head in the sand.' If Labour won the election,

> You will have to form a Government which is at the centre of a great Empire and Commonwealth of Nations, which touches all parts of the world, and which will have to deal, through the diplomatic, commercial and labour machinery with every race and with every difficulty, and everyone of them has a different outlook upon life.[86]

However, the phrase that was remembered was Bevin's claim that 'Left understands Left,' subsequently taken to be a reference to the Soviet Union, though Bevin had actually been talking about the left in France. Attlee, who had recently returned from the difficult negotiations of the San Francisco Conference of the United Nations, told the conference that 'I am afraid sometimes people think that if only we get the nations together they will accept our ideas' but that it was not so easy as this.[87] He was less sanguine than previously about the prospects for world peace and international organisation. Indeed, he and Bevin were far more moderate in their claims about a Labour government having a new approach to foreign policy than most of the rest of the Labour Party.

The 1945 general election

Foreign policy was not at the forefront of the Labour Party's campaign, and people were far more interested in the parties' plans for repairing war-torn Britain than in their plans for British foreign policy. It was found that 'The issues with which the electors felt vitally concerned were domestic issues in the popular, non-political, sense of the term.' Foremost of these was housing. A poll taken by the British Institute of Public Opinion during the election campaign that asked 'what questions do you think will be the most discussed in the General Election?' found that 41 per cent of people answered housing, while only 5 per cent said international security.[88] One interesting aspect of the campaign was that Attlee and Bevin expressed hope that the agreement on foreign policy by the wartime coalition could be continued into peacetime. Bevin declared that 'The foreign policy being pursued at the moment was devised by the Coalition Government, not by the Tory members alone, but by a combined effort and is based upon collective security, a policy for which Labour has always stood. As long as that object is vigorously pursued, then Labour will find an opportunity of co-operating with all other parties.'[89] Furthermore, the 1945 Labour Party election manifesto, *Let Us Face the Future*, did not promise a socialist foreign policy. Rather, it stated that 'We must consolidate in peace the great war-time association of the British Commonwealth with the U.S.A. and the U.S.S.R.'[90] This hardly differed from the Conservative Party's manifesto, which stated that 'Our alliance with Soviet Russia and our intimate friendship with the U.S.A. can be maintained only if we show that our candour is matched by our strength', and that, 'Our prevailing hope is that the foundations [of peace] will be laid on the indissoluble agreement of Great Britain, the United States and Soviet Russia.'[91] The only other Labour Party comment referring to the Soviet Union was, 'Let it not be forgotten that in the years leading up to the war the Tories were so scared of Russia that they missed the chance to establish a partnership which might well have prevented the war.'[92] The Labour Party, it was implied, could handle the Soviet Union, unlike the Conservatives.

This criticism did not commit the Labour Party to any 'socialist' foreign policy. While the Conservative manifesto gave greater emphasis to the British empire and to defence than the Labour one, the lack of comment by the Labour Party meant that it was left with greater freedom of action later on. In fact, Churchill himself had reassured the House of Commons, when he announced that Attlee would accompany him to the Potsdam conference in July, that he and Attlee 'have always in these last few years thought alike on the foreign situation and agreed together'. At the conference 'there will be an opportunity for it to be shown that, although Governments may change and parties may quarrel, yet on some of the main essentials of foreign affairs we stand together'.[93] That the Labour Party leadership was likely to take a strong line on the Soviet Union became clear at Potsdam. James Byrnes, the US Secretary of State, noted that 'Britain's stand on the issues before the (Potsdam) conference was not altered in the slightest, so far as we could discern, by the replacement of Mr. Churchill and Mr. Eden by Mr. Attlee and Mr. Bevin. This continuity of Britain's foreign policy impressed me.' Byrnes also wrote that at the first meeting with Attlee and Bevin, Bevin's manner towards the Soviet demands for East Prussia 'was so aggressive that both the President and I wondered how we would get along with this new Foreign Minister'.[94]

In contrast, those on the Labour left had been busy setting as much distance been a Conservative and a Labour foreign policy as possible. Laski argued that Attlee could not commit the Labour Party to support unconditionally any decisions made by Churchill at Potsdam: 'When we win this election, we want to be free in Socialist terms to make our policy for our own Socialist purposes.'[95] Therefore, the Labour Party could not be committed to any decisions made at Potsdam, which would not have been debated by the party NEC or the Parliamentary Labour Party, for 'Labour has a foreign policy which in many respects will not be continuous with that of a Tory-dominated Coalition. It has, in fact, a far sounder foreign policy.'[96] Of course, hardly anyone on the left actually expected Labour to win. Possibly, for many, it was the case that it was better to lay out a socialist foreign policy in principle, because they would not have to put one into practice. The general election of 5 July 1945, much to the party leaders' amazement, resulted in not only a Labour victory but also a Labour landslide. Labour won 393 seats and 47.8 per cent of the vote. The Conservatives won 213 seats and 39.8 per cent of the vote. The Liberal vote collapsed to 9 per cent, and they gained a meagre twelve seats.[97] The Labour Party had been helped by the strength of the vote received from servicemen overseas, and from those in the electorate for whom this was their first chance to vote, the last election having been held in 1935. It was a 'very surprised' Clement Attlee who went to Buckingham Palace to form a government on 26 July 1945.[98] Bevin the trade union leader, who was expecting the post of Chancellor, was appointed as Foreign Secretary. Dalton the Labour Party intellectual, who had expected this post due to his interest and knowledge in foreign affairs, was appointed as Chancellor.[99] The next day Attlee and Bevin left for the Potsdam conference, the last major Allied conference of the war, replacing Churchill in the negotiations. At this conference an Allied Council of Foreign Ministers was established, consisting of representatives from Britain, the USA, the Soviet Union and France, to draft peace treaties with Germany and Japan.

Both at the time and subsequently, people have been surprised not only that Bevin was made Foreign Secretary, but also that he turned out to be so knowledgeable and adept at it. He was the illegitimate son of a farm-worker who left school at eleven.[100] He had joined the Marxist Social Democratic Federation, but subsequently developed a hatred of communists. He made a name for himself as a union activist, and was the driving force behind the formation of the Transport and General Workers Union in 1922, becoming its General Secretary. This was the largest union in Britain, and came to be remarkably powerful. Bevin's antipathy to communists was due in particular to what he saw as the 'attempt by the Communists to break up the Union that I built'.[101] He spent much of the 1920s and 1930s defending 'his' union against communists. Along with Walter Citrine, he took a leading role in moving the Labour movement to a position of supporting rearmament in the late 1930s. Therefore, he had had years of dealing with recalcitrant trade unionists, and in dealing with his overseas counterparts within the very active and buoyant international trade union movement. He was a forceful individual who did not suffer fools gladly, and anyone who opposed him was seen as a fool or as an enemy. Bevin was not only the first foreign secretary in a majority Labour government, but he is, to date, the longest-serving Labour foreign secretary.

The Second World War marked a decisive break with the past for the Labour Party, as 'The pessimistic mood of the post-1931 period, coloured by talk of class struggle and division, was swept away in the crisis of national survival.'[102] It pointed to the way that Labour governments in the future would approach foreign and defence policy. Labour had rejected appeasement as it did not think that there was any chance of a peaceful settlement with Hitler, thus ending its flirtation of the 1930s with pacifism, and its traditional rejection of the use of force. The war also seemed to vindicate the necessity of policies that Labour had been advocating, such as state planning. It produced a changed ideological climate that made socialism more acceptable, and ideas such as equity and social justice both at home and abroad more prevalent. Unlike the Conservatives, the Labour Party spent much of its time thinking about what would happen when victory was won, and the party's apparatus of committees focused on developing ideas about the future international order. Labour wanted nothing less than the radical restructuring of British society, and the radical restructuring of the international order that had brought about both the world wars. Their vision of a post-war international order was to be based on the acceptance of the idea of subordinating national sovereignty to world institutions and obligations, and on the need for international economic planning. Within the coalition government, Attlee had a significant input into the development of the post-war settlement, especially over Germany. The Labour government ministers were actively involved in planning British post-war foreign policy, whilst the Labour Party planned for their version of the post-war world, based on a complete overhaul of international relations. While Attlee had at first encouraged this perspective, by the end of the Second World War he was distancing himself from some of his earlier claims of a new world order based on socialism and democracy, and calling for the party to have rather more cautious ambitions for both the new world order and the future of British foreign policy. However, by then there was a distinct divergence between the expectations of the Labour Party membership and the expectations of the very top of the Labour Party leadership, and this was to become the main issue of contention for the Attlee government.

Notes

1 Richard Overy, *The Air War, 1939–1945* (London: Europa, 1980) p. 21.
2 Paul Kennedy, *The Rise and Fall of the Great Powers: Economic Change and Military Conflict from 1500 to 2000* (London: Fontana Press, 1989), p. 437.

3 B. H. Liddell Hart, *History of the Second World War* (London: Book Club Associates, 1973), p. 9.

4 *Keesing's Contemporary Archive, vol. 3, 1937–40* (London: Keesing's, 1940), p. 3247.

5 *Labour Party Annual Conference Report*, 1939 (hereafter *LPACR*), National Council of Labour statement, 8 September 1938, p. 14.

6 National Council of Labour statements of 19 and 20 September 1938, cited in *Keesing's Contemporary Archive*, vol. 3, p. 3234.

7 House of Commons Debates (hereafter *H.C. Deb.*), fifth series, vol. 339, cols 51–2, 3 October 1938.

8 *Ibid.*, col. 351, 5 October 1938.

9 *Ibid.*, cols 553–62, 6 October 1938.

10 On the opposition to the government's foreign policy from Conservative MPs, see Neville Thompson, *The Anti-Appeasers: Conservative Opposition to Appeasement in the 1930s* (Oxford: Clarendon Press, 1971).

11 *LPACR*, 1941, p. 142.

12 British Library of Political and Economic Science, London School of Economics (hereafter BLPES), George Lansbury papers, vol. 16, notes on George Lansbury's interview with Hitler, 19 April 1937.

13 BLPES, Lansbury papers, vol. 16, letter from Lansbury to Reginald Clifford Allen, 11 May 1937, italics in original.

14 Museum of Labour History, Manchester, Labour Party archive, LP/ID/INT/1/1, from the Leaders of the Social Democratic Party of Germany to the Labour Party International Department, April 1937.

15 Labour Party, *The Full Facts of the Czech Crisis* (London: Labour Party, 1938), p. 13.

16 *H.C. Deb.*, vol. 342, cols 2503 and 2625–30, 19 December 1938.

17 Kenneth Harris, *Attlee* (London: Weidenfeld and Nicolson, 1982), p. 162.

18 *LPCAR*, 1939, p. 23.

19 Harris, *Attlee*, p. 162.

20 *H.C. Deb.*, vol. 346, cols 1154–5, 26 April 1939.

21 *LPACR*, 1939, p. 289.

22 *Ibid.*, p. 24.

23 *Ibid.*, pp. 215 and 289.

24 *LPACR*, 1940, p. 6. On 27 June 1939, the National Council of Labour appointed Hugh Dalton, Herbert Morrison and Walter Citrine to consult with the Prime Minister on various international matters, including the negotiations on the proposed Anglo-Soviet Pact. See also Hugh Dalton, *The Fateful Years: Memoirs 1945–1960* (Lonson: Mueller, 1962), pp. 246–57.

25 *LPACR*, 1940, p. 8.

26 *Trades Union Congress Annual Report* (hereafter *TUCAR*), 1939, p. 303.

27 *Ibid.*, p. 295.

28 *H.C. Deb.*, vol. 355, col. 291, 30 November 1939.

29 NEC statement of 7 December 1939, in *LPACR*, 1940, p. 13.

30 *LPACR*, 1940, p. 14.

31 Bill Jones, *The Russia Complex: the British Labour Party and the Soviet Union* (Manchester: Manchester University Press, 1977, p. 36.
32 *LPACR*, 1940, p. 8.
33 *LPACR*, 1940, 'Message to the German people', pp. 8–9.
34 *Ibid.*, p. 10.
35 Dalton, *The Fateful Years*, p. 265.
36 Roy Jenkins, *Churchill* (London: Pan Books, 2002), p. 552.
37 *H.C. Deb.*, vol. 351, cols 280–3, 2 September 1939; Dalton, *The Fateful Years*, pp. 264–5.
38 *TUCAR*, 1939, pp. 337–8.
39 NEC statement, *LPACR*, 1941, p. 4.
40 *Ibid.*, p. 5.
41 *LPACR*, 1940, p. 124.
42 *Keesing's Contemporary Archive*, vol. 3, p. 3987.
43 *H.C. Deb.*, vol. 367, cols 695 and 756, 5 December 1940.
44 'Cato', *Guilty Men* (London: Victor Gollancz, 1940); Mervyn Jones, *Michael Foot* (London: Victor Gollancz, 1994), pp. 84–91.
45 *LPACR*, 1941, p. 133.
46 *H.C. Deb.*, vol. 373, col. 1362, 29 July 1941.
47 *H.C. Deb.*, vol. 353, col. 877, 16 November 1940.
48 *LPACR*, 1940, appendix 2, 'Labour, the War, and the Peace'.
49 See Angus Caldor's excellent account of these in *The People's War: Britain 1939–45* (London: Pimlico edition, 1992), chs 1 and 2.
50 *H.C. Deb.*, vol. 360, col. 1150, 7 May 1940.
51 *Ibid.*, col. 1094.
52 *Ibid.*, col. 1283.
53 Hugh Dalton, *The Political Diary of Hugh Dalton: 1918–40, 1945–60*, edited by Ben Pimlott (London: Jonathan Cape, 1986), p. 340.
54 *H.C. Deb.*, vol. 360, cols 1361–6, 8 May 1940. Somewhat confusingly, the numbers given for the voting in this division vary widely according to different accounts of these events.
55 Jorgen Rasmussen, 'Party discipline in war-time: the downfall of the Chamberlain government', *Journal of Politics*, 32:2 (1970), 380.
56 Dalton, *Political Diary*, p. 344.
57 Clement Attlee, *As It Happened* (London: Odhams Press, 1956), p. 158.
58 Winston Churchill, *The Second World War, vol. 1: The Gathering Storm* (London: Cassell, 1948), p. 524.
59 See Peter Clarke, *The Cripps Version: The Life of Sir Stafford Cripps, 1889–1952* (London: Allen Lane/Penguin Press, 2002), parts 3 and 4.
60 John Barnes and David Nicholson, eds, *The Empire at Bay: The Leo Amery Diaries 1929–1945* (London: Hutchinson, 1988), p. 595.
61 Harris, *Attlee*, p. 174.
62 Churchill, *The Gathering Storm*, pp. 523–5.
63 Harris, *Attlee*, p. 188; Michael Foot, *Aneurin Bevan, A Biography: vol. I, 1897–1945* (London: MacGibbon and Kee, 1962), p. 331.
64 Foot, *Bevan*, p. 337.
65 Jones, *The Russia Complex*, p. 75. See ch. 5 for more details of the Second Front Campaign.
66 *H.C. Deb.*, vol. 374, cols 151–2, 9 September 1941.

67 *LPACR*, 1940, appendix 2, 'Labour, the War, and the Peace'.
68 *LPACR*, 1941, p. 3.
69 Steven Fielding, Peter Thompson and Nick Tiratsoo, *'England Arise!'*
    The Labour Party and Popular Politics in 1940s Britain (Manchester:
    Manchester University Press, 1995), p. 79.
70 Harris, *Attlee*, p. 169.
71 *LPACR*, 1940, p. 125.
72 *LPACR*, 1941, p. 4.
73 G. D. H. Cole, *A History of the Labour Party from 1914* (London:
    Routledge and Kegan Paul, 1948), pp. 414–9.
74 *LPACR*, 1942, pp. 151–2.
75 Dalton, *The Fateful Years*, p. 423.
76 *The International Post-War Settlement*, in *LPACR*, 1944, pp. 4–9.
77 *Ibid.*, p. 132.
78 *LPACR*, 1942, pp. 154–5.
79 *LPACR*, 1943, p. 4.
80 Stephen Howe, *Anticolonialism in British Politics: The Left and the End*
    of Empire, 1918–1964 (Oxford: Clarendon Press, 1993), p. 52.
81 The Labour Party, *The Demand for Colonial Territories and Equality*
    of Economic Opportunity (London: Labour Party, 1936).
82 Peter Weiler, *British Labour and the Cold War* (Stanford: Stanford
    University Press, 1988), p. 27. For a less critical perspectives on this, see
    Marjorie Nicholson, *The TUC Overseas: The Roots of Policy* (London:
    Allen and Unwin, 1986), chs 6–7.
83 Alan Bullock, *The Life and Times of Ernest Bevin, vol. 3: Foreign Secretary,*
    1945–1951 (London: Heinemann, 1983), p. 64.
84 Trevor Burridge, *British Labour and Hitler's War* (London: André
    Deutsch, 1976), ch. 8.
85 *LPACR*, 1945, p. 114.
86 *Ibid.*, p. 115.
87 *Ibid.*, pp. 107 and 119.
88 Ronald Buchanan McCallum and Alison Readman, *The British General*
    Election of 1945 (Oxford: Oxford University Press, 1947; reprinted
    London: Frank Cass, 1964), p. 150, citing British Institute of Public
    Opinion poll.
89 *The Times*, 23 June 1946.
90 Labour Party 1945 election manifesto, 'Let us face the future', in F. W.
    S. Craig, ed. and comp., *British General Election Manifestos 1900–1974*
    (London: Macmillan, rev. and enlarged edn, 1975), p. 104.
91 Party 1945 election manifesto, in *ibid.*, pp. 87 and 88.
92 Labour Party 1945 election manifesto, in *ibid.*, p. 104.
93 *H.C. Deb.*, vol. 411, col. 1788, 14 June 1945.
94 James Byrnes, *Speaking Frankly* (London: William Heinemann, 1947),
    p. 79.
95 *The Times*, 20 June 1945.
96 Kingsley Martin, *Harold Laski (1893–1950): A Biographical Memoir*
    (London: Victor Gollancz, 1953), p. 170.
97 Butler and Butler, *British Political Facts*, p. 226.
98 Attlee, *As It Happened*, p. 148.

99 For an explanation of this, see Dalton, *The Fateful Years*, pp. 468, 472 and 474–5.
100 The most detailed and most illuminating source on Bevin is Alan Bullock's remarkable three volumes of his life: Alan Bullock, *The Life and Times of Ernest Bevin*, vols. *1–3* (London: Heinemann, 1960, 1967, 1983).
101 *LPACR*, 1946, p. 167.
102 Stephen Brooke, *Labour's War: The Labour Party during the Second World War* (Oxford: Clarendon Press, 1992), p. 271.

Chapter 7

The Attlee governments

The election of a majority Labour government in 1945 generated great excitement on the left. Hugh Dalton described how 'That first sensation, tingling and triumphant, was of a new society to be built. There was exhilaration among us, joy and hope, determination and confidence. We felt exalted, dedication, walking on air, walking with destiny.'[1] Dalton followed this by aiding Herbert Morrison in an attempt to replace Attlee as leader of the PLP.[2] This was foiled by the bulky protection of Bevin, outraged at their plotting and disloyalty. Bevin apparently hated Morrison, and thought of him as 'a scheming little bastard'.[3] Certainly he thought Morrison's conduct in the past had been 'devious and unreliable'.[4] It was to be particularly irksome for Bevin that it was Morrison who eventually replaced him as Foreign Secretary in 1951.

The Attlee government not only generated great excitement on the left at the time, but since has also attracted more attention from academics than any other period of Labour history. Foreign policy is a case in point. The foreign policy of the Attlee government is attractive to study because it spans so many politically and historically significant issues. To start with, this period was unique in that it was the first time that there was a majority Labour government in British political history, with a clear mandate and programme of reform. Whereas the two minority Labour governments of the inter-war period had had to rely on support from the Liberals to pass legislation, this time Labour had power as well as office. It was also seen as the first time that Labour could really try its hand at international affairs, and certainly Labour's supporters expected a new, more internationalist, socialist and ethical foreign policy from their government. Second, this period was remarkable in that Labour's demand for a new world order, based

on a post-war settlement that included international economic planning and the creation of a more powerful version of the League of
Nations to provide a collective security superstructure, appeared to
have been met. A new international regime was emerging, largely
through Anglo-American collaboration, based on the International
Monetary Fund and the International Bank for Reconstruction and
Development (World Bank), which had been agreed at the Bretton
Woods conference of July 1944, and the United Nations, which had
been established on 26 June 1945. These developments reflected
Labour's vision outlined in its 1942 and 1944 policy documents, *The
Old World and the New Society* and *The International Post-War
Settlement*, for a new multilateral system of organisations to regulate
international relations and the world economy, though the leadership
of the party made no mention of any intention to subordinate national
sovereignty once in power.[5] Labour's vision coincided with America's
concern for an international regime that provided for international
economic growth through the spread of free trade, buttressed by
domestic economic growth, and for a collective security mechanism to
mitigate the more deleterious effects of balance-of-power politics.[6]
During the last eighteen months of the war, Attlee, Bevin and Hugh
Dalton, who had become the President of the Board of Trade in 1942,
had become increasingly involved in the development of the post-war
international order. While Winston Churchill had felt that questions of
the post-war settlement should not distract attention from the prosecution of the war, it had been the Labour ministers who had responded
to the American plans for the establishment of a multilateral regime.[7]
These men also embraced the new economic thinking embodied by
Keynes, who had been a crucial figure in the agreements reached at
Bretton Woods. Thus, Labour's ideas for a new, more regulatory,
framework for international relations coincided with those of the
Roosevelt and Truman administrations, even if they differed somewhat
in their ideological origins, and helped shape the post-1945 international economic order.

Third, this is an interesting period to study in terms of Britain's
changing role in the world. Britain had been the only victorious
European state in the Second World War, which reinforced the
perspective that it was a world leader, and a great and triumphant
power. However, it was at this point in time that it became apparent
for the first time that Britain's pre-eminent position in the world was
being replaced by the United States, and that Britain was, whether it
really wanted to or not, retreating from its previous imperial position.

The great power manoeuvring of the European states was being replaced by the burgeoning contest between the Soviet Union and the USA, the Cold War, in which British foreign policy was to play a more minor, but still significant, role.

There are two main approaches in the extensive literature on the Labour governments' foreign policy between 1945 and 1951. The first is a fairly uncritical approach to what was seen as a surprising degree of realism demonstrated by the Labour ministers, and praise for Bevin in particular in his role in involving the United States in a defensive alliance against the Soviet Union. This is the approach taken in the work by Bullock, Morgan, Ovendale and Pelling.[8] The second is a highly critical approach, seeing the 1945 Labour government as dashing the hopes of those on the left for a new, more internationalist and socialist approach to foreign policy. It presents the Attlee government's foreign policy in terms of a missed opportunity and even a betrayal of the left. This viewpoint can be found in the work of Saville, Schneer and Weiler.[9] This chapter tries to retain a balance between the two approaches, a difficult task made harder by the fact that only a selection of issues can possibly be covered in an overview of this nature. The chapter focuses on two major areas of foreign policy: first, the withdrawal and consolidation of the British empire; and second, the Anglo-American relationship and the emergence of the Cold War. It also outlines the opposition from within the Labour Party towards the government's foreign policy, before finishing with some analysis of Labour's defence policy within the context of competing demands for scarce resources. First, however, it is necessary to point out the context within which the 1945 Labour government had to develop and implement foreign policy, that of economic crisis.

The Attlee government's foreign policy developed within the context of an immediate economic crisis, a recurring theme for Labour governments. During the war defence expenditure had risen from £626 million in 1939 to a peak of £5,125 million in 1944.[10] Britain had used up its financial reserves to finance the war effort, and its manufacturing base had been disrupted. Exports of UK products had fallen from £471 million in 1938 to a low of £234 million in 1943, though had risen to £399 million in 1945.[11] It owed debts to India, Canada and Australia totalling £3,567 million as a result of materials supplied during the war for which payment had been deferred.[12] Millions of homes had been destroyed by German bombing. The USA halted Lend-Lease, the system of American financial aid that had done much to sustain the British war effort, abruptly at the end of the war, which added to the economic problems. The balance of payments deficit had risen from £70 million in 1938 to £875 million in 1945.[13] The national debt had risen from £7,247 million in 1939 to £21,473 million in 1945.[14] Britain managed to negotiate a loan from the USA in 1946, but not on very favourable terms. This situation was compounded by the severe winter of 1947, which resulted in coal shortages. Furthermore, the Labour government was aiming for an export-led recovery at a time of shortages of raw materials and of full employment. This increased the need to demobilise troops as soon as possible. Home consumption was kept low in order to divert goods for export and allow high levels of investment. There was a convertibility crisis in 1947, and sterling had to be devalued in September 1949 by 30 per cent.[15]

In addition to this immediate economic crisis, Britain's relative economic decline meant that it could no longer afford to service its massive empire, and was over-extended in its foreign and defence policy commitments. While the leaders of the Labour government recognised that Britain's power – particularly its economic power – had diminished as a result of nearly six years of war, they did not fully comprehend the extent of its weakened position and the long-term implications Britain's leaders, both Labour and Conservative, contin-ued to maintain that the UK had a leading role in world diplomacy and that Britain was still a great power. Attlee did seek to persuade his Cabinet colleagues that only by reducing global military commitments could economic recovery at home proceed, as there was a shortage of manpower combined with a balance-of-payments deficit.[16] But the problems of maintaining Britain's world role within its straightened economic circumstances did not appear to greatly diminish the objec-tives of British foreign policy, which were to maintain the Common-wealth structure; to ensure that the Middle East and Asia were 'stable, prosperous and friendly'; to maintain a special relationship with the United States of America; to consolidate stability in Western Europe; and to resist the expansion of Soviet communism.[17] However, it was not possible to achieve all these objectives at once, in particular because Britain did not have the resources to implement its global objectives.

Labour and the British empire and commonwealth

When the Labour Party came to power in 1945 one of the major chal-lenges it faced was how to deal with the British empire. This territory,

Table 7.1   *Countries where British forces were stationed in 1945*

Europe	Africa	Middle East	Asia	Americas
Austria	British Somalia	Aden	Burma	Bermuda
Belgium	Ethiopia	Cyprus	Hong Kong	British Guyana
Britain	Gambia	Egypt/Suez	India	British Honduras
France	Ghana	Jordan	Indonesia	Falkland Islands
Germany	Kenya	Libya	Japan	Jamaica
Gibraltar	Mauritius	Muscat/Oman	Malaysia/	
Greece	Nigeria	Palestine	Singapore	
Italy	North Rhodesia	Trucial States		
Netherlands	South Rhodesia			
	Sierra Leone			
	South Africa			
	Tanganyika			
	Uganda			

Source: Table taken from David Sanders, *Losing an Empire, Finding a Role: British Foreign Policy since 1945* (Basingstoke: Macmillan, 1990), p. 50.

made up of colonies such as India, Sierra Leone, Hong Kong, and Commonwealth states such as Canada and Australia, was as extensive as it had been at the height of Britain's power in the world, and manifestly could no longer be maintained. At the end of the war, British troops were stationed in over forty countries across Europe, the Middle East, Africa and Asia, as shown in Table 7.1. There was massive pressure for rapid demobilisation, which was harder for a Labour government to resist than a Conservative one given Labour's traditional rejection of conscription. Furthermore, it was difficult to argue for the need for large-scale troop mobilisation when Britain did not have a history of keeping a large army during peacetime. While Britain ended the war with over five million troops, this was rapidly cut to 3.5 million by December 1945 and to under one million by March 1948.

Labour's policy towards the empire/Commonwealth was based on maintaining a close association with the white Commonwealth states such as Canada, Australia, New Zealand and South Africa, on foreign, defence and trade policy. Care was sometimes taken to inform these states of developments in Britain's foreign policy, and to try to secure their support, for example over Britain's role in Greece.[19] This policy was combined with partial decolonisation.

There were a number of reasons for cutting back on Britain's imperial commitments. First, it was clear that the growing cost of maintaining the empire could not be met and that it was a practical and financial impossibility to keep British forces in so many parts of the world. Second, Britain was under increasing pressure from its allies, in particular the United States, to dismantle an empire that was seen as increasingly anachronistic in the post-war world. Third, the growing strength of nationalist movements in Egypt, parts of West Africa and Asia, and of course India, added to the problems of maintaining British rule. Fourth, the Labour Party's tradition of anti-colonial policy and rhetoric meant that it had high expectations to meet, both from these nationalist movements, and from Labour's supporters at home. Particular individuals had been very interested in colonial questions, such as Hardie, Attlee, Cripps and Arthur Creech Jones, who was Colonial Secretary from 1946 to 1950, and the Labour Party had devoted considerable attention to colonial issues at various points in the past. In 1940, the Fabian Research Bureau had established a Fabian Colonial Research Bureau, which worked hard to develop a credible policy towards the empire/Commonwealth, and which had a considerable impact on the development of the Attlee government's colonial policy. In the case of India, Labour had a historic commitment to independence going back to its 1918 general election manifesto where the party had called for 'freedom' and the right of self-determination.[20] Members of the Labour Party had also lobbied when in opposition for independence for India, and some had links with leaders there such as Nehru. Labour ministers were sensitive to charges of exploitation of the British empire, and in particular were aware of the opportunities for the Soviet Union to use such an accusation for propaganda purposes against a British socialist government.[21]

On the other hand, senior ministers such as Bevin were strongly committed to the British empire, and had not won power in order to dismantle it. Morgan notes that 'Attlee, while capable of penning pungent Cabinet papers which called for imperial retreat and disengagement and the removal of outlying British bases in the new era of long-range air power, was also able to respond to the call of empire.'[22] Bevin had told the 1945 annual Labour Party conference that 'You will have to form a Government which is at the centre of a great Empire and Commonwealth of Nations, which touches all parts of the world.' He was scornful of those in the Labour Party who felt that a socialist government could change the fundamental principles of British foreign policy, for 'Revolutions do not change geography, and revolutions do not change geographical need.'[23] For Bevin, the empire was not only a fundamental part of Britain's history, but also at the heart of its destiny.

There was the enduring belief that Britain was still a great power, and as its empire was the most obvious manifestation of its great power status, this should be protected in order to prevent a loss of prestige which would lead to a decline in Britain's influence more generally.[24] In addition to this, ministers and many civil servants in the Foreign Office and the Colonial Office favoured development projects for the colonies rather than immediate British withdrawal, which, it was argued, would result in political anarchy and economic mismanagement. The empire provided Britain with valuable bases around the world, and with access to economic resources and markets, which might be lost if Britain were to withdraw. There was also concern that the Soviet Union would move into any vacuum left by Britain's withdrawal, which must be avoided at any cost. Bevin had told Byrnes at a meeting of the Council of Foreign Ministers in Moscow in December 1945 that, 'Soviet policy was disturbing. It looked as if the Russians were attempting to undermine the British position in the Middle East.' He said that, 'just as a British admiral, when he saw an island, instinctively wanted to grab it, so the Soviet government, if they saw a piece of land, wanted to acquire it.'[25]

The result of these contradictory motivations was that Britain actually expanded its influence in areas like the Persian Gulf, which had important oil fields, and Cyrenaica, part of the former Italian colony of Libya. The Labour government also actively aided the restoration of colonial rule in French Indo-China. Britain maintained its position in other parts of the empire, for example the Caribbean. In the case of Malaya, the government resisted the communist insurgency, though this situation was not resolved until the end of the 1950s.[26] On the other hand, by 1950, Britain had granted independence to Burma, Ceylon (now Sri Lanka), and India and Pakistan. There were also plans for Sierra Leone, Uganda, Northern Rhodesia (Zambia), Nyasaland (Malawi) and Zanzibar. It is not the intention here to analyse the Attlee government's hand-over of independence to its former colonies as detailed accounts already exist.[27] However, it is worth noting certain aspects of the withdrawal from India and Palestine, as the former was, and is still, generally seen as a success, while the latter, at the time and subsequently, has been regarded as a failure.

Owen notes that 'The ending of British rule in India has been regarded as one of the most decisive achievements of the Attlee governments.'[28] Morgan that 'The independence of India, in particular, became a beacon of freedom for emergent nationalist movements, and a kind of model for peaceful British withdrawal.'[29] Their perspective overlooks the fact that by 1945 independence for India was becoming impossible to resist. The British army would not have been able to quell the nationalist movement in India, and some troops may have mutinied if they had been ordered to attempt to do so, as they expected to be demobilised as quickly as possible and had come to see continued British rule in India as politically and morally anachronistic. Labour's 1945 general election manifesto had contained a commitment to independence for India, and the party had repeatedly passed resolutions at conference committing it to independence for India throughout the 1930s and early 1940s. Therefore, the main problem for the Attlee government was not so much *whether* to grant independence for India, but *how* this was to be done, given the communal divisions between Hindus and Muslims. Partly as a result of these divisions, independence was brought forward, and was granted on 15 August 1947. Partition, with the formation of two separate states of India and Pakistan, was accompanied by intense communal violence. While Churchill lamented Britain's withdrawal from India, there was very little protest from the Conservative Party over it, and it was widely accepted by the public as the retreat from India had long been anticipated. The area where British withdrawal did cause protest in Britain and abroad was Palestine, and this has subsequently been seen by some as Bevin's major foreign policy failure. Avi Shlaim refers to the 'inexcusably abrupt and reckless fashion by which the British government chose to divest itself of the Mandate for Palestine'.[30] Certainly Bevin was criticised simultaneously as being anti-Semitic and as deserting Britain's commitment to an independent Palestine by giving in to pressure for a Jewish homeland. However, just as many authors overly emphasise the success of the role that the Labour government played in granting independence to India, they apportion too much blame to the Labour government, and to Bevin in particular, over its handling of Palestine.

Palestine had become a British mandated territory in 1920 under the auspices of the League of Nations. Britain gave up its mandate in 1947 and withdrew its troops in May 1948. The manner in which this happened, without any resolution of the competing claims for territory, was seen as a humiliation for Britain, which had an ongoing commitment both to the resident Arabs of Palestine and to the immigrant Jewish population. Tensions between both were intensified by the desire for a massive Jewish exodus from Europe to the area following the Holocaust, which Bevin tried to delay as he feared the consequences of immediate mass immigration. Because of this, Bevin (and much of the Foreign Office) was seen as pro-Arab and suspected of anti-Semitism. The issue caused tension between Britain and the United States, with President Truman urging the creation of an independent Jewish state as soon as possible. Britain, however, had long been committed to preserving the state of Palestine and granting it independence under the conditions of its mandate. Bevin feared that the creation of a Jewish state in Palestine would lead to both immediate and prolonged conflict in the Middle East. It would be seen as a betrayal of Britain's responsibilities towards the Palestinian people, and would undermine Britain's relations with Jordan and Iraq (which had also come under British control by the League of Nations mandate in 1920) and cause tension with Egypt, where 100,000 British troops were stationed at the Suez Canal. It would also undermine Britain's relations with the wider Muslim world, which were extensive due to its Commonwealth connections. As Britain was unable to resolve the conflict, and its recommendation for a bi-national state had been rejected, it returned its mandate to the UN in 1947. The UN recommended the partition of Palestine between the Palestinians and the Jews, but both groups also rejected this proposal. Britain withdrew its troops on 14 May 1948, leaving the Jews and the Arabs to settle the matter themselves.[31] David Ben-Gurion immediately declared Israel's independence under his premiership, and President Truman unilaterally recognised the new state of Israel. Intense fighting followed, in which the *de facto* state of Israel was able successfully to defend itself from attack and make further territorial gains, creating hundreds of thousands of Palestinian refugees in the process. Britain's withdrawal – carried out in spite of, and partly because of, the tensions in the area – was seen to have been an ignominious end to its role in Palestine. It was even noted in the House of Commons by Rees-Williams, the Under-Secretary of State for the Colonies, that 'the withdrawal of the British Administration took place without handing over to a responsible authority any of the assets, property or liabilities of the Mandatory Power. The manner in which the withdrawal took place is unprecedented in the history of our Empire.'[32] The Labour government's inability to resolve the Palestinian situation was a failure, but it was one to which previous British governments, an array of British politicians, the actions of other states and the intransigence of both the Palestinians and the Jews all contributed, and which the UN was also unable to resolve. It was also a failure that arose out of Britain's inability to impose a solution on the combatants because of its lack of resources in terms of both military power and political influence.

Palestine is not the only area of criticism of the Labour government's colonial policy, with some authors pointing out that the Labour government continued the tradition of developing policy that was economically beneficial to Britain while taking advantage of the resources of its empire, in particular through the working of the sterling area dollar pool.[33] This meant that certain colonial countries within the sterling area – whose currencies were fixed to the British currency – paid dollars into a central pool of gold and dollars held by the Bank of England, in exchange for sterling. However, this occurred in part because of Britain's economic problems, in particular its balance-of-payments deficit and need for dollars, rather than through the implementation of a traditional imperial foreign and economic policy, and because Labour never really accepted the consequences of Britain's straightened circumstances. Bevin was convinced that Britain was, and should remain, a major force in international politics, admonishing Michael Foot during a debate on foreign affairs and the preparation of a peace treaty with Germany in the House of Commons that,

> His Majesty's Government do [sic] not accept the view … that we have ceased to be a great Power, or the contention that we have ceased to play that role. We regard ourselves as one of the Powers most vital to the peace of the world, and we still have our historic part to play. The very fact that we have fought so hard for liberty, and paid such a price, warrants our retaining that position; and, indeed, it places a duty upon us to continue to retain it. I am not aware of any suggestion, seriously advanced, that, by a sudden stroke of fate, as it were, we have overnight ceased to be a great Power.[34]

However, while Bevin viewed foreign policy as the maintenance of Britain's great power status in the world, many in the Labour Party were calling for a new approach to foreign policy based on international socialist co-operation rather than power politics.

Keep Left and opposition to the Attlee government's foreign policy

One of the biggest challenges faced by the Attlee government was the expectations of change generated by its landslide victory at the election. Many of the rank-and-file of the Labour Party, some of the PLP, and a significant proportion of trade union activists were to the left of the leadership of the Labour government. There were expectations of wide-ranging change amongst the Labour Party's supporters in foreign policy as much as domestic policy. The tension between left and right within the Labour Party and wider labour movement affected perceptions on all policy areas, but 'by far the most contentious areas of policy within the Labour Party itself were foreign affairs and defence'.[35] In the House of Commons 'criticism came more frequently from the Labour left-wingers than from the Conservative benches'.[36] The wartime experiences of the Labour leadership meant that figures such as Attlee had moved from a position of emphasising that 'There is no agreement on foreign policy between a Labour Opposition and a Capitalist Government',[37] to emphasising the need for continuity and stability in foreign policy. However, tensions within the wider party over issues such as Britain's relationship with Soviet Russia and capitalist America, of internationalism versus balance-of-power politics, and of continued high levels of defence expenditure during the post-war peace, had not been resolved.

At the 1946 Labour Party annual conference, out of six resolutions on foreign affairs, only one was positive, and that was on the United Nations. One resolution regretted the 'Government's apparent continuance of a traditionally Conservative Party policy of power politics abroad', and urged 'a return to the Labour Party foreign policy of support of Socialist and anti-Imperialist forces throughout the world'.[38] Criticism was made of the lack of change in Foreign Service personnel; over the barriers of Jewish immigration to Palestine; of the continued diplomatic relations with the Franco regime in Spain; and over relations with the Soviet Union.[39] All the critical resolutions were either withdrawn before being voted upon, or, like the one above, were defeated, but they still carried a worrying message to the government, representing the growing campaign for a 'Third Force' in foreign affairs.

The repeated protest from the left of the PLP was that, 'It is felt that when our policy meets with such hearty approval from the Opposition, there must be something wrong with it. It is felt that if the Tories applaud it, it cannot be a Socialist Foreign Policy.'[40] Instead, the advocates of a Third Force called for a foreign policy which would 'chart a middle way between America and Russia', as Britain's 'historic role' was to 'become the leader of a Third Force in world affairs, politically democratic, economically socialist, capable of mediating between the U.S. and the U.S.S.R.'.[41] The frustration with Bevin's foreign policy reached a climax when in November 1946 fifty-seven back-bench MPs tabled an amendment to the Debate on the King's Speech, laying out the government's legislation for the coming year. Richard Crossman, speaking on behalf of them, expressed,

> the urgent hope that His Majesty's Government will so review and recast its conduct of International Affairs as to afford the utmost encouragement to, and collaboration with, all Nations and Groups striving to secure full Socialist planning and control of the world's resources and thus provide a democratic and constructive Socialist alternative to an otherwise inevitable conflict between American Capitalism and Soviet Communism in which all hope of World Government would be destroyed.[42]

After the debate, which included a strong defence from Attlee on behalf of Bevin who was in the United States at the time, Crossman backed down and unsuccessfully tried to withdraw this amendment. While none of the Labour MPs voted in favour of it, eighty-two of them showed their disapproval of the government's foreign policy by abstaining from the vote.[43] Bevin responded to this episode at the 1947 Labour conference by accusing these rebels of stabbing him in the back. He went on, somewhat disingenuously, 'I do say that if you are to expect loyalty from Ministers, the Ministers – however much they may make mistakes – have a right to expect loyalty in return. I grew up in the trade union, you see, and I have never been used to this kind of thing.'[44]

There was also a growing level of discontent being expressed by the left of the trade union movement, again particularly over foreign policy. At the 1946 TUC conference, only one resolution was forwarded on foreign policy, but this was highly, and extensively, critical of the government. This came from a communist member of the Electrical Trades Union, and stated that 'This Congress views with serious concern aspects of the Government's foreign policy.' This concerned policy regarding Greece, Spain, de-Nazification in Germany, and the Soviet Union, since 'the isolation of the Soviet Union, along with the tying of the economy of Britain with that of Capitalist America is in our view extremely dangerous'.[45] This resolution was defeated by 3,557,000 votes to 2,444,000. However, it sufficiently annoyed the Prime Minister, Clement Attlee, that he made direct reference to it in his speech to the Congress, saying the resolution was 'filled with the kind of misrepresentation to which we have become accustomed from the members of the Communist Party, their dupes and fellow travellers'.[46] The number of critical resolutions being forwarded, combined with criticism from the left of the PLP, caused alarm to the Labour leadership. Denis Healey, the Labour Party's

International Secretary from 1946 to 1951, noted later that 'communist influence in the Labour Party and unions remained a major obstacle in my task of winning support for the Government's foreign policy'.[47]

One particular concern for the labour leadership was the application in 1946 by the CPGB to affiliate to the Labour Party. This was, as expected, rejected at the Labour Party's annual conference. On Healey's suggestion, Herbert Morrison successfully moved an amendment to the party constitution to prevent the situation arising again.[48] This stipulated that political organisations 'having their own Programme, Principles and Policy for distinctive and separate propaganda, or possessing Branches in the Constituencies, or engaged in the promotion of Parliamentary or Local Government Candidatures, or owing allegiance to any political organisation abroad, shall be ineligible for affiliation to the Party'.[49] The aim was 'to end the possibility of communist affiliation once and for all'.[50] As Seyd notes, since individual membership of the party was not possible for anyone belonging to an organisation which was deemed ineligible for party affiliation, this constitutional change also 'provided the Party leadership with the means to control the extent of organised factionalism within the Party'.[51]

This factionalism, organised and unorganised, was a problem for the government. There was a gap between the expectations of the rank-and-file of both the Labour Party and the unions and their respective leaderships. There was also continuing dissent from the left-wing back-bench MPs, who in May 1947 produced the pamphlet *Keep Left*, which by 1950 had sold 30,000 copies. Written by Richard Crossman, Michael Foot and Ian Mikardo, *Keep Left* was critical of the government's domestic, and, in particular, foreign policy, repeating the call for a Third Force. Members of the Keep Left Group included Barbara Castle and Tom Balogh, and after 1950, Fenner Brockway. Richard Crossman chaired its meetings, and was the driving force behind the group.[52] However, the Keep Left Group was careful not to appear to be allying itself with the communist left, and made a point of criticising the Soviet Union while expressing the desire for co-operation with it. No MP who was concerned about their future political career within the Labour government could afford to be accused of co-operating with the Communist Party. The Keep Left initiative, though significant, was to be short lived, for the arguments over foreign policy collapsed with the announcement of Marshall Aid in the summer of 1947. Once the Soviet Union had refused to participate in the

Marshall Plan, it became impossible for the continuation of protest over Bevin's foreign policy for parliamentarians. Crossman stated in the House of Commons that it was the Marshall Plan that changed his opinion over the government's policies: 'I will be frank. My own views about America have changed a great deal in the last six months. Many members have had a similar experience. I could not have believed six months ago that a plan of this sort would have been worked out in detail with as few political conditions.'[53] Thus, the Keep Left rebels came back within the fold, muting their criticism over foreign policy, coming to accept the economic necessity of Marshall Aid, as relations with the Soviet Union deteriorated and avoiding accusations of being a 'fellow-traveller' became increasingly imperative. Cliff and Gluckstein have noted that '*Keep Left* holds the record as the shortest-lived left rebellion in the history of Labour. Marshall Aid from America killed it stone dead.'[54] This is not quite true, for the group did continue to meet until 1952, but certainly it had lost most of its impetus. Only a handful of 'hard left' MPs continued with their criticism of Bevin's foreign policy, most notably Konni Zilliacus, D. N. Pritt, and John Platts-Mills. They were among the six MPs who were either marginalised, expelled by the PLP or denied support for re-election by Labour's NEC.[55]

Morgan has argued that Bevin's foreign policy led to 'an astonishing series of redefinitions, even revolutions, in Labour attitudes towards the world outside'. This required a change in attitudes on the left towards the US, and, 'Most shattering of all, for British socialists committed to a sentimental tenderness for fellow socialist regimes from 1917 onwards, a feeling rekindled by the victories of the Red Army during the war, it implied a stern, unrelenting hostility to the Soviet Union.'[56] However, this study argues that this shift in Labour's foreign policy actually occurred during the second half of the 1930s. It was the Spanish Civil War that destroyed the Labour Party's stance on pacifism and non-intervention, and the rise of Hitler that had paved the way for the acceptance of rearmament and the use of force. The Soviet Union had long been viewed with suspicion by many in the leadership of the party, and the Nazi-Soviet pact and the Soviet invasion of Finland had reinforced this viewpoint. When the Soviet Union joined the allies, this did generate a new wave of hope amongst some sections of the Labour Party that it could forge a new relationship with Russia after the war, but not with government ministers such as Attlee, Bevin and Dalton. They were more focused on working towards the same vision of a post-war multilateral world based on international institutions as the USA, even if this vision arose from very different motivations. The actions of the Soviet Union in refusing to co-operate with Marshall Aid and the developing Cold War meant that this was now accepted by the bulk of Labour's supporters.

Britain, America and the Cold War

One of Bevin's major foreign policy concerns in the immediate post-war period was that the USA would return to an isolationist position. This would be problematic for Britain in three ways. First, Labour's vision of a multilateral world order required leadership from America. Second, in terms of a great power rivalry between the UK and the Soviet Union; whilst the Labour Party had stressed during the 1945 election campaign that it alone could handle the Soviet Union, the Labour government was well aware that it could not handle what it perceived to be an expansionist Soviet Union on its own. Third, Bevin and other ministers were also aware that Britain was not likely to be able to meet all its commitments to maintain stability in Europe, the Middle East and Asia. Thus, Bevin's aim was to maintain the 'special relationship' that had developed from the alliance between Britain and America during the Second World War, and to involve America in European reconstruction as closely as possible.

The situation in Greece was a case in point. Although never part of the British empire as such, Greece had long been considered within the British sphere of influence, and was seen as strategically important in that it intersected lines of communication with the British empire in the Eastern Mediterranean and the Near East. Greece had been polarised politically since the First World War between a largely liberal, republican left and a conservative, monarchist right. This had intensified during the 1930s. In 1936 there was an army coup under General Metaxas, and then Greece was invaded and occupied by the Axis powers during the Second World War. Some of its unpopular right-wing government went into exile, as did the King, who based himself in London. Some of the right-wing stayed in Greece and collaborated with the Germans. Britain supported the underground resistance in Greece, the National Liberation Front (EAM), which included the communist and non-communist left organisations, and the affiliated National Popular Liberation Army (ELAS). This gained in strength to the extent that it seemed likely to win power in the event of an election. At first Britain supported EAM and ELAS, but soon became

concerned about the influence of the communists within it and so
helped nurture the much less popular non-communist resistance, and
in 1943 Britain swapped her support to it. British troops landed in
Greece in October 1944. These troops found themselves not only
fighting the Germans, but also trying to prevent civil war from breaking out.[57]

Britain's policy at the end of the Second World War towards
Greece was to support any government as long as it was not communist. Churchill had been pressing for elections and a plebiscite to be
held as soon as possible, followed by British withdrawal from Greece.
British policy towards the conflict in Greece had been very unpopular
with the Labour Party, and both the party and large sections of the
Greek population expected a change in policy, thinking that a Labour
government would have a more positive attitude towards the
Republicans.[58] However, to a large extent Bevin continued Churchill's
policy. In August he produced a memorandum on Greece recommending to the rest of the Cabinet that the elections and plebiscite
should be held as soon as possible, even though the conditions for free
and fair elections did not exist within the on-going conditions of threat
and violence. The reasons for Bevin's recommendations were that
continuing conflict in Greece would undermine the whole of Britain's
Middle East position;[59] that until the Greek elections were held, 'we
are hampered in pressing for free elections in other Balkan countries';[60]
and that Britain would not be able to withdraw its troops from Greece
until these elections were held.

The Labour government's actions towards Greece were very
unpopular in the Labour Party, and provoked protest from party
members and from within the PLP. Bevin also found that his foreign
policy was being questioned within the government itself. His view
was that,

> The Mediterranean is the area through which we bring influence to bear
> on Southern Europe, the soft underbelly of France, Italy, Yugoslavia,
> Greece and Turkey. Without our physical presence in the Mediterranean,
> we should cut little ice with those States which would fall, like Eastern
> Europe, under the totalitarian yoke. We should also lose our position in
> the Middle East.

Thus, it was 'essential' that Greece remained 'with us politically'.[61]
However, Attlee wrote to Bevin while he was on a trip to New York in
November 1946, laying out his concerns over foreign policy. While he
reassured Bevin 'that there is not much in the complaint that there

have not been full discussions of Foreign Policy in the Cabinet', he went on that,

> I think we have got to consider our commitments very carefully lest we try to do more than we can. In particular I am rather worried about Greece. The Chiefs of staff are suggesting that we must keep our forces there for at least another year. I cannot contemplate the financial and military burden with equanimity. The political and economic situation in Greece shows no improvement. They seem to be unable to get a satisfactory government nor can they do anything but quarrel amongst themselves. Meanwhile we have to accept a good deal of criticism. I feel that we are backing a very lame horse.

Attlee reminded Bevin that 'I have as you know, always considered that the strategic importance of communications through the Mediterranean in terms of modern warfare is very much overrated by our military advisers', and that 'I am beginning to doubt whether the Greek game is worth the candle.' Furthermore, he did not think that the countries bordering Soviet Union's zone of influence, namely Greece, Turkey, Iraq and Persia, could be made strong enough to form an effective barrier, and 'We do not command the resources to make them so.' Instead, Attlee suggested that Bevin try to reach an agreement with Russia that these countries become a neutral zone. He concluded 'that we have got to be very careful in taking on military obligations in Greece and Turkey when the U.S.A. only gives economic assistance'. He complained that 'There is a tendency in America to regard us as an outpost of America, but an outpost that they will not have to defend. I am disturbed by the signs of America trying to make a safety zone around herself while leaving us and Europe in No Man's Land.' His final instruction to Bevin was to find out what the Americans 'are prepared to do', but that 'we should be careful not to commit ourselves'.[62]

This letter from Attlee effectively questioned and challenged Bevin's whole foreign policy stance, recognising the problems inherent in Britain propping up countries in the Mediterranean when it did not have the resources, and questioning Britain's relationship with the USA and the Soviet Union. As far as Bevin was concerned, the Soviet Union was expansionist and had to be stopped whatever the price. Attlee then spoke to Hector McNeil, then a Minister of State at the Foreign Office, who wrote to Bevin in New York asking him if he could 'try to obtain some more definite indication as to what the Americans propose to do for Greece and Turkey'. McNeil warned Bevin that 'I think I should tell you that in my opinion the whole question of our policy towards Greece and Turkey is in the melting pot, and that there is a very great reluctance here to contemplate a continuation of our military, financial and political commitments in Greece.'[63]

Bevin was enraged. He replied that 'I cannot embark on a discussion with Mr. Byrnes on the basis suggested in your telegram. If our policy is under reconsideration it is useless for me to raise Greece and Turkey with him.' Furthermore, McNeil's warning that the policy towards Greek and Turkey was in the melting pot 'has come to me not only as surprise but as a shock'.

> The policy of the Government has been based hitherto on the assumption that Greece and Turkey are essential to our political and strategical [sic] position in the world and I have constantly had that assumption in mind in my conversations both with the United States of American and Russia, and it has been one of the underlying assumptions in our negotiations for the peace treaties ... I really do not know where I stand.[64]

Bevin was not prepared to compromise his position on Greece and the Middle East. This shows a hardening in his position, because he had in fact questioned the government's Middle Eastern policy himself early on in the Attlee government, sending a memo to the Cabinet members in August 1945 requesting their views on the issue. He had asked his colleagues 'to consider the fundamental question of whether we are to continue to assert our political predominance in the Middle East and our overriding responsibility for its defence, or whether, alternatively, it is though to be essential on financial and man-power grounds that we should seek the extensive assistance of other Powers in the defence of the Middle East'.[65] By 1946 he had become convinced of the strategic importance of the Middle East, and of the role that Greece played as an access route to it. However, he had also came to the conclusion that Britain did not have the resources to continue its involvement in Greece, and did turn to the Americans for support. The result was the Truman Doctrine and the policy of containment, as Truman pledged that the USA would 'support free peoples who are resisting attempted subjugation by armed minorities or by outside pressures'. Truman linked aid to Greece and Turkey to the wider fight against communism in order to shock Congress into approving his policy of providing support for these countries and reverse America's traditional policy of non-intervention in European affairs.[66]

The Truman Doctrine was followed by a speech by the Secretary of State, George Marshall, on 5 June 1947 in which he argued that

Europe's political stability depended on its economic stability. He said that 'It is logical that the United States should do whatever it is able to do to assist in the return of normal economic health in the world, without which there can be no political stability and no assured peace'. It was up to the Europeans to come forward with a common programme of their aid requirements.[67] Bevin publicly welcomed the 'inspiring lead' given to Europe in Marshall's proposal.[68] However, privately doubts were expressed about Britain being included on the same basis as continental Europe in any Marshall Aid programme. While Britain was prepared to accept American leadership, it was not prepared to be treated as just another European country. At the first meeting with William Clayton to discuss the Marshall Plan, Stafford Cripps, by then the Chancellor of the Exchequer, pointed out 'that there was a difference between the U.K. and other European countries because of U.K. trade with non-European countries'. Bevin argued that,

> if the U.K. was considered just another European country this would fit in with Russian strategy, namely, that the U.S. would encounter a slump and would withdraw from Europe, the U.K. would be helpless and out of dollars and as merely another European country the Russians, in command of the Continent, could deal with Britain in due course.[69]

Furthermore, the British government did not want to go into the program and 'not do anything', since, it was felt, this 'would sacrifice the "little bit of dignity we have left"'.[70] However, Clayton and other US policy-makers refused to accept that Britain should be treated differently from the rest of Europe, even though Bevin emphasised that Britain was in a unique position to assist in economic revival because of the British empire.

Despite this disagreement between Britain and the USA, events were to move quickly. Bevin met with his French counterpart, Georges Bidault, to discuss a first response to the embryonic Marshall Plan offer on 17–18 June. Molotov, the Soviet Foreign Minister, joined them on 27 June. When Molotov arrived, he found that Bevin and Bidault had already set some of the terms for involvement in the plan, which included treating all the recipient states as part of an economic bloc, thus accepting the multilateral focus of the American offer. This, as Bevin and Bidault presumably realised, would not be acceptable to the Russians, as it would mean opening up the Soviet economy to Western inspection. This would have revealed the full extent of the Soviet's economic weakness, which was not known in the West at this time.

Subsequently, Molotov walked out of the Paris talks after three days, in a fanfare of negative publicity. Bevin and Bidault were presumably relieved, as they had both told the US Ambassador to Paris, Jefferson Caffery, 'that they hope the Soviets will refuse to cooperate' as their participation would greatly complicate things.[71] Albania, Bulgaria, Czechoslovakia, Hungary, Finland, Poland, Romania and Yugoslavia also went on to refuse to participate in the Marshall Plan.

It has been argued by some on the left that the USA used the Marshall Plan to swing Britain towards the American sphere of influence and so alter relations between Britain and the Soviet Union.[72] However, the leaders of the British government had taken a more suspicious stance towards the Soviet Union even before the Second World War was over. This cautious approach to the Soviet Union continued with the election of a Labour government, led by Attlee, Bevin and Dalton who were staunch anti-communists. During 1945 and the first half of 1946, the Americans had in fact resisted what they saw as British attempts to forge an Anglo-American front against the Soviet Union, which included members of the British Embassy making discrete efforts to toughen the American government's attitude towards the Kremlin.[73] Certainly the British Ambassador in Washington was concerned that the Russians have 'found themselves until now in a position where they can manoeuvre at will between the divergent attitudes of Britain and the United States'. Britain has 'tended to be caught in a squeeze play between an expansionist Soviet Union and a United States anxious to compose its own differences with the Russians without due regard for the consequences upon ourselves'. Indeed, the USA should stop 'shilly-shallying' around, as 'The one means of bringing the expansionist moves of the Soviet rulers to a satisfactory halt is to confront them with a joint Anglo-American aggregate of power'. The US government would have to abandon its traditional fear of being accused by its own public of 'ganging up' with the British empire against the Soviet Union. Indeed, 'there seems to be no harm in discreetly exercising our powers of persuasion along these lines on policy-shaping Americans at all levels'.[74]

By the spring of 1946, the American position had changed. According to Gaddis, the turning point in American policy towards the Soviet Union changed in late February and early March of that year. Up until then, attitudes towards the Soviet Union had developed on an *ad hoc* basis, with little consistency besides the assumption of shared basic interests in peace and stability.[75] It was not until after Kennan's Long Telegram of 22 February 1946 that the US fully started to reconsider its position *vis-à-vis* co-operation with the Soviet Union.[76]

Having helped push for the change in the American position towards the Soviet Union, the British government then had to explain to them why it was not being more anti-Soviet in its rhetoric. One of the key reasons for this situation was that the public, and members of the Labour Party, did not share the anti-communism being voiced by the central organs of government, and still regarded the Soviet Union with appreciation for its role in the Second World War. An overt anti-Soviet stance at this point would have created a backlash in the party, which interpreted internationalism as including a strong relationship with the Soviet Union, and might have interpreted an anti-Soviet stance as a rejection of internationalism. Anstey points out that the Foreign Office had the problem of trying to satisfy public opinion in the UK and US at the same time; while the American public was becoming increasingly hostile towards the Soviet Union, the British public still largely desired an alliance with Russia, and so 'aligning rhetoric with reality simultaneously on both sides of the Atlantic became increasingly difficult. An answer of sorts lay in educating the British public to adopt a tougher stand, and in informing American officials of the nature of the Foreign Office's predicament.[77]

While Bevin asked the press to take a tougher anti-Soviet line, Waldemar Gallman, a minister at the American embassy in London, reported the predicament to the American Secretary of State, George Marshall, that,

> Foreign Office officials directly charged with Soviet affairs have recently and repeatedly indicated that while there is no change in substance of United Kingdom policy towards USSR, every move must be carefully considered and planned from point of view of protecting Bevin from Labour Party rebels ... in light of Labour rebellion Bevin and Foreign Office now take greater pains to avoid creating impression he is ganging up with the United States against Russia.[78]

Part of Bevin's problem was that the viewpoint of many Labour Party supporters on foreign policy was to the left of the government's. Since the Labour Party had in the past emphasised its commitment to international socialist co-operation, and had presented the wartime alliance with the Soviet Union as part of a fight against fascism and for working-class values, even a cold war against the Soviet Union was such a *volte-face* that care had to be taken on how it was presented to the public. In addition, many on the left of the Labour Party blamed

Soviet intransigence on its fears of invasion from the West, and its experience of Western intervention to undermine the Soviet revolution, interpreting Soviet actions as defensive rather than offensive.[79] Bevin was helped in this by the Soviet Union's entrenchment of its power in the East. In September 1947 representatives of the communist parties of the USSR, Bulgaria, Romania, Czechoslovakia, Hungary, Poland, France, Italy and Yugoslavia met in Poland to create the Cominform. At this meeting, Zhdanov, the Secretary of the Communist Party of the Soviet Union's Central Committee, made his famous 'two-camps' speech. He argued that Western policies, and especially the Marshall Plan, had split the world into two opposing camps, with the 'antidemocratic' camp led by the imperialist United States, and the other 'democratic' camp led by the Soviet Union.[81] The Cominform was to act as an information bureau, designed to co-ordinate the activities of the communist parties and smooth out differences between them. While Yugoslavia resisted Soviet attempts to centralise control, a series of bilateral treaties were imposed upon Eastern European states during early 1948. In February 1948 a communist coup in Czechoslovakia ousted the coalition government, and the Berlin blockade began in June 1948. This all provided the Labour government with the evidence they needed for their antipathy towards the Soviet Union, and the Cold War became fact rather speculation. The establishment of the Cominform also provided Labour with a perfect excuse for rejecting any co-operation with the CPGB, and launched its own anti-communist campaign.[81] This reflected an increased willingness from the government by spring 1947 publicly to confront their left-wing critics rather than trying to placate them.[82] The Labour back-benchers' *Keep Left* was soon countered by Healey's *Cards on the Table*, an official Labour pamphlet which sought to rebut the criticisms of Bevin's foreign policy. This stated that 'The idea that we should have extricated ourselves from the quarrel between Russia and the USA does not make sense; during the period under review, Britain was the main target of Russian hostility, while until a few months ago America was an undecided spectator.' It argued that it was 'both undesirable and impractical' for Britain to remain completely independent of both Russia and the US after the War since 'Britain herself was too weak to cut herself off from American aid.'[83] The arguments in *Cards on the Table* were reinforced by the unfolding external events of the Marshall Plan, which provided concrete evidence of the difficulties of finding common ground with the Soviet Union. The realities of an increasingly fraught international situation in which it was impossible for Britain to maintain some kind of 'Third Force' or middle way bolstered Bevin's policy of closer relations with the USA.

Defence policy

The Labour government's immediate defence policy had been based on providing armed forces to back up British foreign policy, which included forces in Europe, Africa, the Middle East and East of Suez, within the context of cutting the defence expenditure projections to the £500 million per annum which had been agreed by the wartime coalition government.[84] Initially Attlee acted as Defence Secretary, but with the creation of a separate Ministry of Defence in 1946, he appointed A. V. Alexander to the post of Minister of Defence. Defence policy lacked any overall direction as the Chiefs of Staff had been concerned with winning the Second World War, not planning for the post-war peace. It was also at the centre of a growing division within the Cabinet, as Attlee and his Chancellor of the Exchequer, Hugh Dalton, wanted military cut-backs in the light of the economic crisis, while Bevin and Alexander maintained the necessity of continued military capacity.[85] At the beginning of 1946 Dalton argued that there should a sharp drop in expenditure on defence, as the economic picture 'was a very gloomy one' as Britain was going to be nearly one million men short of the minimum required to revive its export trade. He was very worried by the large military expenditure overseas, and felt that Britain could not possibly afford to continue in this way.[86] Bevin, on the other hand, said that he was nervous of any material cut in the armed forces before the June negotiations with the Soviet Union and the United States, and 'It might be more economical to keep another 100,000 men for a few months if by so doing we avoided much more expensive trouble later on. It was necessary to weigh up whether our future prosperity depended more upon a satisfactory clearing up of the international situation in the coming year, or upon an additional build-up of our productive capacity.'[87] Because of the shortage of troops due to demobilisation, it was agreed in 1946 that conscription would continue for the time being. This was particularly unpopular within the rank-and-file of the Labour Party and trade union movement, given their traditional opposition to conscription, and given the manpower shortages in Britain at this time.

The developing Cold War over the next couple of years served to support Bevin's perspective. At a Cabinet meeting on 5 March 1948

Bevin argued that Soviet activities in Czechoslovakia and Finland 'showed beyond any doubt that there was no hope of reaching a satisfactory settlement' with the Soviet Union and 'that resolute action must be taken to counter the Soviet threat to Western civilisation'. This involved reviewing existing levels of defence expenditure and of the defence measures that would be needed if diplomacy with the Soviet Union failed, launching a propaganda drive to rebut Soviet propaganda that continuously condemned British foreign and defence policy, and completing the North Atlantic Treaty negotiations as a matter of urgency.[88] On 4 March 1947 Britain had signed the Treaty of Dunkirk, a defensive pact with France against an attack from Germany. This was enlarged on 17 March 1948 with the Treaty of Brussels, signed by Britain, France and the Benelux countries, committing them to collective defence against any armed attack for fifty years. Part of the rationale for this treaty was to help President Truman convince the American Congress that Europe was willing to contribute to its own defence, and that the US could therefore join Western Europe in a military alliance. The Labour government feared that if war did break out with the Soviet Union, there would be little chance that either Britain or Europe collectively would be able to resist the Red Army. Thus, Bevin wanted to ensure long-term American military support for Western Europe. A series of Anglo-American talks were held at the end of March 1948 to discuss a collective defence agreement for the North Atlantic, at which a draft treaty was agreed upon. The impetus for this North Atlantic Treaty was increased by the Berlin blockade of June 1948, when the Soviet Union blocked the entry of goods by rail and road from the West into West Berlin in protest against US efforts to centralise the administration of economic policy in the Western sectors of the city. Since Berlin was in the Soviet zone of control, this effectively cut West Berlin off from the rest of the world. In response, Bevin proposed to the British and American Chiefs of Staff that they airlift supplies to both the military and civilian population in Berlin using transport planes.[89] At the same time, Bevin agreed to the stationing of American B-29 bombers, which were capable of carrying atomic weapons, in British bases. Not until 1951 was it made clear that the USA would have to seek permission from Britain before launching an atomic attack from bases in the UK.

While the political division of Europe had occurred during the period from the summer of 1948 to the spring of 1949, the division of Europe into two defensive blocs at the heart of the bi-polar, Cold War world occurred during the period of the Berlin blockade. This ended in May 1949. On 4 April 1949 the USA, Canada, Britain, Belgium, Denmark, France, Iceland, Italy, Luxembourg, the Netherlands, Norway and Portugal signed the North Atlantic Treaty of Mutual Assistance. This in effect committed America to guaranteeing West European defence, for an armed attack against one member state was to be considered as an attack against all. This was then institutionalised into the North Atlantic Treaty Organisation (NATO). In the House of Commons, Bevin was careful to present the treaty as a defensive move, resulting from the failure of the United Nations to prevent Soviet aggression in Eastern Europe, saying:

> [N]o such arrangement as the North Atlantic Treaty would have been found necessary at all if the effectiveness of the Security Council as an instrument for ensuring the immediate defence of any member against aggression had not been undermined by the Soviet use of the veto, and by other actions of the Soviet Government ... That is why we have signed this Treaty; because we must have security and because we have learned by bitter experience that we cannot get it at present through the Security Council.[90]

The treaty was passed by an overwhelming majority in the House of Commons, with only six MPs, four Labour and two Communist, voting against it.[91]

Despite the growing Anglo-American alliance, Britain was reluctant to be too reliant on its allies for its defence needs, and so the decision was made in secret, by Attlee, Bevin and four other members of the Cabinet Defence Committee on 8 January 1947, for Britain to develop an independent nuclear strategy. This decision was made without the knowledge of the rest of the Cabinet, Parliament or the Labour Party. It was made for two reasons. First, for strategic purposes: if other states had so dangerous a weapon, then Britain would need it to deter or retaliate, otherwise Britain would become too dependent on its allies for its defence needs. Second, to halt the image of decline by demonstrating that Britain was still a world power, for 'Nuclear weapons seemed to be the way by which a medium-sized, but technically advanced, nation could retain great power status.'[92] However, these aims were undermined somewhat by the continued reliance on the US for technology and weapons to maintain Britain as a nuclear power. Much to Britain's chagrin, the Soviet Union was the first in the race between the two nations to test an atomic bomb, doing so in August 1949. The first British atomic bomb was not exploded until October 1952, by which time Britain's nuclear strategy, decided in secret, was becoming a highly politicised issue for the Labour Party.

Labour won the election of 23 February 1950, but with a much-reduced majority of only five seats. The government seemed to be suffering from a lack of direction and energy, at a time when international affairs were becoming increasingly tense. The outbreak of the Korean War, when in June 1950 North Korean tanks crossed the thirty-eighth parallel into South Korea, saw another rethink about defence expenditure, galvanising Attlee and Chancellor Stafford Cripps to agree to extra defence provisions. Cripps felt that 'on general economic grounds' the most that Britain could commit to defence over the next three years was £950 million per annum. But, this 'could not be provided without some reduction in Government expenditure, some additional taxation, or some reduction in capital investment or a combination of all three'. The Cabinet approved Cripps' proposals for increased expenditure as ministers pointed out that 'the fact was that our forces were insufficiently equipped to meet the dangers with which we were now faced. It was abundantly clear that we must spend substantially more on defence.' It was decided that Britain would inform the US that 'We considered on general economic grounds an annual expenditure of £950 million on defence was the most we could afford in 1951–52 and in the following two years.'[93] Labour's defence and foreign policy were criticised at the Labour Party conference, to the extent that Bevin felt it necessary to speak on behalf of the NEC's report on the international situation, despite his failing health. At what was to be Bevin's last conference appearance, he spoke in defence of the NEC's report on the international situation, saying that Labour's foreign policy was based on collective security through the United Nations. He argued that they must give the UN the necessary power and defence arrangements so that aggression could never succeed, for 'A few failures by the aggressor will mean … the triumph of peace over the sadistic desire for war and destruction.'[94]

Ernest Bevin's health had been failing for some time, but he wished to continue as Foreign Secretary until the next election, which would not be far off given Labour's small majority. Attlee, however, felt that the post was now too demanding for Bevin. On 9 March 1951, the day of Bevin's seventieth birthday, Attlee requested that he resign. Both worn-out and devastated at his loss of power, he died on 14 April.[95] Herbert Morrison replaced him, but remained Foreign Secretary only until Labour's election defeat in October 1951. Morrison's Principle Private Secretary at the Foreign Office has said

that 'This relatively short period amply sufficed to show up his inade-
quacy for the job' and that 'One unexpected complication was
Morrison's extraordinary ignorance of most of the Foreign Office
problems of the moment.'[96] The choice of Morrison to be Bevin's
successor was unusual in that Morrison did not have any particular
experience of foreign affairs, nor had he demonstrated any particular
flair for dealing with such policy issues. It perhaps reflected the declining health, vigour and power of the government and its leading
members, though at the time the appointment was 'widely
acclaimed'.[97] Certainly Morrison's brief time at the Foreign Office was
marked by failure both at home and abroad to maintain the influence
that Bevin had achieved. Morrison did not have the influence with the
Americans that Bevin had had, nor did he have as much influence
within the Labour Party. Foreign and defence policy was again becoming highly politicised and contentious within the Labour Party, particularly over the issue of British rearmament.

The result of the increased defence expenditure was that cuts
would have to be made in public spending. The rather inexperienced
Hugh Gaitskell, who had taken over as Chancellor on 19 October
1950, proposed in the spring of 1951 that charges be introduced in the
National Health Service for teeth and spectacles. This rather prosaic
choice of spending cuts was to result in a very embarrassing debacle.
Nye Bevan, who was upset at Gaitskell's appointment as well as this
particular decision, resigned in protest, and Harold Wilson and John
Freeman joined him.[98] Many in the party felt that Labour had gone
back on a commitment to one of their most popular policies, free
health care, as well as feeling that the commitment to such a huge rearmament policy would undermine the British economy. The party was
demoralised, Bevin was gone, and Attlee was unwell and unable to
exert his leadership to contain the row. The Gaitskell/Bevan split was
to permeate the Labour Party until 1957, with foreign and defence
policy being the main issue of contention. This all occurred as the
Labour government was seen to be stalling, exhausted from its years in
power, with its main achievements now in the past.

When the Labour Party assumed power in 1945 there were high
expectations of what it could achieve in international affairs. However,
the government found that there was a disjunction between what it
saw as Britain's leading role in the world, and Britain's ability to meet
its existing foreign and defence requirements. Despite trying to cling
to its role as one of the 'big three' of the wartime alliance, it was
becoming clear that Britain's power was declining, in particular in

relation to the power and reach of the US. The Attlee years saw a period of retrenchment from the empire, which was to be continued, though reluctantly, by successive post-war governments. Britain's hasty withdrawal from Palestine in particular reflected a pragmatic and even unpropitious response to a difficult problem. The central conundrum that had to be faced was how to cut back expenditure while continuing to have as powerful a role in the world as possible. Somewhat surprisingly given the focus of sections of the party on the inter-linking of economic and political issues, the Labour Party was often just as reluctant as its opponents to admit to Britain's decline, or to be open about its inability to afford a world-wide role in security issues. Its response to its problems was to turn to the USA for support, as Britain could no longer afford to maintain its world role unaided. As Porter puts it, '[Britain's] superstructure had come to rest on someone else's base.'[99] Bevin in particular predicated his foreign policy on a close relationship with the US, as America's involvement in Europe became institutionalised through the Marshall Plan and NATO. To a certain extent the Labour government's foreign policy of 1945–1951 was Bevin's foreign policy, with Attlee allowing him a remarkable degree of freedom. No other Labour foreign secretary has had the impact that Ernest Bevin had, either on Labour's foreign policy or Britain's role in the world. However, while Bevin was implementing what he saw as Labour's foreign policy, his critics on the left felt that the party had wasted its opportunity to change the nature of British foreign policy. The battle against the Labour Party's pacifism in the early 1930s; the battle for rearmament in the face of the threat from Hitler in the late 1930s; disgust at the Nazi-Soviet pact; and experience of coalition government, meant that there had already been a remarkable shift in attitudes of the Labour leadership away from socialist internationalism and towards balance-of-power politics. For these men, Labour's internationalism was being met through the new post-war regime based on the UN and the institutions of the Bretton Woods agreement, and through Britain's remaining global commitments. For them, international solidarity did not mean co-operating with the Soviet Union. However, for many in the rank-and-file of the party, their hopes for a post-war Labour foreign policy were based on a continuation of the wartime alliance with the Soviet Union, and internationalism and international solidarity meant working with Russia, not capitalist America. The criticisms over the Labour government's foreign policy were muted by the onset of the Cold War, but they never really went away, and this period saw the division between left and right of the party on foreign policy solidify into a division between Atlanticists and those suspicious of the USA, which continues to this day.

Notes

1 Hugh Dalton, *High Tide and After: Memoirs, 1945–1960* (London: Muller, 1962), p. 3.
2 Bernard Donoughue and George Jones, *Herbert Morrison: Portrait of a Politician* (London: Weidenfeld and Nicolson, 1973), pp. 340–3.
3 *Ibid.*, citing interview with Sir Trevor Evans, p. 346.
4 Roderick Barclay, *Ernest Bevin and the Foreign Office, 1932–1969* (London: Roderick Barclay, 1975), p. 78.
5 Labour Party, *The Old World and the New Society* (London: Labour Party, 1942); 'The Post-War International Settlement', in *Labour Party Annual Conference Report* (hereafter *LPACR*), 1944, pp. 4–9.
6 John Gerard Ruggie, *Constructing the World Polity: Essays on International Institutionalization* (London: Routledge, 1998), p. 123
7 Richard Gardner, *Sterling-Dollar Diplomacy: Anglo-American Collaboration in the Reconstruction of Multilateral Trade* (Oxford: Clarendon Press, 1956), pp. 24–5.
8 Alan Bullock, *The Life and Times of Ernest Bevin, vol. 3: Foreign Secretary, 1945–1951* (London: Heinemann, 1983); Kenneth O. Morgan, *Labour in Power 1945–51* (Oxford: Oxford University Press, 1985); Henry Pelling, *The Labour Governments, 1945–51* (London: Macmillan, 1984); Ritchie Ovendale, *The English Speaking Alliance: Britain, the United States, the Dominions and the Cold War 1945–51* (London: Allen and Unwin, 1985).
9 John Saville, 'Labour and foreign policy, 1945-1947', *Our History Journal*, Journal of the History Group of the Communist Party, no. 17 (May 1991), 18–32, and Saville, *The Politics of Continuity: British Foreign Policy and the Labour Government, 1945–46* (London: Verso, 1993); Jonathan Schneer, 'Hopes deferred or shattered: the British Labour Left and the Third Force movement, 1945–49', *Journal of Modern History*, 56:2 (1984), 197–226, and Schneer, *Labour's Conscience: The Labour Left 1945–51* (Boston: Unwin Hyman, 1988); Peter Weiler, 'British Labour and the Cold War: the foreign policy of the Labour governments, 1945–1951', *Journal of British Studies*, 26:1 (1987), 54–82, and Weiler, *British Labour and the Cold War* (Stanford: Stanford University Press, 1988).
10 David Butler and Gareth Butler, *British Political Facts, 1900–1985* (London: Macmillan, 6th edn, 1986), p. 390.
11 *Annual Abstract of Statistics, no. 88, 1938–1950* (London: HMSO, 1952), table 217, p. 207.
12 David Sanders, *Losing an Empire, Finding a Role: British Foreign Policy since 1945* (Basingstoke: Macmillan, 1990), p. 47.
13 Butler and Butler, *British Political Facts*, p. 386.
14 *Annual Abstract of Statistics*, table 267, p. 256.

15 For information on the economic situation, see Alec Cairncross, *Years of Recovery: British Economic Policy 1945–51* (London: Methuen, 1985); and George Worswick and Peter Ady, eds, *The British Economy, 1945–1950* (Oxford: Clarendon Press, 1952).

16 Public Record Office, London (hereafter PRO), CAB 131/1 DO (46) 1, 3 and 5, minutes of meetings of 1st, 3rd and 5th meetings of the Cabinet Defence Committee, 11 January, 21 January and 15 February 1946.

17 *Documents on British Policy Overseas*, series 2, vol. 2, 1950 (London: HMSO, 1987), memorandum for the Permanent Under-Secretary's Committee, 'British overseas obligations', 27 April 1950, p. 158.

18 Sanders, *Losing an Empire, Finding a Role*, p. 49, referring to *CMND 6743, Statement Relating to Defence* (London: HMSO, February 1946) and *CMND 7327, Statement Relating to Defence* (London: HMSO, February 1948).

19 PRO, CAB 129/1/CP (45) 107, memorandum by the Foreign Secretary, 'Greece', 11 August 1945.

20 F. W. S. Craig, ed. and comp., *British General Election Manifestos 1900–1974* (London: Macmillan, rev. and enlarged edn, 1975), p. 31.

21 Comments by Bevin, PRO, CAB 129/23, CP (48) 7, July 1948.

22 Morgan, *Labour in Power*, pp. 192–3.

23 *LPACR*, 1945, p. 115.

24 *Documents on British Foreign Policy Overseas*, series 2, vol. 2, 1950, memorandum for the Permanent Under-Secretary's Committee, 'British overseas obligations', 27 April 1950, p. 171.

25 *Documents on British Policy Overseas*, series 1, vol. 2, 1945 (London: HMSO, 1985), Record of a conversation at the US Ambassador's residence, Moscow, 17 December 1945, pp. 733–5.

26 See article by the Labour Colonial Secretary, 'British colonial policy, with particular reference to Africa', *International Affairs*, 17:2 (April 1951), 176–83.

27 For example, Partha Sarathi Gupta, *Imperialism and the British Labour Movement, 1914–1964* (London: Macmillan, 1975); Stephen Howe, *Anticolonialism in British Politics: The Left and the End of Empire, 1918–1964* (Oxford: Clarendon Press, 1993); *Robin Moore, Making the New Commonwealth* (Oxford: Clarendon Press, 1987).

28 Nicholas Owen, '"Responsibility without power": The Attlee governments and the end of the British rule in India', in Nick Tiratsoo, ed., *The Attlee Years* (London: Pinter, 1991), p. 167.

29 Morgan, *Labour in Power*, p. 228.

30 Avi Shlaim, 'Britain and the Arab-Israeli War of 1948', in Michael Dockrill and John Young, eds, *British Foreign Policy, 1945–56* (New York: St. Martin's Press, 1989), p. 77.

31 See *ibid.*, and W. Roger Louis and Robert Stookey, eds, *The End of the Palestine Mandate* (London: I. B. Taurus, 1986).

32 *House of Commons Debates* (hereafter *H.C. Deb.*), fifth series, vol. 461, col. 2050, 24 February 1949.

33 Mark Curtis, *The Ambiguities of Power: British Foreign Policy since 1945* (London: Zed Books, 1995), p. 12; David Fieldhouse, 'The Labour governments and the Empire-Commonwealth, 1945–1951', in Ritchie

Ovendale, ed., *The Foreign Policy of the British Labour Governments, 1945–1951* (Leicester: University of Leicester Press, 1984), pp. 95–8; Partha Sarathi Gupta, 'Imperialism and the Labour government', in Jay Winter, ed., *The Working Class in Modern British History* (Cambridge: Cambridge University Press, 1983), pp. 94 and 110.

34 *H.C. Deb.*, vol. 437, col. 1965, 16 May 1947.

35 Henry Pelling and Alastair Reid, *A Short History of the Labour Party* (Basingstoke: Macmillan, 11th edn, 1996), p. 91. See also David Coates, *The Labour Party and the Struggle for Socialism* (Cambridge: Cambridge University Press, 1975), p. 190.

36 Barclay, *Ernest Bevin and the Foreign Office*, p. 82.

37 Clement Attlee, *The Labour Party in Perspective* (London: Victor Gollancz, 1937), p. 227.

38 *LPACR*, 1946, p. 151.

39 *Ibid.*, pp. 152–7.

40 *H.C. Deb.*, vol. 419, col. 1322, 21 February 1946.

41 Schneer, 'The British Labour left and the Third Force movement', p. 198.

42 *H.C. Deb.*, vol. 430, col. 526, 13 November 1946.

43 *Ibid.*, cols 591–2; Tribune, 22 November 1946, p. 3.

44 *LPACR*, 1947, p. 179.

45 *Trades Union Congress Report* (hereafter *TUCR*), 1946, p. 469.

46 *Ibid.*, p. 416.

47 Denis Healey, *The Time of My Life* (London: Michael Joseph, 1989), p. 75.

48 *Ibid.*

49 *LPACR*, 1946, p. 174.

50 Healey, *The Time of My Life*, p. 75.

51 Patrick Seyd, *The Rise and Fall of the Labour Left* (London: Macmillan, 1987), p. 7.

52 Modern Records Centre, University of Warwick (hereafter MRC), Richard Crossman papers, MSS 154/3/KL/1-4, Keep Left Group.

53 *H.C. Deb.*, vol. 446, col. 566, 23 January 1948.

54 Tony Cliff and Donny Gluckstein, *The Labour Party: A Marxist History* (London: Bookmarks, 2nd edn, 1996), p. 284.

55 Schneer, 'The British Labour left and the Third Force movement', pp. 213–14.

56 Kenneth O. Morgan, *Labour People: Leaders and Lieutenants, Hardie to Kinnock* (Oxford: Oxford University Press, 1987), p. 154.

57 For readings on the history of the Greek Civil War see Richard Clogg, *A Short History of Modern Greece* (Cambridge: Cambridge University Press, 1979); David Close, ed., *The Greek Civil War, 1943–1950: Studies of Polarization* (London: Routledge, 1993); John Iatrides, ed., *Greece in the 1940s: A Nation in Crisis* (Hanover, NH, and London: University Press of New England, 1981). On Britain's role see Thanasis Sfikas, *The British Labour Government and the Greek Civil War 1945–1949: The Imperialism of 'Non-Intervention'* (Keele: Ryburn/Keele University Press, 1994).

58 Documents on British Policy Overseas, series 1, vol. 1, telegram from Mr Caccia (Athens) to Anthony Eden, reporting meeting of Caccia with the Greek Regent (Damaskinos), 27 July 1945, p. 1157.

59 PRO, CAB 129/1/CP (45) 107, memorandum by the Foreign Secretary, 'Greece', 11/8/1945.

60 PRO, FO 371/48276/R13689, Pierson Dixon note on discussion with Bevin on 'Balkan Problems', 14/8/1945.

61 PRO, CAB 131/2/DO (46) 40, Memorandum by Bevin, 13/3/1946.

62 PRO, Bevin Papers, FO 800/475/ME/46/22, Attlee to Bevin, 1/12/1946.

63 PRO, Bevin Papers, FO 800/468/GRE/46/39, McNeil (Minister of State) to Bevin, 4/12/1946.

64 PRO, Bevin Papers, FO 800/468/GRE/46/40, Bevin to McNeil, 5/12/46.

65 PRO, Bevin Papers, FO 800/475/ME/45/11, Memorandum by Bevin to members of Cabinet, 28/08/1945.

66 See John Lewis Gaddis, The United States and the Origins of the Cold War, 1941–1947 (New York: Columbia University Press, 1972), ch. 10; Joseph Jones, The Fifteen Weeks: February 21–5 June, 1947 (New York: Harcourt, Brace and World, 1955).

67 Foreign Relations of the United States (hereafter FRUS), 1947, vol. 3, Remarks by the Honourable George Marshall, Secretary of State, at Harvard University on June 5, 1947, p. 237.

68 Bevin's address to the Foreign Press Association in London, 13 June 1947.

69 FRUS, 1947, vol. 3, Memorandum of conversation by the First Secretary of the Embassy in the UK (Peterson), of the first meeting of Under Secretary of State for Economic Affairs (Clayton) and ambassador with British cabinet members, 24 June 1947, p. 271.

70 Ibid., Memorandum of second meeting of Clayton with British cabinet ministers, 25 June 1947, p. 277.

71 FRUS, 1947, vol. 3, Caffery to Secretary of State Marshall, 18 June 1947 at 11.00am and 18 June 1947 at 4.00pm, p. 258 and 260.

72 For example, Willie Thompson, The Good Old Cause: British Communism, 1920–1991 (London: Pluto Press, 1992), p. 78.

73 See Caroline Anstey, 'The projection of British socialism: Foreign Office publicity and American opinion, 1945–50', Journal of Contemporary History, 19:3 (1984), 417–51.

74 PRO, FO 115/4270, the British Ambassador in Washington, the Earl of Halifax, to Bevin, 19 February 1946, enclosing a 'Note on Mr. Davies' Memorandum', by John Balfour and Isaiah Berlin, of 18 February 1946.

75 Gaddis, The United States and the Origins of the Cold War, pp. 312–13.

76 See George Kennan, Memoirs 1925–1950 (New York: Pantheon, 1967), Appendix C, 'Excerpts from telegraphic message from Moscow of February 22, 1946', p. 557.

77 Anstey, 'The projection of British socialism', p. 434.

78 US National Archives II, College Park, Maryland, State Department RG59, W. Gallman to G. Marshall, 3 February 1947, 841.00/2-3-47.

79 See Dan Keohane, *Labour Party Defence Policy since 1945* (Leicester: Leicester University Press, 1993), pp. 6–7.
80 See Anna Di Biagio, 'The Marshall Plan and the founding of the Cominform, June–September, 1947', in Francesca Gori and Silvio Pons, *The Soviet Union and Europe in the Cold War, 1943–53* (Basingstoke: Macmillan, 1996), pp. 208–21.
81 See Rhiannon Vickers, *Manipulating Hegemony: State Power, Labour and the Marshall Plan in Britain* (London: Macmillan, 2000), pp. 70–3.
82 Michael Gordon, *Conflict and Consensus in Labour's Foreign Policy 1914–1965* (Stanford, CA: Stanford University Press, 1969), p. 139.
83 Denis Healey, *Cards on the Table* (London: Labour Party, 1947).
84 PRO, FO 800/351, Bevin to Attlee, 3 September 1945; and Attlee to Bevin, 5 September 1945.
85 See Anthony Gorst, '"We must cut our coat according to our cloth": the making of British defence policy, 1945–1948', in Richard Aldrich, ed., *British Intelligence, Strategy and the Cold War* (London: Routledge, 1992), pp. 143–65.
86 PRO, CAB 131/1 DO (46) 3, minutes of meeting of Cabinet Defence Committee, 21 January 1946; and PRO CAB 131/ DO (46) 1, minutes of meeting of Cabinet Defence Committee, 11 January 1946.
87 PRO, CAB 131/1 DO (46) 3, minutes of meeting of Cabinet Defence Committee, 21 January 1946.
88 PRO, CAB 128/12, CM (48), 19, minutes of meeting 5 March 1948.
89 See Bullock, *Ernest Bevin, vol. 3*, pp. 574–7.
90 *H.C. Deb.*, vol. 464, col. 2019, 12 May 1949.
91 *Ibid.*, col. 2128.
92 Margaret Gowing, 'Britain, America and the bomb', in Michael Dockrill and John Young, eds, *British Foreign Policy, 1945–56* (New York: St. Martin's Press, 1989), pp. 39–40.
93 PRO CAB 128/18, CM (50), 52, minutes of meeting 1 August 1950.
94 *LPACR*, 1950, pp. 146–50.
95 For poignant accounts of Bevin's death, see Bullock, *Ernest Bevin, vol. 3*, pp. 832–5; Francis Williams, *Ernest Bevin: Portrait of a Great Englishman* (London: Hutchinson, 1952), pp. 271–2.
96 Barclay, *Ernest Bevin and the Foreign Office*, pp. 94 and 96.
97 Donoughue and Jones, *Herbert Morrison*, p. 479.
98 See Michael Foot, *Aneurin Bevan: A Biography, vol. 2, 1945–1960* (London: Davis-Poynter, 1973), ch. 8.
99 Bernard Porter, *Britain, Europe and the World, 1850–1986: Delusions of Grandeur* (London: George Allen and Unwin, 2nd edn, 1987), p. 148.

Chapter 8

Conclusion

The nature of Labour's foreign policy remains under-analysed and under-theorised. This is partly due to an academic division of labour: academics who study the Labour Party come from a domestic politics background, while International Relations scholars tend to focus on the state, and not party politics. It is also because the Labour Party itself has had great difficulty theorising and analysing the nature of its ideological stance on foreign policy. The differing ideological streams of the Labour Party, outlined in the previous chapters, have complicated attempts to produce overall analyses of Labour's view of foreign policy. In addition, the Labour Party itself has tended to see particular foreign policy problems discretely.[1] Thus, there is no major work by the party on the theoretical basis of its foreign policy; instead there are many speeches and documents that relate to specific responses to concrete situations, sometimes couched within the context of Labour's view of Britain's role in the world. However, it is possible to delineate an outline of the main theoretical perspective of a Labour Party foreign policy. To date, this has been done within the context of developing a typology of a 'socialist' foreign policy. The most interesting attempts to do this are by Michael Gordon in *Conflict and Consensus in Labour's Foreign Policy: 1914–1965*, Kenneth Miller in *Socialism and Foreign Policy*, which examined the period up to 1931, and Eric Shaw, who focused on the Attlee governments.[2]

This study takes a different approach from that of Gordon, Miller and Shaw, and argues that as far as foreign policy was concerned, it is not clear that the Labour Party ever had any socialist ideology as such. Sections of the Labour Party did at times offer a socialist critique of some of the liberal internationalist assumptions of the party's foreign policy perspective, which sometimes combined with the more radical liberal critiques, but the socialist standpoint only usually had minority support within the party, certainly from 1937 onwards with its accept-ance of rearmament in the face of a rising European fascist threat. Labour sought to offer an alternative to the traditional, power politics or realist approach of British foreign policy, which had stressed national self-interest. This alternative was internationalism, which stressed cooperation and interdependence, and a concern with the international as well as the national interest. In this, the most important influence on Labour's foreign policy were liberal views of international relations, but Labour's internationalism also arises from certain meta-principles of Labour's ideology, which have influenced Labour's external princi-ples and policies as much as its domestic ones. These are a belief in progress and change, influenced by the Enlightenment tradition with its teleology of progress, and an optimistic view of human nature. This view of human nature has been influenced by Kant and Rousseau rather than Hobbes, and can be extrapolated to the nature of relations between states. This is that human nature is capable of positive, rational, co-operative, fraternal and moral thought and action. Man is naturally sociable, and is capable of solidarity with the rest of mankind, and this solidarity overcomes national boundaries. If people are capable of behaving rationally and co-operatively, then so too are states as they are governed by such people. Systems of production such as capitalism might encourage militarism and conflict, but this is due to the system of production rather than a system of sovereign states.

The principles of Labour's foreign policy

Internationalism is the over-riding principle upon which Labour's foreign policy has been based. The party has had a commitment to internationalism throughout its history, and internationalism has been espoused by Labour leaders from Keir Hardie to Tony Blair. Internationalism, broadly defined, is the desire to transcend national boundaries in order to find solutions to international issues. However, there are different strands of internationalism, and it is not a world-view that is the preserve of the Labour Party. Much of the party's thinking on internationalism was shaped by radical liberal thinking, and has also been influenced by a Christian-socialist, Nonconformist streak amongst party members. Leonard Woolf noted that 'Historically, the Labour Party inherited its foreign policy from Cobden and Bright through Gladstonian liberalism.'[3] In addition, internationalism does not necessarily provide clear policy solutions in the face of particular policy problems. Internationalism is an impulse that can be used to prescribe non-intervention in the pursuit of peace, or intervention for military or humanitarian means. This is because as a concept, internationalism is very vague, and has sometimes meant different things at different times in history. Despite the problems of definition, for the purpose of this study it is possible to outline a framework that helps us analyse the nature of Labour's foreign policy through the concept of internationalism. At the heart of this framework is the fundamental belief that while states are sovereign entities, the peace and stability of any one state and the peace and stability of the international system as a whole are inexorably linked.

The Labour Party's own particular brand of internationalism is largely in line with a Kantian perspective, and this has emphasised certain aspects of internationalist thought.[4] These are, first, that while states operate in a system of international anarchy, fundamental reform of the system is possible because states have common interests and values. This change is only likely to be secured through the construction of international institutions to regulate economic, political and military relations between states. Second, linked to this is a sense of belonging to an international community, and each state has a responsibility to work towards the common good of the international system, to work in the 'international' interest rather than purely in what it perceives to be its national interest. Third, international policy and governance should be based on democratic principles and universal moral norms. Fourth, collective security is better than secret bilateral diplomatic treaties or balance-of-power politics, which are self-defeating in terms of generating conflict. Fifth, armaments and arms races can destabilise the international system, and the proliferation or arms should be limited, the arms trade regulated, and disarmament, in principle, is desirable. In addition to these five largely liberal internationalist principles is one additional socialist aspect of Labour's international thought, and this has been a belief in international working-class solidarity, especially with socialist states.

Within the Labour Party there have always been divisions over how these principles should be interpreted, which of them should be prioritised, and which were achievable in the real world. Tensions have existed 'between those believing in the need to transform international relationships by pursing principled positions involving cooperation and harmony between states and those observing the competitive nature of international politics and concluding that realism rather than idealism must be the guide'.[5] Thus, for some in the Labour Party, collective security should be sought through the United Nations, whereas for others, collective security is assured through the establishment of NATO. For some in the Labour Party, disarmament is a tenet of faith, and should be sought at all times, whereas for others, disarmament is desirable in principle but unrealisable in practice because of the potential danger of aggressor states. For some, the use of force and military intervention is to be avoided in the pursuit of peace, whereas for others, the use of force and intervention is sometimes the 'right' thing to do for humanitarian reasons as well as being a valuable instrument of foreign policy in the longer-term pursuit of peace. The acceptance of a near pacifist position in the early 1930s when it was still believed that the League of Nations could deter aggression; the shift in opinions about the validity of non-intervention with regard to the Spanish Civil War; to the acceptance of rearmament and military strength in the late 1930s when it became clear that the League of Nations could not deter the threat of fascism, were all different ways of interpreting the principles of Labour's internationalism, rather than a rejection of them.

The first of the two principles highlighted above are closely inter-twined; namely the belief in the reform and regulation of the system through international institutions. It was the belief in internationalism and an international community that underpinned Labour's call for an 'international authority to settle points of difference among the nations by compulsory conciliation and arbitration, and to compel all nations to maintain peace'.[6] This led Labour to support the establishment of the League of Nations following the First World War, and to pursue its League of Nations policy under Ramsay MacDonald and Arthur Henderson in the 1929–31 minority government, even if the party was at times critical of the form that the League of Nations took and the way that it operated. Belief in the international community was even written into the Labour Party's constitution, with the commitment 'for the establishment of suitable machinery for the adjustment and settlement of international disputes by conciliation or judicial arbitration and for such other international legislation as may be practicable'.[7] The Labour Party was the most wholehearted supporter amongst the British political parties for the establishment of international organisations to regulate and arbitrate world affairs, and it spent the years during the First and Second World Wars thinking about the post-war settlement and the maintenance of peace through international institutions. Indeed, during the Second World War the party argued in its report *The Old World and the New Society* that national sovereignty would have to be given up, with a new, much stronger version of the League of Nations forming a superstructure through which a new World Society could be established, founded upon democratic Socialist ideas.[8] A new international organisation was required, 'possessing many powers hitherto exercised by a competing anarchy of national sovereignties'.[9] The party's document on The International Post-War Settlement argued that,

> [W]e must begin, without delay, to build a World Order, in which all people unite to pursue their common interests. We are confident that the vital interests of all nations are the same. They all need Peace; they all need security and freedom; they all need a fair share in that abundance which science has not put it into our power to create.[10]

This commitment to internationalism has continued throughout the twentieth century with Labour's commitment to international agreements and regulation, and has been particularly noticeable more recently in the speeches of Tony Blair, where he has repeatedly stressed that 'We are all internationalists now, whether we like it or not.' This is because 'Interdependence is the core reality of the modern world.'[11] In recent years, internationalism has also been linked with the Labour Party's embrace of globalisation, as 'We recognise that globalisation demands a new internationalism, and our internationalism recognises that we cannot deliver our domestic programme working alone in the world.'[12]

These elements of internationalism have been present throughout the whole of the Labour Party's history. However, while they provide the guiding principles behind Labour's foreign policy, they do not necessarily imply policy solutions to concrete problems, and so are the backdrop to many of Labour's internal splits over international policy. In addition, Labour's commitment to internationalism has sometimes been in conflict with its view of Britain's role as a leading international actor. Labour has been just as reluctant as its opponents to give up the trappings of a world power. It was the Attlee government that decided to go ahead with the atom bomb, and Labour has retained the commitment to an independent nuclear deterrent for all of the post-war period apart from the periods of 1960–61 and 1983–89. In terms of Britain's imperial role, the Commonwealth was seen for both the left and the right of the party as a means of continuing British influence, and carried an implicit assumption of Britain's leadership.[13] Indeed, the Labour Party has often emphasised that a Labour government can give

Britain 'the moral leadership of the world',[14] and be a 'force for good in the world'.[15] Throughout the twentieth century Labour has stressed the potential for Britain to play a leadership role in international disarmament (including nuclear disarmament) and control of the arms industry. During the Cold War Labour emphasised the role that Britain could play in acting as a bridge between East and West and resolve deadlocks between the two. This moral imperative has been highlighted at various times by all sections of the party. Richard Taylor argues that,

> [The] Labour left belief in Britain's 'moral lead' stemmed in part from the long tradition of quasi-pacifist internationalism which had formed a persistent minority dimension of the Labour left from the early years of the ILP onwards … And yet this tradition embodied also a moral nationalism, a position stemming from the nineteenth-century radical ideological framework, emphasizing the importance of national sovereignty, parliamentary democracy, and the rights of free individuals and free nations to determine their futures.[16]

Thus, Labour's commitment to working in the international good, to work in the 'international' interest rather than purely in what it perceives to be its national interest has often been based on the idea of Britain's leadership in the world. This reflects the context within which the Labour Party developed, as well as its tendency to have a missionary zeal to reform and shape the world in its likeness, which has sometimes been at odds with its commitment to working through international institutions.

This belief in Britain's moral leadership role under a Labour government not only arises from the fact that the party developed within the context of Britain as a superpower, but also reflects the third of its principles of internationalism, namely that there are universal moral principles. For Labour, domestic and foreign policy are seen as parts of a whole, as inextricably linked, and as impacting on each other. Arthur Henderson said that there is an 'intimate' connection between Labour's home and foreign policy.[17] Policies pursued externally should help, or at least not hinder, the kind of society being build domestically. In addition, principles valued domestically, such as democracy and human rights, should be reflected externally and pursued in relations with other states. Keir Hardie, when criticising the suppression of trade union action and the introduction of martial law in South Africa in 1914, argued that the Liberal government should refuse to condone the actions of the government in South

Africa. 'They had to realise that the cause of democracy was the same
everywhere, and if they tolerated injustice and oppression in any part
of the earth, sooner or later it was bound to come home to themselves.'[18] The key to international peace was social justice at home and
abroad. This was strongly emphasised during the Second World War,
with Attlee arguing that 'the world that must emerge from this war
must be a world attuned to our ideals'.[19]

Linked to the idea of universal moral norms is a belief in a democratic foreign policy, and a rejection of secret diplomacy. This was an
issue that was particularly popular within the Labour Party in the years
before and after the First World War. At the 1912 annual conference a
resolution was unanimously agreed that 'protests against secret diplomacy and urges that no treaty, agreement, understanding, or entente
be entered into with any foreign Power by any person whatsoever on
behalf of the British State until such proposals shall have been brought
before the House of Commons'.[20] This became a staple demand for
the Labour Party. Ramsay MacDonald, in *Labour and International
Relations*, argued that 'A difference between the democratic system of
foreign policy and an aristocratic one is that under a democracy we
always strive for co-operation, under an aristocracy we only prepare for
war. Co-operation on the one hand, militarism on the other.'[21] This
view was further entrenched by the involvement of Liberals such as E.
D. Morel in the Labour Party. The Union of Democratic Control saw
the outbreak of the Great War as the failure of diplomacy, arguing that
the Foreign Department was 'avowedly and frankly autocratic'.[22] They
saw the war as the failure of diplomacy, and 'Instead of taking advantage of the marked growth in the pacific inclinations of the peoples of
the world', statesmen 'have insisted on encouraging between the
Governments of Europe the most deadly and determined competition
in preparation for war that the world has ever known'.[23] The Labour
Party itself saw the war as the result of 'Foreign Ministers pursuing
diplomatic polices for the purposes of maintaining a balance of power',
and condemned Sir Edward Grey for committing 'without the knowledge of our people the honour of the country to supporting France in
the event of any war'.[24] It was one of the achievements of the 1924
minority Labour government that it fulfilled its manifesto pledge to
open secret diplomatic agreements, by announcing that it would inau-
gurate a new practice of laying all treaties with other nations on the
table of the House of Commons for a period of twenty-one days,
after which the treaty would be ratified. This would strengthen the
control of Parliament over the conclusion of international treaties and

agreements, allow discussion of them, and 'By this means secret Treaties and secret clauses of Treaties will be rendered impossible.'[25]

The 1929–31 Labour government also advocated a democratic foreign policy. While Prime Minister Ramsay MacDonald and Foreign Secretary Arthur Henderson had their differences over policy, exacerbated by their mutual dislike and distrust of each other, both believed in the role of public opinion. Henderson argued that 'the public opinion of nations has always been ahead of what the Governments were prepared to do'.[26] Linked to this was the view that the Foreign Office was the preserve of the upper-class elite. Both secret diplomacy and 'the oligarchical character of foreign services increased the likelihood of armed conflict'.[27] Following both the world wars there were calls for the labour movement to be given a direct voice in foreign policy, as world affairs were seen as too important to be left to the diplomats and politicians. Again, Labour has not always stuck to the principle in practice, and has carried out its own secret negotiations, for example, on the establishment of US bases in Britain, and the development of nuclear weapons.

A related aspect of the belief in a democratic foreign policy was that democratic states were more peaceable than authoritarian ones, and the greater the democratic control over foreign policy-making, the more rationally and peacefully a state would behave. As a consequence, democratic states were far less likely to go to war with each other, and democratic governments would have more to lose from conflict, an early form of the 'democratic peace' theory developed by Doyle.[28] Hence, states had much to benefit from good relations with other states, and from encouraging democracy in other states. This was stated in Labour's *Memorandum on War Aims*, written by Ramsay MacDonald, Arthur Henderson and Sidney Webb at the end of the First World War. This declared that the establishment of lasting peace was the principal war aim of British Labour, and 'As a means to this end the British Labour Movement relies very largely upon the complete democratisation of all countries'.[29] The modern equivalent for the calls for a democratic foreign policy has been an acceptance that public opinion has a role to play in foreign policy, and that the foreign policy-making should include some kind of an input from non-traditional foreign policy circles, such as non-government organisations.

Linked in with the belief that international policy and governance should be based on democratic principles and universal moral principles, has been the fourth aspect of Labour's internationalism, that

collective security is better than secret bilateral diplomatic treaties or
balance-of-power politics, which are self-defeating in terms of generating conflict. The League of Nations, it was hoped, would by-pass the
need for balance-of-power politics, and Labour had envisaged a
League that was 'so strong in its representative character and so dignified by its powers and respect that questions of national defence sink
into the background of solved problems'.[30] The belief in collective
security was one of the reasons that Labour tended to vote against the
government's defence estimates. Labour's position following the First
World War was that the party, 'whether in power or in opposition,
supports *some* expenditure on Armaments', but that it 'believes that
the present expenditure could be drastically reduced'. The party line
was that,

> Support of some expenditure on armaments is based on the assumption
> that the Covenant of the League [of Nations] is taken seriously. The plea
> that our forces are used only to maintain peace, if not hypocritical, means
> that we repudiate the use of force to press purely British claims ... Our
> policy is the maintenance of peace: the pre-war policy was the pursuit of
> national advantage.[31]

The party's attitude towards the nature of the armed forces was that a
national military capability was only acceptable to the extent that it
formed part of an international military force that could be used for
international intervention, under the control of the League of Nations,
in the last resort. As shown in Chapter 4, support for collective security against aggression lay behind Labour's League of Nations foreign
policy in the second minority government. The failure of the League
of Nations over the Manchurian crisis in 1931 discredited the League
somewhat, and started to undermine the belief in the system of collective security that had been developed with the Covenant of the League
of Nations and the Geneva Protocol. The Labour Party came very
close to briefly embracing pacifism instead of collective security as its
leaders, Lansbury, Attlee and Cripps, rejected the existing system of
international relations and advocated their own visions of Labour's
foreign policy. For Attlee, this was based on a system of pooled security through a new organisation, such as a world commonwealth,
which could provide collective security through an international military force. The tensions over whether to continue with support for
collective security or adopt a more pacifist position lead to the resignation of George Lansbury from the leadership of the Labour Party
in 1935, and paved the way for the acceptance of British rearmament

in the face of threat of fascism in the second half of the 1930s. As outlined in Chapter 6, the Munich crisis galvanised the Labour Party into urging collective action with France and the Soviet Union against Hitler, and a renewed call for collective security through the League of Nations. Labour's 1944 policy document, *The International Post-War Settlement*, which was largely written by Hugh Dalton, went so far as to say that pacifism had been proved to be 'an unworkable basis of policy'. Instead, 'Strength is essential to safety and, as we now know, there are terrible risks in being weak. It is better to have too much armed force than too little.'[32] The experience of the Second World War led to a further shift away from international collective security and towards a more traditional balance-of-power politics, as exemplified through Britain's role in Greece, and an Anglo-American alliance institutionalised through the establishment of NATO in the face of the threat posed by the Soviet Union within the context of the developing Cold War.

The fifth principle of Labour's internationalism has been one that has been strongly influenced by both Labour's liberal and socialist heritage, and this has been its belief in 'anti-militarism'. This has been manifested in many different ways. It includes a commitment to collective security, arms control, regulation of the arms industry, opposition to conscription, support for arbitration, and a suspicion of the use of force as a foreign policy instrument. These commitments were particularly strong in the years just before and just after the First World War and in the early 1930s. Annual conference regularly passed resolutions condemning militarism and war. Many in the party believed that war could be avoided through the avowed rejection of armaments and the use of force. The preparation for war was seen as one of the major causes of war, as this destabilised the international system by causing suspicion between states. As Marquand puts it, the Labour Party had 'inherited the anti-militaristic attitudes of the nineteenth century Radicals who were its real intellectual ancestors'.[33] It was strongly influenced by the pacific outlook of the Independent Labour Party, who believed that 'War is the result of the preparation for war.'[34] According to Arthur Henderson, 'The alternative to the arms race and Armageddon is to make a reality of the collective peace system to which we are bound by solemn treaty obligations ...' And, 'An integral part of the peace-keeping system is the obligation to reduce and limit arms.'[35] The arms trade in general should be regulated and limited as the production and sale of arms was part of the problem. In particular, it was argued that the profit motive of capitalists and the production of

weapons and subsequent arms races resulted in conflict. In this way
war, militarism and capitalism were related: war was a result of
economic factors as much as political or diplomatic ones.

Again, here was an example of Labour's international perspective
being determined by both radical liberal and socialist perspectives. J. A.
Hobson, a radical Liberal economist who later joined the Labour
Party, published a study on imperialism in 1902 that was to have a
major impact on the way the party thought about the international
system. He argued that the under-consumption of capital domestically
led to the need for capitalists to export surplus capital by investing
profits abroad, and this resulted in war, militarism and a 'spirited
foreign policy'.[36] Furthermore, 'Imperialism makes for war and for
militarism, and has brought a great and limitless increase of expenditure of national resources upon armaments. It has impaired the independence of every nation which has yielded to its false glamour.'[37]
Hobson provided an explanation for international relations and the
causes of war for both Labour and the radical Liberals, as well as
impacting on the Marxist understanding of international conflict
through the subsequent study by Lenin on *Imperialism, the Highest
Stage of Capitalism*. This perspective also tied in with Norman Angell's
work, *The Great Illusion*, which explained that the motivation for the
international rivalry in armaments was due to the view that military
and political power gave a nation commercial advantage, and the
illusion that it was to a state's economic advantage to subjugate a
weaker one.[38]

Labour's anti-militarist tendencies manifested themselves in a
number of ways. First, there was a commitment to controlling the
proliferation of weapons, especially weapons of mass destruction,
through multilateral negotiations. Labour supported the organisation
of disarmament conferences domestically and internationally, and
presented itself as the party able to reach agreement internationally.
The 1929–31 Labour government had called for a World Disarmament Conference to be convened by the League of Nations, and it
was Arthur Henderson who was subsequently invited to be the
president of it, for which he received the Nobel Peace Prize. Labour's
disarmament impulse was multilateral rather than unilateral – the
policy of unilateral nuclear disarmament briefly embraced in the early
1960s and again in the 1980s was unusual, and not the norm.

Second, Labour sought ways to control the arms trade, sharing the
view of the Liberals that trading in arms leads to militarism and hence
war. However, the party has always faced the problem that the arms

trade was a major British employer. Third, Labour expressed the desire on many occasions to cut defence budgets. It was Labour Party practice up until 1937 to vote against the government's defence estimates (apart from when they were in power). Despite this, some still lobbied ministers to build arms in their constituencies. For example, Sir Thomas Inskip, who was the Minister for the Co-ordination of Defence, said in the House of Commons in 1936 that MPs from both the front and back-benches had 'besought me to place orders for munitions of war in their constituencies'.[39] This was at a time when the Parliamentary Labour Party voted against increases in the defence estimates. Fourth, the Labour Party rejected compulsory national service and conscription. Numerous resolutions were passed at annual conferences on compulsory national service alone.[40] Conscription during wartime was only accepted reluctantly.

Labour when in power, however, tended to view Britain's need for a strong military in much the same way as its opponents did. To some extent, it had to be more hard-line when in government than the Conservatives because of its apparent weakness in the eyes of the electorate on the issue of defence. Thus, while Labour's instinct has been for anti-militarism, its policies have not. For instance, it was Ramsay MacDonald who initially blocked the signing of the Geneva Protocol; it was Labour who urged a policy of rearmament in the face of threat posed by Hitler; and it was Labour who escalated defence expenditure in peace time in the late 1940s and the beginning of the 1950s.

While some of the Labour Party's members have held pacifist views, it never whole-heartedly embraced pacifism. The party vehemently denounced militarism in the run-up to the outbreak of the First World War, but once war was declared the party's policy was to support the government and not threaten the war effort. As was discussed in Chapter 3, the party flirted with various forms of pacifism in the early 1930s, but this was rejected in the face of the rising threat of fascism. Certainly the party has tended to be against the use of force while in opposition, seeing it as resulting in war, but this policy was discredited by the failure of the non-intervention pact on the Spanish Civil War. Resolutions were forwarded on occasion that called for support for a general strike if Britain were about to engage in war in order to prevent the outbreak of hostilities, within the context of similar action being taken overseas,[41] but this was never adopted as formal party policy. The most common form of expression of anti-militarism has been in resolutions to conference condemning the actions of governments in encouraging war through the pursuit of traditional power politics and through the destabilising effects of the arms trade and arms races.

In addition to the above five 'internationalist' principles is one additional aspect of Labour's internationalist thought that is a direct result of its socialist heritage, and this has been a belief in international working-class and socialist solidarity. A belief in international socialist solidarity underlay British socialist thinking from the start, but has been manifested in different ways over the years. This was expressed in Labour's early years through a commitment to the international social-ist and trade union movements. As outlined in Chapter 3, the Socialist Internationals provided the Labour Party with the opportunity to join like-minded socialist parties in a common cause, and a forum within which discussions on foreign affairs and the causes of war were of central importance. It was within the context of the Second International that the divisions within the British Labour Party between those who supported the calling of a general strike and mass popular resistance to prevent the outbreak of war and those who did not, were played out. However, the International also demonstrated the inability of socialist parties to transcend national loyalties in order to reach the goal of international solidarity, with the Second International collapsing with the outbreak of the First World War in August 1914. This, in turn, lead to a renewed belief in the importance of the international socialist movement, and to the commitment to international socialist co-operation and the establishment of an inter-national body for the socialist parties being written into the Labour Party's constitution in 1918. The Internationals also provided social-ists with the opportunity to institutionalise divisions within their ranks, with the Second International deciding to exclude anarchists and anti-parliamentarians from its meetings during its first congress in Paris in 1889, and competing for power against the Communist, or Third, International, after it was reconvened in 1920.

Another example of international solidarity in action has been the numerous appeals by the Labour Party to their members to lobby and to raise money for labour movements overseas. In 1913 an appeal was launched in the name of international solidarity following a request from the Bulgarian and Serbian Socialist Parties 'to assist our fellow workers in the Balkans' in the hardships they were enduring as a result of the Balkan war.[42] Unlike internationalism as such, socialist interna-tionalism has been 'an interventionist doctrine, holding that it was a duty of the oppressed in one nation to aid those in another', what could be called 'popular solidarity'.[43] The Spanish Civil War caused huge divisions within the Labour Party and wider labour movement, and led to the rejection of the position of pacifism that the party had been moving towards in the early 1930s. The policy of non-intervention, which was pursued by the National government, and officially supported at first by the Labour Party leadership, was bitterly resented by many in the party. Aid for Spain campaigns sprang up around the country, and of course some in the labour movement expressed their solidarity for Spain by joining the International Brigades. However, the Spanish Civil War demonstrated clearly the dilemmas that Labour faced in reconciling its views on non-intervention, anti-militarism and international working-class solidarity.

A third aspect of Labour's international socialist solidarity arose with the advent of the Russian Revolution and the establishment of the Soviet Union. Arthur Henderson noted that '[T]he international outlook of the rulers of the Soviet Union is based on the fundamental belief of all Socialists everywhere that the ultimate guarantee of peace must be the drawing together of the nations of the world into one Commonwealth, and that this can come about only through Socialism.'[44] Events in Russia radicalised the Labour Party internally, in that it provided a socialist 'utopia' for those on the far left to look to, work with and emulate. The establishment of the Bolshevik regime also provided a communist foe for those on the centre and centre-right of the labour movement to be fearful of, thus deepening existing divisions between the revolutionary and the parliamentary left. This tension was given an added dimension when the British Socialist Party, along with some smaller parties, formed the Communist Party of Great Britain on 1 August 1920. The instructions from Moscow were for the CPGB to affiliate to the Labour Party and convert the bulk of the party to the communist cause. Before the Bolshevik Revolution, the issue of whether party members were Marxists was a matter for individuals; after it became a matter of party unity and control. Externally, the establishment of the Soviet Union added a new dimension to Labour's foreign policy, for while in theory Labour wanted to work with the Soviet Union, in practice the party leadership saw the Soviet Union as a threat. The party's 1936 document on *British Labour and Communism* pointed out that the sympathetic interest that British labour had shown in the Soviet Union 'has been qualified by growing resentment against Russian effort through the Communist Inter-national to establish and finance revolutionary Communist Parties in other countries with the object of destroying existing democratic industrial and political Labour Movements, and of bringing about the overthrow of the existing social system by violence'.[45]

The Russian Revolution also had a particular impact on Labour's thinking on foreign policy in that it provided a major issue of contention between Labour and its Liberal and Conservative opponents. British foreign policy towards Russia following the revolution of October 1917 was based on non-recognition of the Soviet Union, and limited intervention. The Labour Party bitterly opposed this, seeing it as the cause for bad relations between the Soviet Union and Europe, for 'By maintaining troops against Russia, the Allied Governments violate in their most flagrant manner the right of the Russian people to dispose of themselves ... They are thereby multiplying the reasons for civil war in Russia.'[46] The Labour Party launched a manifesto in January 1920 that called for the 'Complete raising of the Blockade and a complete peace with Russia.' It also called for full recognition of the Soviet government, while pointing out that 'Such a formal recognition of a Government would no more imply moral approval of it than did our formal recognition of the Tsar's Government.'[47] One of the main actions of the first Labour government of 1924 was to recognise the Soviet Union. However, Labour was suspicious of the Soviet Union, and large sections of the party quickly came to see it as a source of conflict in foreign policy, most obviously during the Attlee governments and the developing Cold War, as Ernest Bevin worked to involve the United States in a defensive alliance against the Soviet Union. This position was never fully accepted by many in the party, for whom co-operation with the Soviet Union was the touchstone of international socialist solidarity.

Finally, another aspect of Labour's international socialist solidarity has been a concern more generally with the international working class. Feelings of kinship with workers overseas were engendered not only from a socialist belief in the need for international working-class solidarity, but also from the impact of Nonconformist beliefs in the brotherhood of man. This led to a concern with imperialism and of conditions in the British empire. The Independent Labour Party proposed a resolution at the first annual Labour Party conference in 1901 that referred to imperialism as a 'reversion to one of the worst phases of barbarism', which 'is inimical to social reform and disastrous to trade and commerce, a fruitful cause of war, destructive of freedom, fraught with menace to representative institutions at home and abroad, and must end in the destruction of democracy'.[48] Feelings of kinship for workers overseas led to Labour Party support for nationalist movements and for national self-determination, which was often at odds with Labour's belief in Britain's continuing world and imperial role. Indeed, Labour's policy on colonial affairs was usually confused and always inconsistent, calling at times for self-government and Dominion status for India but not other countries; calling at times for self-government for all the colonies; and sometimes going further by demanding the 'freedom' or complete independence for the colonial states. It was usually assumed, however, that Britain's colonies, even if they were given independence, would choose to remain within the Commonwealth, and 'under the guidance of the Mother Country.'[49]

To conclude, while there are many problems inherent in analysing the nature of Labour's foreign policy, it is possible to identify certain key principles. Overall, Labour has had an internationalist world-view, and within this internationalist perspective, it has emphasised six key issues: first, that fundamental reform of international relations is possible through the establishment of international institutions to regulate the anarchic international system; second, that states belong to an international community, and have a commitment to work in the international interest rather than just the national interest; third, that international policy should be based on democratic principles and universal moral norms; fourth, that collective security is better than secret bilateral diplomatic treaties or balance-of-power politics; fifth, that armaments and arms races can destabilise the international system, and that the proliferation of arms should be limited, the arms trade regulated, and that disarmament, in principle, is desirable. In addition to these five largely liberal internationalist principles is one additional socialist aspect of Labour's international thought, and this has been a belief in international working-class solidarity, especially with socialist states. However, the Labour Party has suffered from severe and recurring intra-party conflict over its foreign policy, because these principles can sometimes conflict, and are open to a range of interpretations in terms of policy solutions to particular problems. In addition, Labour has often found itself unable to transcend national barriers in order to meet its commitment to internationalism. These themes will be continued in the second volume of this study, which begins with the Labour Party's loss of power in 1951, and which will also assess the contribution that Labour's particular world-view and foreign policy doctrine has made to the nature of British foreign policy.

Notes

1 Richard Taylor, 'The Labour Party and CND: 1957 to 1984', in Richard Taylor and Nigel Young, eds, *Campaigns for Peace: British Peace Movements in the Twentieth Century* (Manchester: Manchester University Press, 1987), p. 124.

2 Michael Gordon, *Conflict and Consensus in Labour's Foreign Policy, 1914–1965* (Stanford, CA: Stanford University Press, 1969); Kenneth Miller, *Socialism and Foreign Policy: Theory and Practice in Britain to 1931* (The Hague: Martinus Nijhoff, 1967); Eric Shaw, 'British Socialist Approaches to International Affairs, 1945–1951', M.Phil thesis, University of Leeds, 1974.

3 Leonard Woolf, *Foreign Policy – The Labour Party's Dilemma* (London: Labour Party, 1947), p. 7.

4 Immanuel Kant, 'Perpetual peace: a philosophical sketch', in *Kant's Political Writings*, edited by Hans Reiss (Cambridge: Cambridge University Press, 2nd enlarged edn, 1991). See also James Bohman and Matthias Lutz-Bachmann, eds, *Perpetual Peace: Essays on Kant's Cosmopolitan Ideas* (Cambridge, MA: Massachusetts Institute of Technology Press, 1997); Howard Williams and Ken Booth, 'Kant: Theorist beyond limits', in Ian Clark and Iver Neumann, eds, *Classical Theories of International Relations* (Basingstoke: Macmillan/St Anthony's College, Oxford, 1996), pp. 71–98.

5 Patrick Seyd, *The Rise and Fall of the Labour Left* (London: Macmillan, 1987), p. 2.

6 *Labour Party Annual Conference Report* (hereafter *LPACR*), 1916, p. 32.

7 *LPACR*, 1918, p. 141.

8 See G. D. H. Cole, *A History of the Labour Party from 1914* (London: Routledge, 1948), pp. 414–19.

9 *LPACR*, 1941, p. 4.

10 *LPACR*, 1944, pp. 4–9.

11 Tony Blair, 'Doctrine of international community', speech to the Economic Club of Chicago, 22 April 1999; Tony Blair, 'At our best when at our boldest', speech to the Labour Party Annual Conference, 1 October 2002.

12 Robin Cook, speech to 1999 Labour Party Annual Conference, *LPACR*, 1999, p. 52.

13 Caroline Knowles, *Race, Discourse and Labourism* (London: Routledge, 1992).

14 The 1931 Labour Party general election manifesto, in F. W. S. Craig, ed. and comp., *British General Election Manifestos 1900–1974* (London: Macmillan, rev. and enlarged edn, 1975), p. 97.

15 Robin Cook, 'Mission Statement for the Foreign and Commonwealth Office', FCO, London, 12 May 1997.

16 Richard Taylor, *Against the Bomb: The British Peace Movement, 1958–1965* (Oxford: Clarendon, 1988), p. 305.

17 Arthur Henderson, *Labour's Way to Peace* (London: Methuen, 1935), p. 30.
18 *LPACR*, 1914, p. 95.
19 *LPACR*, 1940, p. 125.
20 *LPACR*, 1912, p. 91.
21 J. Ramsay MacDonald, *Labour and International Relations* (Derby: Derby and District ILP Federation, 1917), p. 5.
22 Union of Democratic Control, *The Morrow of War* (London: UDC, pamphlet no. 1, 1914), p. 4.
23 Arthur Ponsonby, *Parliament and Foreign Policy* (London: UDC, pamphlet no. 5, 1914), p. 1.
24 Museum of Labour History, Manchester, Labour Party archive, NEC minutes, 5 August 1914, pp. 86–7.
25 House of Commons Debates (hereafter *H.C. Deb.*), fifth series, vol. 171, cols 2001–3, 1 April 1924.
26 Arthur Henderson, *Consolidating World Peace* (London: Burge Memorial Lecture, 1931), p. 26.
27 Shaw, 'British Socialist Approaches to International Affairs 1945–51', p. 10.
28 Michael Doyle, 'Kant, Liberal Legacies and Foreign Affairs' Parts 1 and 2, *Philosophy and Public Affairs*, 12:3 (Summer 1983), 205–35; and 12:4 (Autumn 1983), 323–53.
29 Labour Party, *Memorandum on War Aims* (London: Labour Party, 1918).
30 J. Ramsay MacDonald, *A Policy for the Labour Party* (London: Leonard Parsons, 1920), pp. 131, 161 and 172.
31 Modern Records Centre, University of Warwick, TUC archive, MSS 292/906/1, Labour Party International Department, Advisory Committee on International Questions, C. Delisle Burns, 'Note on the estimates for the armed forces', no. 367, May 1927.
32 *LPACR*, 1944, pp. 4–9.
33 David Marquand, *Ramsay MacDonald* (London: Jonathan Cape, 1977), p. 169.
34 MacDonald, *Labour and International Relations*, 5.
35 Henderson, *Labour's Way to Peace*, p. 42.
36 J. A. Hobson, *Imperialism: A Study* (London: George Allen and Unwin, 3rd rev. and reset edn, 1938), p. 106.
37 *Ibid.*, p. 138.
38 Norman Angell, *The Great Illusion: A Study of the Relation of Military Power in Nations to their Economic and Social Advantage* (London: Heinemann, 1912, 3rd edition), p. xi.
39 *H.C. Deb.*, vol. 315, col. 74, 20 July 1936.
40 See, for example, *LPACR*, 1912, pp. 99–100; *LPACR*, 1914, p. 121; *LPACR*, 1916, pp. 116–17; *LPACR*, 1939, p. 289.
41 At the 1911 annual conference a resolution proposing an inquiry into the 'utility of the general strike' was defeated; at the 1912 conference a similar resolution was passed, but a resolution to actually support a general strike was not. See *LPACR*, 1912, p. 101. The issue was returned to in the mid-1920s, rather ironically just after the failure of the 1926

general strike, and a resolution supporting the concept of a general strike against war was passed at the 1926 annual conference, *LPACR*, 1926, p. 256.

42 *LPACR*, 1913, p. 99.
43 Shaw, 'British Socialist Approaches to International Affairs 1945–51', p. 17.
44 Henderson, *Labour's Way to Peace*, p. 84.
45 *LPACR*, 1936, 'British Labour and Communism', pp. 296–7.
46 *LPACR*, 1919, Special resolution on 'Intervention in Russia', p. 225.
47 Labour Party, *Labour's Russian Policy: Peace with Soviet Russia* (London: Labour Party, 1920), p. 3, held in the University of Leeds Library, Brotherton Collection, Mattison, LAB.
48 *Report of the First Annual Conference of the Labour Representation Committee*, 1901, p. 20.
49 *LPACR*, 1943, p. 4.

Bibliography

Manuscript collections

Public Record Office, London

Cabinet Office, CAB 128-131; Foreign Office, FO 115, FO 371 General Correspondence, FO 800 Private Collections (including Bevin papers); Ramsay MacDonald Papers, PRO 30/69

US National Archives, College Park Maryland

US National Archives II, State Department RG59

Archives

Labour Party (Museum of Labour History, Manchester)
Trades Union Congress (Modern Records Centre, University of Warwick)

Private papers

Ernest Bevin (Churchill College, Cambridge)
Brotherton Collection (University of Leeds Library)
Richard Crossman (Modern Records Centre, University of Warwick)
Hugh Dalton (British Library of Political and Economic Science, London School of Economics)
George Lansbury (British Library of Political and Economic Science, London School of Economics)
E. D. Morel (British Library of Political and Economic Science, London School of Economics)

Published documents

Annual Abstract of Statistics, no. 88, 1938–1950 (London: HMSO, 1952)
British Documents on the Origin of the War 1898–1914, vol. 3, edited by George Gooch and Harold Temperly (London: HMSO, 1928)
British Foreign Policy in the Second World War, 5 vols, edited by Sir Ernest Llewellyn Woodward (London: HMSO, 1970-1976)
Documents on British Policy Overseas, series 1 and 2, various vols (London: HMSO, 1985–1991)
Documents on European Recovery and Defence, March 1947–April 1949 (London: Royal Institute of International Affairs, 1949)
Foreign Relations of the United States, various vols (Washington DC: Department of State, various)
House of Commons Debates (*Hansard*), series 4 and 5, various vols (London: HMSO, various)
Keesing's Contemporary Archive, various vols (London: Keesing's, various)
Labour Party Annual Conference Reports, various vols (London: Labour Party, various)
Report of the Inaugral Conference of the Labour Representation Committee (London: Labour Representation Committee, 1900)
Trade Union Congress Annual Reports, various vols (London: TUC, various)
The Transfer of Power, various vols, editor-in-chief Nicholas Mansergh (London: HMSO, 1970-83)
Twenty First Abstract of Labour Statistics of the United Kingdom, 1919–1933 (London: HMSO, 1934)

Unpublished work

Rose, Richard, 'The Relation of Socialist Principles to British Labour Foreign Policy, 1945–51', D.Phil. thesis, University of Oxford, 1959
Shaw, Eric, 'British Socialist Approaches to International Affairs, 1945–1951', M.Phil. thesis, University of Leeds, 1974

Published pamphlets

Brailsford, H. N., *The Origins of the Great War* (London: UDC, pamphlet no. 4, 1914)
Hardie, J. Keir, *India: Impressions and Suggestions* (London: ILP, 1909).
Healey, Dennis, *Cards on the Table* (London: Labour Party, 1947)
Hyndman, H. M., *The Coming Revolution in England* (London: William Reeves, 1883)
——, *The Unrest in India: Verbatim Report of the Speech delivered on 12th May 1907* (London: Twentieth Century Press, 1907)
——, *The Emancipation of India* (London: Twentieth Century Press, 1911)
Labour Party, *Memorandum on War Aims* (London: Labour Party, 1918)
——, *Labour's Russian Policy: Peace with Soviet Russia* (London: Labour Party, 1920)

——, *The 'National' Government's Disarmament Record* (London: Labour Party, 1935)

——, *The Demand for Colonial Territories and Equality of Economic Opportunity* (London: Labour Party, 1936)

——, *What Spanish Democracy is Fighting For* (London: Labour Party, 1938)

——, *The Full Facts of the Czech Crisis* (London: Labour Party, 1938)

——, *The Old World and the New Society* (London: Labour Party, 1942)

MacDonald, J. Ramsay, *Labour and International Relations* (Derby: Derby and District ILP Federation, 1917)

——, *The History of the ILP* (London: ILP, 1921)

——, *Protocol or Pact: The Alternative to War* (London: Labour Party, 1925)

Morel, E. D., *War and Diplomacy* (London: UDC, pamphlet no. 11, 1915)

Ponsonby, Arthur, *Parliament and Foreign Policy* (London: UDC, pamphlet no. 5, 1914)

Russell, Bertrand, *War, the Offspring of Fear* (London: UDC, pamphlet no. 3, 1914)

Shaw, G. Bernard, ed., *Fabianism and the Empire: A Manifesto by the Fabian Society* (London: Fabian Society, 1900)

Union of Democratic Control, *The Morrow of War* (London: UDC, pamphlet no. 1, 1914)

Woolf, Leonard, *Foreign Policy – The Labour Party's Dilemma* (London: Labour Party, 1947)

Speeches

Blair, Tony, 'Doctrine of international community', speech to the Economic Club of Chicago, 22 April 1999

——, 'At our best when at our boldest', speech to the Labour Party Annual Conference, 1 October 2002

Cook, Robin, 'Mission statement for the Foreign and Commonwealth Office', FCO, London, 12 May 1997

Published work

Adamthwaite, Anthony, 'Britain and the world, 1945–9: the view from the Foreign Office', *International Affairs*, 61:2 (1985), 223–36

Addison, Paul, *The Road to 1945: British Politics and the Second World War* (London: Quartet Books, 1977)

Angell, Norman, *The Great Illusion: A Study of the Relation of Military Power in Nations to their Economic and Social Advantage* (London: Heinemann, 3rd edn, 1912)

——, *Foreign Policy and our Daily Bread* (London: Collins, 1925)

——, *The Unseen Assassins* (London: Hamilton, 1932)

——, *After All: The Autobiography of Norman Angell* (London: Hamish Hamilton, 1951)

Anstey, Caroline, 'The projection of British socialism: Foreign Office publicity and American opinion, 1945–50', *Journal of Contemporary History*, 19:3 (1984), 417–51

Attlee, Clement, *The Labour Party in Perspective* (London: Victor Gollancz, 1937)
——, *As It Happened* (London: Odhams Press, 1956)
Bairoch, Paul, 'International industrialization levels from 1750 to 1980', *Journal of European Economic History*, 11:2 (1982), 269–333
Barclay, Roderick, *Ernest Bevin and the Foreign Office, 1932–1969* (London: Roderick Barclay, 1975)
Barnes, John and David Nicholson, eds, *The Empire at Bay: The Leo Amery Diaries 1929–1945* (London: Hutchinson, 1988)
Barnes, Trevor, 'The secret Cold War: the CIA and American foreign policy in Europe, 1946-1956: Part I', *Historical Journal*, 24:2 (1981), 399–415
Bartlett, C. J., *British Foreign Policy in the Twentieth Century* (London: Macmillan, 1989)
Bassett, Reginald, *Nineteen Thirty-One: Political Crisis* (London: Macmillan, 1958)
Bealey, Frank, ed., *The Social and Political Thought of the British Labour Party* (London: Weidenfeld and Nicolson, 1970)
Bealey, Frank and Henry Pelling, *Labour and Politics, 1900–1906: A History of the Labour Representation Committee* (London: Macmillan, 1958)
Bell, Geoffrey, *Troublesome Business: The Labour Party and the Irish Question* (London: Pluto Press, 1982)
Bennett, Edward, *Germany and the Diplomacy of the Financial Crisis* (Cambridge, Mass: Harvard University Press, 1962)
Bennett, Gill, at the Foreign and Commonwealth Office, 'A Most Extraordinary and Mysterious Business': The Zinoviev Letter of 1924 (London: FCO, 1999)
Berger, Stefan, *The British Labour Party and the German Social Democrats* (Oxford: Oxford University Press, 1994)
Berkeley, Humphry, *The Myth that Will Not Die: The Formation of the National Government 1931* (London: Croom Helm, 1978)
Bogdanor, Vernon, '1931 revisited: the constitutional aspects', *Twentieth Century British History*, 2:1 (1991), 1–25
Bogdanor, Vernon and Robert Skidelsky, eds, *The Age of Affluence 1951–1964* (London: Macmillan, 1970)
Bohman, James and Matthias Lutz-Bachmann, eds, *Perpetual Peace: Essays on Kant's Cosmopolitan Ideas* (Cambridge, MA: Massachusetts Institute of Technology Press, 1997)
Brailsford, H. N., *The War of Steel and Gold: A Study of the Armed Peace* (London: Bell and Sons, 3rd edn, 1915)
Brand, Carl, *The British Labour Party: A Short History* (Stanford, CA: Hoover Institution Press, revised edn, 1974)
Branson, Noreen, *History of the Communist Party of Great Britain, 1941–1951* (London: Lawrence and Wishart, 1997)
Braunthal, Julius, *History of the International, vol. 1, 1864–1914*, translated by Henry Collins and Kenneth Mitchell (London: Thomas Nelson, 1966)
——, *History of the International, vol. 2, 1914–1943*, translated by John Clark (London: Thomas Nelson, 1967)
British Labour and the Russian Revolution. The Leeds Convention, A report from the *Daily Herald*, with an introduction by Ken Coates (London: Bertrand Russell Peace Foundation/Spokesman, no date)
Brooke, Stephen, *Labour's War: The Labour Party during the Second World War* (Oxford: Clarendon Press, 1992)
Buchanan, Tom, *The Spanish Civil War and the British Labour Movement* (Cambridge: Cambridge University Press, 1991)

Buchanan McCallum, Ronald and Alison Readman, *The British General Election of 1945* (Oxford: Oxford University Press, 1947; reprinted London: Frank Cass, 1964)

Bullock, Alan, *The Life and Times of Ernest Bevin, vol. 1: Trade Union Leader, 1881–1940* (London: Heinemann, 1960)

——, *The Life and Times of Ernest Bevin, vol. 2: Minister of Labour, 1940–1945* (London: Heinemann, 1967)

——, *The Life and Times of Ernest Bevin, vol. 3: Foreign Secretary, 1945–1951* (London: Heinemann, 1983)

Burgess, Simon, *Stafford Cripps: A Political Life* (London: Victor Gollancz, 1999)

Burridge, Trevor, *British Labour and Hitler's War* (London: André Deutsch, 1976)

Busch, Gary, *The Political Role of International Trade Unions* (Basingstoke: Macmillan, 1983)

Butler, David and Gareth Butler, *British Political Facts, 1900–1985* (London: Macmillan, 6th edn, 1986)

Byrnes, James, Speaking Frankly (London: William Heinemann, 1947)

Cairncross, Alec, *Years of Recovery: British Economic Policy 1945–51* (London: Methuen, 1985)

——, *The British Economy since 1945: Economic Policy and Performance, 1945–1995* (Oxford: Blackwell, 2nd edn, 1995)

Caldor, Angus, *The People's War: Britain 1939–45* (London: Pimlico edition, 1992)

Callaghan, John, *Socialism in Britain* (Oxford: Basil Blackwell, 1990)

Carew, Antony, *Labour under the Marshall Plan* (Manchester: Manchester University Press, 1987)

Carlton, David, *MacDonald versus Henderson: The Foreign Policy of the Second Labour Government* (London: Macmillan, 1970)

Carr, E. H., *The Twenty Years' Crisis, 1919–1939* (London: Papermac/ Macmillan, 2nd edn, 1981)

'Cato', *Guilty Men* (London: Victor Gollancz, 1940)

Chesterton, A. K., *Oswald Mosley: Portrait of a Leader* (London: Action Press, 1937)

Churchill, Winston, *The Second World War, vol. 1: The Gathering Storm* (London: Cassell, 1948)

Citrine, Walter, *Two Careers: A Second Volume of Autobiography* (London: Hutchinson, 1967)

Clarke, Peter, *The Cripps Version: The Life of Sir Stafford Cripps, 1889–1952* (London: Allen Lane/Penguin Press, 2002)

Clegg, Hugh, Alan Fox and A. Thompson, *A History of British Trade Unions since 1889, vol. 1, 1889–1910* (Oxford: Clarendon Press, 1964)

Cliff, Tony and Donny Gluckstein, *The Labour Party: A Marxist History* (London: Bookmarks, 2nd edn, 1996)

Cline, Catherine Ann, *Recruits to Labour: The British Labour Party, 1914–1931* (Syracuse, NY: Syracuse University Press, 1963)

Clogg, Richard, *A Short History of Modern Greece* (Cambridge: Cambridge University Press, 1979)

Close, David, ed., *The Greek Civil War, 1943–1950: Studies of Polarization* (London: Routledge, 1993)

Clough, Robert, *Labour: A Party Fit for Imperialism* (London: Larkin Publications, 1992)

Coates, David, *The Labour Party and the Struggle for Socialism* (Cambridge: Cambridge University Press, 1975)

Coates, David and Peter Lawler, eds, *New Labour in Power* (Manchester: Manchester University Press, 2000)

Cole, G. D. H., *British Working Class Politics, 1832–1914* (London: Routledge, 1941)

——, *Fabian Socialism* (London: George Allen and Unwin, 1943)

——, *A History of the Labour Party from 1914* (London: Routledge, 1948)

——, *A History of Socialist Thought, vol. 3, parts 1 and 2, The Second International, 1889–1914* (London: Macmillan, 1956)

——, *A History of Socialist Thought, vol. 4, part 2, Communism and Social Democracy 1914–1931* (London: Macmillan, 1958)

Cole, Margaret, *The Story of Fabian Socialism* (London: Heinemann, 1961)

Cox, Robert, 'Labour and transnational relations', special issue of *International Organization*, 25:3 (1971), 554–84

——, *Production, Power and World Order: Social Forces in the Making of History* (New York: Columbia University Press, 1987)

Craig, F. W. S., ed. and comp., *British General Election Manifestos 1900–1974* (London: Macmillan, rev. and enlarged edn, 1975)

Creech Jones, Arthur, 'British colonial policy, with particular reference to Africa', *International Affairs*, 17:2 (1951), 176–83

Cripps, R. Stafford, 'Alternatives before British Labour', *Foreign Affairs*, 13:1 (1934–35), 122–32

Crofts, William, *Coercion or Persuasion? Propaganda in Britain after 1945* (London: Routledge, 1989)

Cronon, E. David, ed., *The Political Thought of Woodrow Wilson* (Indianapolis: Bobbs-Merrill, 1965)

Cross, Colin, *The Fascists in Britain* (London: Barrie and Rockliff, 1961)

Crossman, R. H. S., 'British political thought in the European tradition', in J. P. Mayer *et al.*, *Political Thought: The European Tradition* (London: Dent, 1939), pp. 171–204

——, ed., *New Fabian Essays* (London: Turnstile Press, 1952)

Curtis, Mark, *The Ambiguities of Power: British Foreign Policy since 1945* (London: Zed Books, 1995)

Dale, Iain, ed., *Labour Party General Election Manifestos* (London: Routledge, 2000)

Dalton, Hugh, *Towards the Peace of Nations: A Study in International Politics* (London: Routledge, 1928)

——, *Call Back Yesterday: Memoirs 1887–1931* (London: Muller, 1953)

——, *The Fateful Years: Memoirs 1931–1945* (London: Mueller, 1957)

——, *High Tide and After: Memoirs 1945–1960* (London: Mueller, 1962)

——, *The Political Diary of Hugh Dalton: 1918–40, 1945–60*, edited by Ben Pimlott (London: Jonathan Cape, 1986)

Dangerfield, George, *The Strange Death of Liberal England* (London: Constable and Co., 1936)

Davies, Andrew, *To Build a New Jerusalem: The British Labour Party from Keir Hardie to Tony Blair* (London: Abacus, 1996)

Di Biagio, Anna, 'The Marshall Plan and the founding of the Cominform, June-September 1947', in Francesca Gori and Silvio Pons, *The Soviet Union and Europe in the Cold War, 1943–53* (Basingstoke: Macmillan, 1996), pp. 208–21

Dilks, David, ed., *Retreat from Power. Studies in British Foreign Policy of the Twentieth Century, vols 1 and 2* (London: Macmillan, 1981)

Dockrill, Michael and John Young, ed., *British Foreign Policy, 1945–56* (London: St Martin's Press, 1989)

Donoughue, Bernard and George Jones, *Herbert Morrison: Portrait of a Politician* (London: Weidenfeld and Nicolson, 1973)

Dowse, Robert, *Left in the Centre: The Independent Labour Party 1893–1940* (London: Longmans, 1966)

Doyle, Michael, 'Kant, liberal legacies and foreign affairs', parts 1 and 2, *Philosophy and Public Affairs*, 2:3 (Summer 1983), 205–35; and 12:4 (Autumn 1983), 323–53

Drennan, James (W. E. D. Allen), *B.U.F. – Oswald Mosley and British Fascism* (London: John Murray, 1934)

Duverger, Maurice, *Political Parties: Their Organization and Activity in the Modern State*, 1st English language edn (London: Methuen, 1954)

Dyer, Hugh, *Moral Order/World Order* (London: Macmillan, 1997)

Fabian Society, *Fabianism and the Empire* (London: Fabian Society, 1900)

Fieldhouse, David, 'The Labour governments and the Empire-Commonwealth, 1945–1951', in Ritchie Ovendale, ed., *The Foreign Policy of the British Labour Governments, 1945–1951* (Leicester: University of Leicester Press, 1984), pp. 83–120

Fielding, Steven, Peter Thompson and Nick Tiratsoo, *'England Arise!' The Labour Party and Popular Politics in 1940s Britain* (Manchester: Manchester University Press, 1995)

Foot, Michael, *Aneurin Bevan, A Biography: vol. I, 1897–1945* (London: MacGibbon and Kee, 1962)

——, *Aneurin Bevan: A Biography, vol. 2, 1945–1960* (London: Davis-Poynter, 1973)

Foote, Geoffrey, *The Labour Party's Political Thought* (New York: St Martin's Press, 3rd ed., 1997)

Frankel, Joseph, *British Foreign Policy 1945–1973* (Oxford: Oxford University Press, 1975)

Friedberg, Aaron, *The Weary Titan: Britain and the Experience of Relative Decline, 1895–1905* (Princeton, NJ: Princeton University Press, 1988)

Fyrth, Jim, ed., *Labour's High Noon: The Government and the Economy 1945–51* (London: Lawrence and Wishart, 1993)

Gaddis, John Lewis, *The United States and the Origins of the Cold War, 1941–1947* (New York: Columbia University Press, 1972)

——, *The Long Peace: Inquiries into the History of Cold War* (Oxford: Oxford University Press, 1987)

Gamble, Andrew, *Britain in Decline: Economic Policy, Political Strategy and the British State* (London: Macmillan, 4th edn, 1994)

Gardner, Richard, *Sterling-Dollar Diplomacy: Anglo-American Collaboration in the Reconstruction of Multilateral Trade* (Oxford: Clarendon Press, 1956)

Godson, Roy, *American Labor and European Politics: The AFL as a Transnational Force* (New York: Crane, Russak and Co., 1976)

Gordon, Michael, *Conflict and Consensus in Labour's Foreign Policy, 1914–1965* (Stanford, CA: Stanford University Press, 1969)

——, 'Domestic conflict and the origins of the First World War: the British and German cases', *Journal of Modern History*, 46:2 (1974), 191–226

Gori, Francesca and Pons, Silvio, *The Soviet Union and Europe in the Cold War, 1943–53* (London: Macmillan, 1996)

Gorst, Anthony, '"We must cut our coat according to our cloth": the making of British defence policy, 1945–1948', in Richard Aldrich, ed., *British Intelligence, Strategy and the Cold War* (London: Routledge, 1992), pp. 143–65

Gowing, Margaret, 'Britain, America and the bomb', in Michael Dockrill and John Young, eds, *British Foreign Policy, 1945–56* (New York: St. Martin's Press, 1989), pp. 31–45

Graham, Gordon, *Ethics and International Relations* (Oxford: Blackwell, 1997)

Graubard, Stephen Richards, *British Labour and the Russian Revolution, 1917–1924* (Cambridge, Mass: Harvard University Press, 1956)

Gupta, Partha Sarathi, *Imperialism and the British Labour Movement, 1914–1964* (London: Macmillan, 1975)

——, 'Imperialism and the Labour government', in Jay Winter, ed., *The Working Class in Modern British History* (Cambridge: Cambridge University Press, 1983), pp. 99–124

Hamilton, Mary Agnes, *Arthur Henderson: A Biography* (London; Heinemann, 1938)

Hardach, Gerd, *The First World War 1914–1918*, translated by Peter and Betty Ross (London: Allen Lane, 1977)

Harris, Kenneth, *Attlee* (London: Weidenfeld and Nicolson, 1982)

Harris, Sally, *Out of Control. British Foreign Policy and the Union of Democratic Control 1914–1918* (Hull: University of Hull Press, 1996)

Harrison, Martin, *Trade Unions and the Labour Party Since 1945* (London: Allen and Unwin, 1960)

Healey, Denis, 'The International Socialist Conference, 1946–1950', *International Affairs*, 26:3 (1950), 363–73

——, 'Power politics and the Labour Party', in Richard Crossman, ed., *New Fabian Essays* (London: Turnstile Press, 1952), pp. 161–79

——, *The Time of My Life* (London: Michael Joseph, 1989)

Henderson, Arthur, *Consolidating World Peace* (London: Burge Memorial Lecture, 1931)

——, *Labour's Way to Peace* (London: Methuen, 1935)

Hermassi, Elbaki, 'Towards a comparative study of revolutions', *Comparative Studies in Society and History*, 18:2 (April 1976), 211–35

Hinton, James, *Labour and Socialism: A History of the British Labour Movement 1867–1974* (Brighton: Wheatsheaf, 1983)

——, *Protests and Visions: Peace Politics in Twentieth Century Britain* (London: Hutchinson, 1989)

Hobsbawm, Eric, *Industry and Empire. An Economic History of Britain since 1750* (London: Penguin, 1968)

Hobson, J. A., *Imperialism: A Study* (London: George Allen and Unwin, 3rd rev. and reset edn, 1938)

Howard, Michael, *The Continental Commitment* (London: Temple Smith, 1972)

——, *War and the Liberal Conscience* (London: Temple Smith, 1978)

Howe, Stephen, *Anticolonialism in British Politics. The Left and the End of Empire, 1918–1964* (Oxford: Clarendon Press, 1993)

Howell, David, *British Social Democracy: A Study in Development and Decay* (London: Croom Helm, 1976)

——, *British Workers and the Independent Labour Party 1888–1906* (Manchester: Manchester University Press, 1983)

Hyndman, H. M., *The Bankruptcy of India* (London: Swann Sonnenschein, 1886)

——, *The Record of an Adventurous Life* (London: Macmillan, 1911)

——, *Further Reminiscences* (London: Macmillan, 1912)

Iatrides, John, ed., *Greece in the 1940s: A Nation in Crisis* (Hanover, NH, and London: University Press of New England, 1981)

James, Alan, *Peacekeeping in International Politics* (London: Macmillan for the International Institute for Strategic Studies, 1990)

Jenkins, Roy, *Asquith* (London: Papermac/Macmillan edn, 1986)

——, *Churchill* (London: Pan Books, 2002)

Joll, James, *The Second International, 1889–1914* (London: Routledge and Keegan Paul, rev. and extended edn, 1974)

——, *The Origins of the First World War* (London: Longman, 1984)

Jones, Bill, *The Russia Complex: The British Labour Party and the Soviet Union* (Manchester: Manchester University Press, 1977)

Jones, Joseph, *The Fifteen Weeks, February 21–5 June, 1947* (New York: Harcourt, Brace and World, 1955)

Jones, Mervyn, *Michael Foot* (London: Victor Gollancz, 1994)

Jupp, James, *The Radical Left in Britain, 1931–1941* (London: Frank Cass, 1982)

Kampfner, John, *Robin Cook* (London: Victor Gollancz, 1988)

Kant, Immanuel, 'Perpetual peace: a philosophical sketch', in *Kant's Political Writings*, edited by Hans Reiss (Cambridge: Cambridge University Press, 2nd enlarged edn, 1991)

Kendall, Walter, *The Labour Movement in Europe* (London: Allen Lane, 1975)

Kennedy, Paul, *The Rise and Fall of British Naval Mastery* (London: Allen Lane, 1976)

——, *The Rise of Anglo-German Antagonism 1860–1914* (London: Macmillan, 1980)

——, *The Realities Behind Diplomacy. Background Influences on British External Policy, 1865–1980* (London: Fontana Press, 1981)

——, *The Rise and Fall of the Great Powers. Economic Change and Military Conflict from 1500 to 2000* (London: Fontana Press, 1989)

Kennan, George, *Memoirs 1925–1950* (New York: Pantheon, 1967)

Keohane, Dan, *Labour Party Defence Policy since 1945* (Leicester: Leicester University Press, 1993)

——, *Security in British Politics, 1945–99* (London: Macmillan, 2000)

Knowles, Caroline, *Race, Discourse and Labourism* (London: Routledge, 1992)

Laybourn, Keith, *Philip Snowden: A Biography, 1864–1937* (London: Temple Smith, 1988)

Leffler, Melvyn, *A Preponderance of Power: National Security, the Truman Administration and the Cold War* (Stanford, CA: Stanford University Press, 1992)

Lenin, V. I., *Imperialism, the Highest Stage of Capitalism: A Popular Outline* (New York: International Publishers, revised translation, 1939)

——, *British Labour and British Imperialism: A Compilation of Writings by Lenin on Britain* (London: Lawrence and Wishart, 1969)

Leventhal, F. M., *Arthur Henderson* (Manchester: Manchester University Press, 1989)

Liddell Hart, B. H., *A History of the World War 1914–1918* (London: Faber and Faber, 1934)

Little, Richard, and Mark Wickham-Jones, *New Labour's Foreign Policy: A New Moral Crusade?* (Manchester: Manchester University Press, 2000)

Lorwin, Lewis, *The International Labor Movement: History, Policies, Outlook* (New York: Harper, 1953)

Ludlam, Steve and Martin Smith, eds, *New Labour in Government* (London: Macmillan, 2001)

Lukes, Stephen, *Power: A Radical View* (London: Macmillan, 1974)

Lyman, Richard, *The First Labour Government, 1924* (London: Chapman Hall, 1957)

MacDonald, J. Ramsay, *Labour and the Empire* (London: George Allen, 1907)

——, *The Government of India* (London: Swarthmore Press, 1919)

——, *A Policy for the Labour Party* (London: Leonard Parsons, 1920)

MacShane, Denis, *International Labour and the Origins of the Cold War* (Oxford: Clarendon Press, 1992)

Marquand, David, *Ramsay MacDonald* (London: Jonathan Cape, 1977)

Martin, Kinglsey, *Harold Laski (1893–1950): A Biographical Memoir* (London: Victor Gollancz, 1953)

Martin, Laurence and John Garnett, *British Foreign Policy: Challenges and Choices for the 21st Century* (London: Pinter/RIIA, 1997)

McBriar, Alan, *Fabian Socialism and English Politics, 1884–1918* (Cambridge: Cambridge University Press, 1962)

McKenzie, Robert, *British Political Parties: The Distribution of Power within the Conservative and Labour Parties* (London: Heinemann, 1955)

Meynell, Hildemarie, 'The Stockholm conference of 1917', *International Review of Social History*, 5 (1960), 1–25 and 202–25

Miliband, Ralph, *Parliamentary Socialism: A Study in the Politics of Labour* (London: Allen and Unwin, 1961)

Miller, Kenneth, *Socialism and Foreign Policy: Theory and Practice in Britain to 1931* (The Hague: Martinus Nijhoff, 1967)

Miller, Steven, Sean Lynn-Jones and Stephen Van Evera, eds, *Military Strategy and the Origins of the First World War* (Princeton: Princeton University Press, 1985)

Minkin, Lewis, *Labour Party Conference: A Study in the Politics of Intra-Party Democracy* (Manchester: Manchester University Press, 1980)

——, *The Contentious Alliance: Trade Unions and the Labour Party* (Edinburgh: Edinburgh University Press, 1992)

Moore, Robin, *Making the New Commonwealth* (Oxford: Clarendon Press, 1987)

Morel, E. D., *Morocco in Diplomacy* (London: Smith, Elder, 1912)

Morgan, Kenneth O., *Keir Hardie: Radical and Socialist* (London: Weidenfeld and Nicolson, 1975)

——, *Labour in Power 1945–51* (Oxford: Oxford University Press, 1985)

——, *Labour People: Leaders and Lieutenants, Hardie to Kinnock* (Oxford: Oxford University Press, 1987)

Mosley, Oswald, *My Life* (London: Nelson, 1968)

Muir, Ramsay, *The Record of the National Government* (London: Allen and Unwin, 1936)

Naylor, John, *Labour's International Policy: The Labour Party in the 1930s* (London: Weidenfeld and Nicolson, 1969)

Nicholson, Marjorie, *The TUC Overseas: The Roots of Policy* (London: Allen and Unwin, 1986)

Nicolson, Harold, *King George the Fifth: His Life and Reign* (London: Constable, 1952)

Northedge, F. S., *British Foreign Policy: The Process of Readjustment 1945–1961* (London: Allen and Unwin, 1962)

Northedge, F. S. and Audrey Wells, *Britain and Soviet Communism: The Impact of a Revolution* (Basingstoke: Macmillan, 1982)

Nossal, Kim Richard, *The Politics of Canadian Foreign Policy* (Scarborough, Ontario: Prentice-Hall, 2nd edn, 1989)

Ovendale, Ritchie, *The English Speaking Alliance: Britain, the United States, the Dominions and the Cold War 1945–51* (London: Allen and Unwin, 1985)

——, ed., *The Foreign Policy of the British Labour Governments, 1945–1951* (Leicester: University of Leicester Press, 1984)

Overy, Richard, *The Air War, 1939–1945* (London: Europa, 1980)

Owen, Nicholas, '"Responsibility without power". The Attlee governments and the end of the British rule in India', in Nick Tiratsoo, ed., *The Attlee Years* (London: Pinter, 1991), pp. 167–89

Panebianco, Angelo, *Political Parties: Organization and Power* (Cambridge: Cambridge University Press, 1988)

Pease, Edward Reynolds, *The History of the Fabian Society* (London: Fabian Society, 1916)

Pelling, Henry, 'Governing without power', *Political Quarterly*, 32:1 (1961), 45–52

——, *A History of British Trade Unionism* (London: Macmillan, 1963)

——, *The Origins of the Labour Party, 1880–1900* (Oxford: Clarendon Press, 2nd edn, 1965)

——, *Winston Churchill* (London: Macmillan, 1974)

——, *The Labour Governments, 1945–51* (London: Macmillan, 1984)

Pelling, Henry and Alastair Reid, *A Short History of the Labour Party* (London: Macmillan, 11th edn, 1996)

Pierson, Stanley, *Marxism and the Origins of British Socialism: The Struggle for a New Consciousness* (Ithaca, NY: Cornell University Press, 1973)

Pimlott, Ben, *Hugh Dalton* (London: Papermac/Macmillan, 1985)

Porter, Bernard, *Critics of Empire: British Radical Attitudes to Colonialism in Africa 1895–1914* (London: Macmillan, 1968)

——, *Britain, Europe and the World, 1850–1986: Delusions of Grandeur* (London: George Allen and Unwin, 2nd edn, 1987)

Rasmussen, Jorgen, 'Party discipline in war-time: the downfall of the Chamberlain government', *Journal of Politics*, 32:2 (1970), 379–406

Reed, Bruce, and Geoffrey Williams, *Denis Healey and the Politics of Power* (London: Sidgwick and Jackson, 1971)

Ruggie, John Gerard, *Constructing the World Polity: Essays on International Institutionalization* (London: Routledge, 1998)

Sanders, David, *Losing and Empire, Finding a Role: British Foreign Policy since 1945* (Basingstoke: Macmillan, 1990)

Saville, John, *The Labour Movement in Britain: A Commentary* (London: Faber and Faber, 1988)

——, 'Labour and foreign policy, 1945–1947', *Our History Journal*, Journal of the History Group of the Communist Party, no. 17 (May 1991), 18–32

——, *The Politics of Continuity: British Foreign Policy and the Labour Government, 1945–46* (London: Verso, 1993)

Schneer, Jonathan, 'Hopes deferred or shattered: the British Labour left and the Third Force movement, 1945–49', *Journal of Modern History*, 56:2 (1984), 197–226

——, *Labour's Conscience: The Labour Left 1945–1951* (Boston: Unwin Hyman, 1988)

Scott Lucas, W. and C. J. Morris, 'A very British crusade: the Information Research Department and the beginning of the Cold War', in Richard Aldrich, ed., *British Intelligence, Strategy and the Cold War, 1945–51* (London: Routledge, 1992), pp. 85–110

Seyd, Patrick, *The Rise and Fall of the Labour Left* (London: Macmillan, 1987)

Sfikas, Thanasis, *The British Labour Government and the Greek Civil War 1945–1949: The Imperialism of 'Non-Intervention'* (Keele: Ryburn/Keele University Press, 1994)

Shaw, Eric, *Discipline and Discord in the Labour Party: The Politics of Managerial Control in the Labour Party, 1951–87* (Manchester: Manchester University Press, 1988)

——, *The Labour Party since 1945: Old Labour: New Labour* (Oxford: Blackwell, 1996)

Shaw, George Bernard, *et al.*, *Fabian Essays in Socialism* (London: Walter Scott, 1889)

Shlaim, Avi, 'Britain and the Arab-Israeli war of 1948', in Michael Dockrill and John Young, eds, *British Foreign Policy, 1945–56* (New York: St. Martin's Press, 1989), pp. 77–100

Skidelsky, Robert, *Politicians and the Slump: The Labour Government of 1929–1931* (London: Macmillan, 1967)

——, *Oswald Mosley* (London: Papermac/Macmillan, 3rd edn, 1990)

Skocpol, Theda, *States and Social Revolutions: A Comparative Analysis of France, Russia and China* (Cambridge: Cambridge University Press, 1979)

Smith, Lyn, 'Covert British propaganda: the Information Research Department: 1947-77', *Millennium: Journal of International Studies*, 9:1 (1980), 67–83

Smith, Michael, Steve Smith and Brian White, eds, *British Foreign Policy: Tradition, Change and Transformation* (London: Unwin Hyman, 1988)

Smith, Raymond, and John Zametica, 'The Cold Warrior: Clement Attlee reconsidered, 1945-7', *International Affairs*, 61:2 (1985), 237–52

Snowden, Philip, *An Autobiography, vol. 2* (London: Nicholson and Watson, 1934)

Steiner, Zara, *The Foreign Office and Foreign Policy, 1898–1914* (Cambridge: Cambridge University Press, 1969)

——, *Britain and the Origins of the First World War* (London: Macmillan, 1977)

Stewart, William, *J. Keir Hardie. A Biography* (London: Cassell, 1921)

Swartz, Marvin, *The Union of Democratic Control in British Politics during the First World War* (Oxford: Clarendon Press, 1971)

Taylor, A. J. P., *The Trouble Makers: Dissent Over Foreign Policy 1792–1939* (London: Hamish Hamilton, 1957)

Taylor, Philip, 'The projection of Britain abroad, 1945–51', in Michael Dockrill and John Young, eds, *British Foreign Policy, 1945–56* (New York: St Martin's Press, 1989), pp. 9–30

Taylor, Richard, *Against the Bomb: The British Peace Movement, 1958–1965* (Oxford: Clarendon, 1988)

——, 'The Labour Party and CND: 1957 to 1984' in Richard Taylor and Nigel Young, eds, *Campaigns for Peace: British Peace Movements in the Twentieth Century* (Manchester: Manchester University Press, 1987)

—— and Nigel Young, eds, *Campaigns for Peace: British Peace Movements in the Twentieth Century* (Manchester: Manchester University Press, 1987)

Thomas, Mark and Guy Lodge, eds, *Radicals and Reformer: A Century of Fabian Thought* (London: Fabian Society, 2000)

Thompson, Neville, *The Anti-Appeasers: Conservative Opposition to Appeasement in the 1930s* (Oxford: Clarendon Press, 1971)

Thompson, Willie, *The Good Old Cause: British Communism, 1920–1991* (London: Pluto Press, 1992)

Thorne, Christopher, *The Limits of Foreign Policy: The West, the League and the Far Eastern Crisis of 1931–1933* (London: Hamish Hamilton, 1972)

Thurlow, Richard, *Fascism in Britain: A History 1918–85* (Oxford: Blackwell, 1987)

Tsuzuki, Chushichi, *H. M. Hyndman and British Socialism*, edited by Henry Pelling (Oxford: Oxford University Press, 1961)

Toynbee, Arnold, ed., *Survey of International Affairs, 1924* (Oxford: Oxford University Press, 1926)

Vickers, Rhiannon, *Manipulating Hegemony: State Power, Labour and the Marshall Plan in Britain* (London: Macmillan, 2000)

——, 'Labour's search for a Third Way in foreign policy', in Richard Little and Mark Wickham-Jones, eds, *New Labour's Foreign Policy. A New Moral Crusade?* (Manchester: Manchester University Press, 2000), pp. 33–45

——, 'Understanding the Anglo-American Council on Productivity: Labour and the politics of productivity', *Labour History Review*, 66:2 (2001), 207-22

Wallace, William, 'World status without tears', in Vernon Bogdanor and Robert Skidelsky, *The Age of Affluence 1951–1964* (London: Macmillan, 1970), pp. 192–220

Waltz, Kenneth, *Foreign Policy and Democratic Politics: The American and British Experience* (London: Longmans, 1968)

Wark, Wesley, 'Coming in from the Cold: British propaganda and Red-Army defectors, 1945–1952', *International History Review*, 9:1 (1987), 48–72

Watt, Donald Cameron, *Succeeding John Bull: America in Britain's Place, 1900–1975* (Cambridge, Cambridge University Press 1984)

Webb, Beatrice, *Beatrice Webb's Diaries, 1912–1924, vol. 1*, ed. by Margaret Cole (London: Longmans, 1952)

Webb, Sidney, 'The first Labour government', *Political Quarterly*, 32:1 (1961), 6–44

Weiler, Peter, 'British Labour and the Cold War: the foreign policy of the Labour governments, 1945–1951', *Journal of British Studies*, 26:1 (1987), 54–82

——, *British Labour and the Cold War* (Stanford: Stanford University Press, 1988)

——, *Ernest Bevin* (Manchester: Manchester University Press, 1993)

Wheeler, Nicholas and Tim Dunne, 'Good international citizenship: a Third Way for British foreign policy', *International Affairs*, 74:4 (1998), 847–70

White, Stephen, 'Soviets in Britain: the Leeds Convention of 1917', *International Review of Social History*, 19:2 (1974), 165–93

Williams, Andrew, *Labour and Russia: The Attitude of the Labour Party to the USSR, 1924–34* (Manchester: Manchester University Press, 1989)

Williams, Francis, *Ernest Bevin: Portrait of a Great Englishman* (London: Hutchinson, 1952)

Williams, Howard, and Ken Booth, 'Kant: Theorist beyond limits', in Ian Clark and Iver Neumann, eds, *Classical Theories of International Relations* (Basingstoke: Macmillan/St Anthony's College, Oxford, 1996), pp. 71–98

Windmuller, John, *American Labor and the International Labor Movement, 1940–1953* (Ithaca, NY: Cornell University Press, 1954)

——, The International Trade Union Movement (Deventer: Kluwer, 1980)

Windrich, Elaine, *British Labour's Foreign Policy* (Stanford, CA: Stanford University Press, 1952)

Winkler, Henry, *The League of Nations Movement in Great Britain, 1914–1919* (New Brunswick, NJ: Rutgers University, 1952)

——, 'The emergence of a Labor foreign policy in Great Britain, 1918–1929', *Journal of Modern History*, 28:3 (1956), 247–58

Winter, J. M., 'Arthur Henderson, the Russian Revolution and the reconstruction of the Labour Party', *The Historical Journal*, 15:4 (1972), 733–73

Worswick, George and Peter Ady, eds, *The British Economy, 1945–1950* (Oxford: Clarendon Press, 1952)

Wrench, David, 'The parties and the National government, August 1931– September 1932', *Journal of British Studies*, 23:2 (1984), 135–53

Wright, Quincy, *A Study of War* (Chicago: University of Chicago Press, 2nd edn, 1965)

Young, John, 'Foreign, defence and European affairs', in Brian Brivati and Tim Bale, eds, *New Labour in Power: Precedents and Prospects* (London: Routledge, 1997), pp. 137–55

Index